Parties and Leaders

in the

Postreform House

American Politics and Political Economy Series

Edited by Benjamin I. Page

Parties and Leaders in the Postreform House

David W. Rohde

The University of Chicago Press
Chicago and London

The University of Chicago Press, Chicago 60637
The University of Chicago Press, Ltd., London
© 1991 by The University of Chicago
All rights reserved. Published 1991
Printed in the United States of America

00 99 98 97 96 95   5 4 3

Library of Congress Cataloging in Publication Data

Rohde, David W.
    Parties and leaders in the postreform house / David W. Rohde.
        p.   cm. — (American politics and political economy series)
    Includes bibliographical references and index.
    ISBN 0-226-72406-9. — ISBN 0-226-72407-7 (pbk.)
    1. United States. Congress. House—Leadership.   2. Political
parties—United States.   3. United States—Politics and
government—20th century.   I. Title.   II. Series: American
politics and political economy.
JK1411.R64   1991
328.73′0769—dc20   90-22984
                                                                      CIP

For Barb, Jennie, and Maggi

All together now . . . and then.

Contents

Preface   ix

Acknowledgments   xi

1 Parties in the House of Representatives   1
    Parties in the House before Reform 3
    The Decline in Party Voting 8
    The Reform Era and Its Consequences 11
    Partisanship in the House: Decline and
       Resurgence 13

2 Reform and Its Consequences: A Closer Look   17
    The Motivations for House Reform 17
    Three Tracks of Reform 20
    House Reform and Member Goals 28
    The Gradual Impact of Reform 34

**3 The Democratic Caucus: Membership Change and
Organizational Developments**   40
    Some Perspectives on Roll-Call Voting 40
    Variations in Homogeneity among House
       Democrats 45
    Some Specific Issue Perspectives 58
    The Changing Role of the Democratic
       Caucus 65

The Democratic Caucus and Collective
        Control 69

**4 The Democratic Leadership: Party Agents and
   Agenda Management**   82
        The Evolution of Leadership Activities 82
        Employing the Fruits of Reform: The
           Leadership and Agenda Management 93
        Leadership at Full Tide: The Wright
           Speakership 105
        Some Conclusions 118

**5 Republican Reactions, Presidential Agendas, and
   Legislative Consequences**   120
        House Republicans 120
        Presidents and Partisanship 138
        Some Legislative Consequences 151
        Summary 160

6 Conclusions and Future Prospects   162
        Theory and Evidence: A Summary 162
        Changing Perspectives on Politics in the
           House 169
        Future Prospects 179
        Conclusion 192

   Notes   193

   References   213

   Index   225

Preface

The analysis presented in this book grew out of a set of longstanding and interrelated interests: in factional divisions within congressional parties, in the organization and leadership of those parties, in the impact of electoral forces on Congress, and in the effects of congressional reforms on behavior and outcomes. Each of these interests is a facet of the discussion that follows.

The more immediate impetus for this work came from a recognition that there has been a resurgence of partisanship in Congress (particularly apparent in floor voting), and that the earlier research on the decline of partisanship in Congress neither anticipated nor appeared able to explain this resurgence. There seemed, moreover, to be an incomplete understanding in the congressional literature of the causes and effects of the reforms in the House during the 1970s. It will be argued below that the reforms in the House and the growth of partisanship are systematically related, and that both are in turn related to important electoral changes. The analysis will seek to provide theoretical support and empirical evidence for this perspective.

Virtually all research builds on the work of other scholars, but the approach taken here depends on previous research to a greater degree than is usual. There has been a great deal of superb research on the House of Representatives over the last twenty-five years, and this discussion will draw on it extensively, blending earlier findings with original work done specifically for this study. Thus the abnormally large set of references is not merely a long series of courtesy listings, but rather a recounting of the elements that went into what is intended to be a synthesis of the relevant research. That synthesis is linked to new theoretical arguments and evidence to provide a (hopefully) thorough account of the resurgence of partisanship in the House since reform.

The mode of presentation of research results will vary with the nature of the target audience. The structure of this presentation reflects the belief that the theoretical arguments and empirical findings to be discussed would potentially be of interest not only to research specialists on the internal workings of Congress, but also to scholars with broader interests in American politics, and to students. For example, there is a tension between accessibility of the discussion and completeness. We argue that the resurgence of partisanship is the consequence of a fairly complex set of influences and interactions. A full and complete consideration of all of these elements would probably have produced a manuscript two to three times the current length. This would have limited (if not eliminated entirely) the readership.

We chose, therefore, to treat the issues and evidence with sufficient detail to make a convincing case, and leave fuller considerations to other current and future analyses. As a consequence of this choice, even the extensive list of references employed is not exhaustive. There are many relevant pieces of research which could not be considered within these self-imposed limits. Similarly, a complete consideration of the questions on which we focus would necessitate analysis of the Senate as well as the House, but that expansion would also require far more space than is feasible. Moreover, the time for data collection would have been multiplied as well, with a corresponding delay in presentation of the results. We will briefly discuss some Senate comparisons at a few points, particularly in chapter 6, but a full analysis will have to wait for the future.

Another reflection of the desire to widen the accessibility of the discussion is the decision to present the theoretical arguments in segments at appropriate points in the analysis, rather than together at the outset. We felt that the continued interaction among theory, description, and evidence would provide a more interesting treatment for the non-specialist. However, the concluding chapter includes a section that seeks to draw together and integrate theoretical considerations and empirical results. It is hoped that in this way, the interests of all types of readers will be adequately served.

Acknowledgments

Any research project incurs a series of debts, and large projects of long duration incur the most. That was certainly true in this case. In the five years since I began the research of which this book is a part, many organizations and individuals have provided support and advice. Early funding for research assistance was provided by the Department of Political Science at Michigan State University, and the university's All-University Research Initiation Grant Program. The greater share of support for data gathering and analysis came from the National Science Foundation through grant SES-89-09884. All of the funds for the interviews with members of the House were received through two grants from the Everett M. Dirksen Congressional Leadership Research Center. I am most grateful for all of this support. I am certain that this project could not have been developed and completed without it. The roll-call data, the survey data, and some of the information on electoral patterns employed in this project were made available by the Interuniversity Consortium for Political and Social Research, which is not responsible for any of the analyses conducted or conclusions reached. Some of the arguments and evidence contained in this book were initially presented in a paper titled "Democratic Party Leadership, Agenda Control, and the Resurgence of Partisanship in the House," which was delivered at the 1989 annual meeting of the American Political Science Association.

Another substantial debt is owed to my research assistants. James Meernik joined the project during its early stages, and cheerfully endured the burdens of seemingly endless data collection, coding, and analysis. His efforts were always excellent. More recently, Renée Smith provided valuable help in developing the many data bases used in the project. In addition, assistance was provided at various times by Stephen Burgess, Joseph Ignagni, and Blair Stieber. I am happy to take this opportunity to thank all of them for their efforts.

I have also benefited from the encouragement and advice of many friends and colleagues. Ken Shepsle and John Aldrich were willing to listen to me try to sort out my ideas from the earliest stages of the project to the present. Their positive feedback helped me to continue to believe that the work was worthwhile, but they also raised useful questions, and even dissented when they thought it was warranted. I continue to believe that my work and my life are better for the benefits of their friendship. Many congressional scholars read and commented on individual chapters or the papers and articles that were incorporated in them, including Stan Bach, Joe Cooper, Gary Cox, Dick Fenno, Evelyn Fink, Rick Hall, Brian Humes, Gary Jacobson, Chuck Jones, Mike Malbin, Mat McCubbins, Norm Ornstein, Barb Sinclair, Barry Weingast, and Joe White. Special thanks are due to L. Sandy Maisel and to Steven S. Smith, who read and critiqued a draft of the full manuscript. They offered many useful suggestions that improved the final product, although I (alas) am responsible for any problems that remain.

I am grateful to my editor, John Tryneski, for making my interaction with the University of Chicago Press such a pleasant experience. He understood what I wanted to accomplish in this book, and helped me to achieve it. Thanks are also due to Rhonda Burns, who typed the entire manuscript with her usual skill, and under frequently unreasonable deadlines.

Finally, I want to express my appreciation to my wife, Barbara, and to my daughters, Jennifer and Margaret. This book consumed a great deal of what might have been "free time"—time I could otherwise have spent with them. Yet I never received anything other than tolerance and encouragement as the project progressed. I am most grateful for that, and for everything else, and it gives me great pleasure to dedicate this book to them.

Parties in the House of Representatives

Analysis of the organization and influence of political parties in the House of Representatives was an early and persistent interest of political scientists who studied the Congress. In *Congressional Government* (1885), Woodrow Wilson discussed the role of party leadership within what he termed the system of "committee government" in the House. Stuart Rice's (1928) analysis of party voting was one of the earliest applications of quantitative techniques to American politics. Later, Turner (1951) and Truman (1959) substantially advanced our knowledge about Congress in the early years of the behavioral era by their focus on parties and partisanship, followed in the 1960s by the work of scholars like Jones (1968), Patterson (1963), Peabody (1967), and Ripley (1964, 1967). More recently, however, interest in these subjects has declined. For example, Collie (1986, p. 91) examined publications in four major journals during 1985–86, and found only "three articles [that] dealt with congressional parties and two of them suggested that parties weren't particularly important to an understanding of what happens in the contemporary Congress."

Why this shift in interest? The early focus on parties was due to a combination of belief that they *could* play an important role in the operation of Congress, and a desire to explore and describe the role they actually *did* play. The waning of interest seems to have been the consequence of the early research that showed that parties were relatively weak in Congress, and of later work that convinced scholars that changes in the congressional context—particularly the evolution of electoral circumstances and congressional reforms—had made parties even weaker and condemned them to remain so.

In this chapter, we will briefly consider some of this research. The picture of congressional parties derived from this work will provide a basis for our subsequent analysis of their changing impact in the House during the last two decades. Before beginning that discussion, it is important to be clear about what we mean by the term *partisanship* in the House. It refers to the impact and influence of political parties on the operation of the House and the behavior of its members. Thus partisanship is a matter of degree; we can speak of some aspect of congressional operation being more or less partisan compared to another aspect, or compared to the same aspect at a different point in time. Or we can refer to some activity, institutional arrangement, or individual as partisan (or nonpartisan), indicating that the connection to political parties is relatively strong (or weak).

For example, we can speak of the House as partisan, and mean that parties (and particularly the majority party) are important influences on the institution's mode of operation and on the decisions of the representatives who serve in it. The characterization would also imply that conflict within the House would tend to divide along partisan lines. If, on the other hand, we labeled the House bipartisan (or nonpartisan), we would imply that parties are not especially influential, and that disagreements over policy are mostly shaped by other considerations.

Similarly, we can say that an action or activity is partisan, meaning that it is designed to benefit one party (usually, but not always, at the expense of the other). A visible example is the choice of which party's leader will be Speaker of the House, a choice made at the beginning of every Congress. The votes on this decision fall exactly along party lines, with all the Democrats voting for their leader and the Republicans voting for theirs. Thus we would refer to the choice of a Speaker as a partisan decision.

Finally, we can talk of an individual as partisan. Here we mean that this person feels a strong connection to a party, or that the person's decisions and behavior are greatly influenced by his or her party affiliation. So in later chapters we will characterize Speaker James Wright as partisan because much of his leadership activity was directed at securing adoption of legislation favored by Democrats and at blocking alternatives supported by Republicans.

Our discussion of parties and partisanship, then, will deal with the links between individuals and their parties and how those links affect behavior, with the organization of the parties and their impact on the organization and operation of the House, and with the effects these considerations have on the pattern of legislative outcomes within the institution.

Parties in the House before Reform

For many early students of Congress, their perceptions of political parties (and frequently their preferences about them) were shaped by the way parties operated in the parliamentary systems of other countries. In those systems, parties usually took clear positions on issues, and different parties offered sharply contrasting policy platforms to the voters. The voters (at least theoretically) selected the party that offered the most attractive platform by giving it a majority of seats in parliament, and that party then organized the government and enacted its platform. When specific pieces of government-sponsored legislation were considered, the parties were generally true to their previous positions: almost all members of the majority voted for the proposed law, with members of the minority voting in opposition. The loyalty of individual members to party positions was reinforced by the fact that each party generally controlled who was allowed to run for office under its label.

It was this pattern of government—policy-oriented parties with strong leaders and loyal members—that Woodrow Wilson had in mind when he wrote *Congressional Government* over one hundred years ago. Compared to this standard, the Congress was found wanting in all respects: parties did not offer distinct policy agendas, leaders were not powerful, members were not loyal. In Wilson's view, "the great need is, not to get rid of parties, but to find and use some expedient by which they can be managed and made amenable from day to day to public opinion" (1885, pp. 79–80). Without responsibility to public opinion, there was no party program, and the various components of the party simply went their own way. "There is within Congress no *visible*, and therefore no *controllable* party organization. . . . The legislation of a session is simply an aggregate of the bills recommended by Committees composed of members from both sides of the House . . ." (1885, p. 80).

To Wilson, the chief reason for the weakness of the parties was that "there are in Congress no authoritative leaders who are the recognized spokesmen of their parties" (1885, p. 76). While the Speaker of the House was the closest thing to a leader the Congress had, his power (according to Wilson) did not extend much beyond naming the members of the committees that considered legislation. Unlike parliamentary systems, where the Prime Minister really was the single party leader and spokesperson, "The leaders of the House are the chairmen of the principal Standing Committees. Indeed, to be exactly accurate, the House has as many leaders as there are subjects of legislation; for there are as many Standing Committees as there are leading classes of legislation . . ." (Wilson, 1885, p. 58). Hence Wilson's characterization of the congressional process as "committee government."[1]

Wilson's view of the Congress was, of course, shaped by the patterns that were visible when he wrote, and the party politics of the 1870s and 1880s were rather chaotic, with frequent shifts of party control of the House. However, within a few years of Wilson's writing, Thomas B. Reed rose to the speakership of the House, and a few years after Reed came Speaker Joseph G. Cannon. The period during which "Boss" Reed and "Czar" Cannon led the House was very different from that characterized by Wilson, and it set the standard for a strong party leadership for congressional scholars ever since.[2]

Thomas Reed was elected to the House as a Republican in 1876. He served on the Rules Committee, and was intensely interested in House rules and governance. During the 1880s, a decade of mostly Democratic majorities, Reed became convinced that the rules permitted a minority of members to frustrate the passage of legislation. When he became Speaker in 1889, he engineered the adoption of a major revision of the House's rules and practices. These changes, which came to be known as the "Reed rules," strengthened the hand of the majority party and particularly that of the Speaker, while reducing the ability of the minority to block or delay legislation. He appointed allies as chairmen of major committees, and he and the chairmen of Ways and Means and Appropriations constituted the Republican majority of the Rules Committee. With these institutional powers and the disciplined support of the Republican majority, he secured the passage of a wide range of new domestic legislation.

Joseph Cannon, also a Republican, became Speaker in 1903. He built on the practices followed by Reed, serving as chairman of Rules and ensuring that his closest supporters headed the other major committees. He used his power to appoint all Republican committee members as a vehicle for rewarding allies and punishing dissidents. Control of the Rules Committee permitted him to determine which bills got to the floor, and his powers as presiding officer enabled him generally to dictate their fate once there. All of these institutional powers were buttressed by Cannon's position as leader of his party and by the strong party discipline among House Republicans. As Cooper and Brady (1981, p. 413) said, "The House of Reed and Cannon contained a highly centralized power structure with control resting essentially in the hands of the Speaker. The key to the Speaker's power lay not simply in his prerogatives under rules, nor in his position as party chief, but rather in the manner in which these two sources of leverage reinforced one another. . . ." These arrangements were, however, not to last. In 1910 insurgent progressive Republicans, who had been blocked from having any influence over outcomes by Cannon's domination, joined with the Democratic minority to strip the Speaker of most of his institutional powers, particularly the ability to appoint the Rules Committee and to serve on it (see Jones, 1968, pp. 619–36).

In succeeding years the influence of party leaders continued to decline, and over time the House largely reverted to the pattern of "committee government." This was, to be sure, a gradual process. Immediately after the revolt against Cannon, when the Democrats assumed majority control, they vested substantial power in their party caucus, which could bind members to vote a certain way on the floor, and in their majority leader, who also chaired the Ways and Means Committee and the party's committee on committees. These practices were discarded within a few years, however, as policy divisions within the Democratic party revealed themselves (Cooper and Brady, 1981, pp. 416–17). Other mechanisms for party control declined as well. In both parties, positions of influence within the committee system were distributed on the basis of seniority, generally without regard to a member's policy views or party loyalty (Polsby, 1968; Polsby, Gallaher, and Rundquist, 1969).

Thus from the revolt in 1910 to the assumption of the speakership by Sam Rayburn in 1940, the organization of the House passed "from hierarchy to bargaining" (Cooper and Brady, 1981, p. 417). The party leadership had lost control over committee assignments and the Rules Committee, and their ability to reward or punish individual members also declined. During the early years of Rayburn's leadership, moreover, the divisions within his party became more sectional in character, with northern Democrats disagreeing more often with their southern colleagues. The "conservative coalition"—the voting alignment of a majority of Republicans and a majority of southern Democrats against a majority of northern Democrats—appeared more frequently on the House floor, and became an important element in conflict over policy (Manley, 1973; Brady and Bullock, 1980, 1981). Over time the majority leadership had greater difficulty securing the cooperation of committees and their chairmen, and this was particularly true on the crucial Rules Committee, where the conservative coalition frequently controlled outcomes (Robinson, 1963; Bolling, 1966; Jones, 1968).

These changes did not render parties and their leadership inconsequential, but they did alter the impact of parties and the style of leaders. Committees and committee chairmen became a rival power center to the party leadership, and Rayburn and his successor, John McCormack (who served until the beginning of the reform era), were compelled to deal with committee leaders. They were rarely in a position to force the committees to do anything. Party leaders "had to function largely as petitioners of committee support and floor managers of committee legislation" (Cooper and Brady, 1981, p. 419). And on the floor the leadership had to build supporting coalitions issue by issue, because they did not have a large enough bloc of votes across issues on which they could depend to carry the day. Because of the changed context, Cooper and Brady argued, Rayburn's approach was markedly different from that of Cannon and Reed. He accepted party irregularity and sought to limit partisanship and conflict. Rayburn was cautious in pursuing party goals, and usually declined to challenge the other power centers in the House. "In short, then, Rayburn was far more inclined to accept the defeat of party programs than to risk his influence and prestige in battles to attain them" (Cooper and Brady, 1981, p. 421). In many ways the House had reverted to the patterns of behavior described by Wilson over a half-century earlier.

Of course many people, including certain political scientists and members of Congress, were not pleased with these developments. For some political scientists, the changes in Congress were just specific reflections of the general decline of the potency of political parties in American politics, which they regarded negatively. This viewpoint received its greatest visibility in the 1950 report of the Committee on Political Parties of the American Political Science Association (APSA) titled "Toward a More Responsible Two-Party System." Echoing the criticisms of Woodrow Wilson, the report claimed (p. v) that at the national level the two major parties were just loose confederations of state and local organizations, and therefore "either major party, when in power, is ill-equipped to organize its members in the legislative and executive branches into a government held together and guided by the party program." The report went on to offer a wide range of suggestions designed to strengthen the parties. Regarding Congress, these included national party councils, which would screen potential congressional candidates, and a return to using party caucuses to bind members to support party positions on the floor. This report provoked much debate within the profession.[3] Some critics shared the view that parties should be more responsible, but didn't think there was any practical way to bring this about, particularly because voters did not make their choices based on issues or ideological orientations. Others claimed that parties were more responsible than the APSA committee believed, or argued that for various reasons a shift in the direction of party responsibility was undesirable. This debate and its echoes continued throughout the 1950s and beyond.[4]

Among members, probably the most visible and articulate critic of the organizational structure of the House and the role of parties in it was Richard Bolling of Missouri. Bolling was an ally of Sam Rayburn and a member of the Rules Committee. He was also one of the founders in 1959 of the Democratic Study Group (DSG), an organization of liberal and mostly northern Democrats in the House.[5] In *House Out of Order* (1966), Bolling offered a detailed critique of what was wrong with the House: "In the many years I have been a Member of Congress, the House has revealed itself to me as ineffective in its role as a coordinate branch of the federal government, negative in its approach to national tasks, generally unresponsive to any but parochial economic interests" (p. 221).

Why was this the case? In Bolling's view, the "entire function of the House is determined by the effective action of a majority. Yet the majority of House Democrats has not had effective control of the House" (p. 223). This in turn was the consequence of the seniority system's granting of control of House committees to conservative southern Democrats. To break this pattern, Bolling proposed increasing the powers of the Speaker, under the control of the Democratic Caucus to prevent the kind of autocratic rule exhibited by Cannon. The changes he called for included letting the Speaker nominate (for Caucus ratification) all the Democratic members of Ways and Means (who also served as the party's committee on committees) and Rules, as well as the chairmen of all committees. Bolling's goal in all of this was clear: to strengthen the parties and enhance their responsibility. "The one purpose of the changes is to make the committee system of the House more representative of the majority views of the two parties. This should, as a consequence, increase the party's leadership and the individual Member's responsibility for legislative action and his accountability to the country and to his constituency" (p. 229).

Thus by the 1960s the House was characterized by a system of committee government, dominated by a working coalition of southern Democrats and Republicans. The majority party leadership was not without resources, but it generally lacked the institutional tools, the numerical support, and the personal inclination to confront and defeat the committee leadership. But the House is not a static institution, and during the 1960s some significant changes became apparent. There was a large influx of northern liberal Democrats into the House as a result of the 1958 election. Indeed, the presence of this group was one of the reasons for the founding of the DSG in 1959. Some of these newcomers lost in subsequent elections, but others survived, and their numbers were reinforced by another large group of liberal northerners in the 1964 Goldwater landslide. About half of the 1964 freshmen lost in 1966, but the remainder, coupled with members from previous elections, left the junior ranks of the House Democrats with a markedly liberal cast.

These changes, however, expanded the ideological gap between junior and senior Democrats about which Bolling complained. The conservative southerners who dominated the committee leadership stood in the way, in the view of junior members, of the passage of legislation favored by the party's liberal majority. The liberals' appetite, moreover, had been whetted by the range of "Great Society" legislation passed under Lyndon Johnson's leadership in the Eighty-ninth Congress. But after the 1966 election, substantial Republican gains meant that the liberals no longer had the numbers to simply overwhelm conservative opposition. They believed that their preferred policies could still command majority support if given a fair chance, but now southern committee leaders were able to use the power granted to them through the seniority system to block that chance. The frustration of junior members was reinforced by the judgment that many committee chairmen, conservative or not, used their powers in an autocratic fashion.

In many ways this situation was reminiscent of the House in 1910 under Cannon: members of the majority party were frustrated by the arbitrary exercise of institutional power which prevented them from securing the passage of policies they supported. And what occurred next had certain analogues to the 1910 result, although it took more time. During the early 1970s, the House was swept by a series of institutional reforms which vastly changed the ways the body operated. Before we consider those reforms and their consequences, however, it will be useful to look at another set of analyses that considered the changing impact of party in the House. These studies dealt with the declining role of partisanship in floor voting.

The Decline in Party Voting

In the discussion above, we talked about parties in terms of the degree to which they support contrasting policy positions, and the amount of support members provide for those party positions. Analysts have developed a set of measures that permit one to describe the amount of disagreement that exists between parties on roll-call votes in a legislature, and the amount of agreement within a party on those votes. The most commonly used measure of disagreement is the frequency of *party voting*, which indicates the proportion of a set of votes on which a majority of one party voted in opposition to a majority of the other party.[6] This is not an entirely satisfactory measure because it counts a vote on which the parties unanimously opposed one another the same as one on which only 51 percent majorities disagreed. To compensate for this problem, the *average party difference* can be used. This measure computes on each vote the absolute value of the difference in the proportion of each party voting aye. Thus when both parties are unanimously opposed, the difference is 100 points; on the other hand, with 51 percent of each party on opposite sides, the difference is only 2 points. These differences are then averaged across the set of votes in question.

To measure intraparty agreement, two indexes are commonly used. The *index of cohesion* computes the absolute difference between the proportion of a party's members voting aye and the proportion voting nay on a given vote. Thus the index can range from 100 (when the party is unanimous) to 0 (when 50 percent of the party is on each side of the vote). For a set of votes, one takes the average of these calculations to indicate the degree to which a party's members vote together. The other measure is the *party-unity index,* which employs a set of party votes, as described above. The index value for a given member is the proportion of those votes on which he or she supports the party position. Individual scores are then averaged for a party or some subset of it.

Employing these measures, researchers have been able to describe and analyze the changing patterns of partisanship in congressional voting. This research has largely been the account of party decline. Brady, Cooper, and Hurley (1979) demonstrated that there was a long-term decline in party voting in the House from the strong-party era of Reed and Cannon through 1968. Collie and Brady (1985) offered a similar analysis from the New Deal era through 1980.

The common theme in the literature on party decline is that party voting is the consequence of influences inside and outside the Congress, and that both were related to the decline. For example, Collie and Brady (1985, p. 283) argued that "salient partisan voting coalitions result from an electorate that votes for parties rather than for individual personalities and from an institutional arrangement that vests party leaders with an authority recognized by the rank-and-file party membership in the Congress." That is, party voting will tend to be high when voters choose congressional candidates on the basis of their party affiliation, and when party leaders are granted strong institutional powers. Like the analysts we discussed above, Collie and Brady too argued that the House had become decentralized institutionally since the 1910 revolt, and that since the New Deal the link between party and voting within the electorate had declined. They attributed the latter trend to the use of the direct primary to nominate candidates, to the fact that candidates' campaign organizations tend to be independent of party, and to the weakened effect of party identification on voters' choices. Due to these factors, they contended (p. 284), "by the 1970s, the 'average' Democrat or Republican in the House was not encumbered by either electoral or institutional sanctions." As a consequence, party voting declined.

Brady, Cooper, and Hurley (1979) offered parallel arguments in a study that provided a statistical analysis of the changes in party voting.

They employed four variables related to the external environment and two indicators of internal institutional arrangements to analyze party decline from 1887 through 1968. The external variables were (1) the proportion of freshmen in the House, as an indicator of the extent of electoral change, (2) a variable to indicate whether the House and the presidency were controlled by the same party, (3) a measure of the amount of conflict between the parties on economic issues, derived from an analysis of party platforms, and (4) the degree to which each party's House delegation was dominated by members from one region. The last variable was intended as an indicator of the homogeneity of preferences within the party, and the regional breakdowns were northern versus southern/border Democrats, and eastern versus noneastern Republicans. The idea is that party members from different regions will have less in common politically than members from the same region. Finally, to measure internal structure, the authors employed variables to indicate time periods that capture the decline of centralization of parties discussed above, specifically the change from strong to weak Speakers and the shift away from use of the party caucus to shape the substance of policy.

The dependent variables in their analysis included measures of party voting and of party cohesion. The relationship between the external variables and the party measures varied, but overall Brady, Cooper, and Hurley concluded (p. 391) that the "long-run decline in party strength in the House is clearly related to the increased stability of the membership, a decline in electoral party homogeneity and conflict, and an increasing tendency to have a president of one party and a Congress of the other party." They also concluded that the changes regarding the Speaker's powers and the strength of the party caucus also were related to party decline.

Other studies provided additional perspectives on the impact of external forces on partisanship. Cooper and Brady (1981), for example, sought to measure the differences in the constituency bases of the two parties by calculating the degree to which each congressional party represented agricultural as opposed to industrial districts. They found that between 1881 and 1921, when the constituency bases of the parties were different from one another, the level of party voting was high. Brady and Ettling (1984) focused on the shifting relationship between region and party success since the Civil War. They argued that since 1938 the relationship between North and South in the Democratic party has been only electoral, and that party cohesion has been weakened by disagreement on a range of issues.[7]

More detailed consideration of the sectional roots of the divisions in the Democratic party have been provided in the studies of the conservative coalition, noted above, and in Barbara Sinclair's analyses (1978, 1982) of various issue dimensions in congressional voting.[8] In a study of House voting from 1933 through 1956, Sinclair (1978) showed that by the mid-1940s, voting alignments were less dominated by party than before. Specifically, two new policy dimensions—international involvement and civil rights—arose, and they cut across party lines. In addition to the new dimensions, however, Democratic splits developed on the more traditional dimensions of social welfare and government management. Sinclair argued that by the 1950s, the sense of crisis that had fostered cohesion during the New Deal had dissipated. By then, "each party represented a conglomeration of particularized interests, and, as such interests cut across the party's coalitions, the parties fragmented along regional, particularized constituency lines" (1982, pp. 145–46).

To summarize, the research on the decline of partisanship in House voting through the 1970s has attributed it to two root causes: the reduction of partisan influences in the electorate and the weakening of party organization within the institution. With the external and internal changes we have discussed as background, we can now turn to a consideration of the institutional reforms that were adopted by the House in the 1970s.

The Reform Era and Its Consequences

A detailed account of specific reforms will be reserved for the next chapter. At this point we want to give only sufficient background to present some perspectives on the consequences of the reforms for congressional parties.

The most visible reforms were related to committees and their chairmen. They moved the House away from a rigid adherence to seniority in choosing chairmen, permitting the rejection of the most senior member by the Democratic Caucus in a secret-ballot vote. Other reforms restricted the powers of chairmen within their committees, removing the ability to determine committee members' subcommittee assignments or to juggle the jurisdictions of subcommittees. A chairman's ability to block the consideration of legislation was also reduced, and subcommittee chairs were guaranteed staff of their own. The visibility of House proceedings was fostered by another set of reforms which put members on the record on votes within committee, permitted recorded votes on amendments on the floor, and required most committee meetings to be open to the public. A third set of changes enhanced the powers of the Democratic party leadership by transferring committee assignment powers to the Steering and Policy Committee (a majority of which is made up of party leaders and the Speaker's appointees), by granting the Speaker the power to choose the Democrats on the Rules Committee, and by permitting the Speaker to refer bills to more than one committee.

The most widely shared view regarding the consequences of these reforms is that they further decentralized power and policy-making in the House.[9] If the post-Cannon era can be characterized as the transition to "committee government," the postreform period has been described as the transition to "subcommittee government" (Davidson, 1981). Davidson said that since the reforms, "the chief impression is of buzzing confusion. . . . In place of party labels there are individual politicians in business for themselves, and a series of shifting coalitions around specific issues. Instead of a few leaders or checkpoints for legislation, there are many" (p. 131).

To many observers, the reduction of the power of committee chairmen and the guarantees provided to subcommittees increased decentralization and legislative fragmentation. Subcommittee growth and independence increased workloads and reliance on staff, and may have resulted in a decrease in specialization and expertise (Rieselbach, 1986, p. 88). In the view of Dodd and Oppenheimer (1981, p. 49),

> Problems have been created that, if left unresolved, could cripple the legislative process in the House.
>
> At its heart, subcommittee government creates a crisis of interest aggregation in the House. . . . It has led to increased dominance of committee decisionmaking by clientele groups, particularly single-interest groups. . . . The responsibility for saving subcommittee government from itself . . . thus falls largely to the party and party leadership.

However, most analysts also concluded that the reforms were inadequate or irrelevant to this leadership task. Few believed that parties had been strengthened in any meaningful way. Rieselbach argued that "in neither house has reform produced significantly stronger parties, better able to move their programs forward," and that "procedural reforms have produced only minimal and often unanticipated effects" (1986, pp. 107, 108). Similarly, Collie and Brady (1985, p. 275) claimed that "the renewed institutional strength of party in the House has been more than counterbalanced by the trend toward fragmentation and dispersal of power."

Most students of congressional politics were also convinced that the reform measures enhancing the majority leadership's powers were not very consequential.[10] Rieselbach concluded that "House leaders' new powers have proven inadequate to overcome the decentralizing forces that the reform movement unleashed" (1986, p. 107). Cooper and

Brady pointedly argued that "it is doubtful that O'Neill can be as strong a Speaker as Rayburn whatever the level of skill he possesses, given the increased fractionalization in both the formal and party systems that has occurred in the past two decades" (1981, p. 423). Indeed, at least one analyst (Waldman, 1980, p. 373) concluded that "the majority-party leadership may well have grown weaker as compared with the 1960s and continues to be quite constrained and limited. . . ."[11] In Waldman's view, the changes which increased members' independence "seem to have more than countered leadership gains" (p. 392).

The analyses of declining party voting we discussed above generally agreed that that trend was due to changes in the political environment in addition to changes in the institutional structure. In the postreform era, there has been widespread agreement that further environmental changes, particularly related to congressional elections, have had an additional negative effect on partisanship in Congress.[12] Beginning in the late 1960s, the margins by which House incumbents won reelection grew substantially (Mayhew, 1974b). The linkage for voters between party identification and the choice of congressional candidates became weaker (Ferejohn, 1977). Incumbents were more visible to voters than were challengers, and were perceived more positively (Mann and Wolfinger, 1980). This was due in part to the inability of challengers to raise adequate amounts of campaign funds (Jacobson, 1985), and in part to incumbents' performing various types of services for their constituents (Fiorina, 1977; Cain, Ferejohn, and Fiorina, 1987).

The consequence of these trends was that members had achieved a great deal of electoral independence and wanted to maintain it. Mayhew (1974a, pp. 99, 101) contended that

> the enactment of party programs is electorally not very important to members. . . .
>
> What is important to each congressman, and vitally so, is that he be free to take positions that will serve his advantage. . . . [A] member can build a quite satisfactory career within either congressional party regardless of his issue positions.

Collie and Brady (1985, p. 282) listed the following electoral influences that contributed to the decline of partisan voting in the House: the rise of primary elections to select candidates, nonpartisan constituency services by incumbents, the decline of partisan voting behavior in the electorate, and the rise of candidate-centered campaign organizations.

Partisanship in the House: Decline and Resurgence

To summarize the discussion to this point, there was a decline in the impact of parties and leaders within the House after the revolt against

Speaker Cannon. In the view of many analysts this decline was exacerbated by the institutional changes of the reform era and by changes in the electorate at that time. Through the beginning of the Reagan presidency, most scholars shared the view that parties had come to have relatively little impact on policy-making in the House, because party leaders were generally unable to marshal the support of rank-and-file members behind a definable party program. This was evidenced by the long-term decline in party voting on the House floor.

Specific evidence on the decline in partisan voting can be seen in table 1.1, which lists annual figures on party voting and party unity in the House. Through the mid-1970s, the decreasing potency of party is apparent. In 1970 and 1972, party voting reached a low point of only 27 percent of votes cast. Average party-unity scores declined too, with southern Democrats exhibiting the most striking decrease.[13] During the 1950s, unity scores for southern Democrats were in the 60 to 70 percent range. However, by the 1970s, when the reform movement was passing its rules changes, scores were below 50 percent. That is, the average southerner supported his or her party less than half the time.

Yet despite all the arguments we have seen about the continuing weakening of party inside and outside the institution, the decline did not persist. Instead the late 1970s and the 1980s witnessed a striking resurgence of partisanship. Party voting peaked at 64 percent of the votes taken in 1987, more than double the 1970/1972 low point. Democratic party unity, which had declined to a range of 70 to 72 percent in the four years of Nixon's first term, climbed sharply to a maximum of 88 percent in 1987 and 1988. To find a Congress in which Democratic unity was higher than that, one has to go back to the Sixty-first Congress (1909–1911), when "Boss" Cannon was Speaker.[14] Republican unity also increased, albeit not so sharply, from 71 percent in 1969 to 80 percent in 1988.

The purpose of this book is to explore the reasons for the remarkable resurgence of partisanship in the House, in floor voting and in other areas. In particular, the argument will be made that the reform movement, rather than weakening the impact of parties on policy-making, had as its purpose and effect the fostering of the majority party's ability to enact a party program. During the 1960s, liberal strength grew substantially among House Democrats. The pressure for reform came from these members, because they believed that institutional arrangements (particularly within the committee system) unfairly blocked the achievement of their policy goals. Through the passage of various reforms, the liberals sought to reduce the power of committee chairmen, to strengthen the party leadership, and to guarantee that the will of the majority of Democrats was not overridden. Afterwards, the House

Table 1.1 Party Votes and Party-Unity Scores in the House, 1955–1988

	Party Votes (Percent)	Party-Unity Scores (Percents)[a]		
		All Democrats	Southern Democrats	Republicans
1955	41	84	68	78
1956	44	80	79	78
1957	59	79	71	75
1958	40	77	67	73
1959	55	85	77	85
1960	53	75	62	77
1961	50	n.a.	n.a.	n.a.
1962	46	81	n.a.	80
1963	49	85	n.a.	84
1964	55	82	n.a.	81
1965	52	80	55	81
1966	41	78	55	82
1967	36	77	53	82
1968	35	73	48	76
1969	31	71	47	71
1970	27	71	52	72
1971	38	72	48	76
1972	27	70	44	76
1973	42	75	55	74
1974	29	72	51	71
1975	48	75	53	78
1976	36	75	52	75
1977	42	74	55	77
1978	33	71	53	77
1979	47	75	60	79
1980	38	78	64	79
1981	37	75	57	80
1982	36	77	62	76
1983	56	82	67	80
1984	47	81	68	77
1985	61	86	76	80
1986	57	86	76	76
1987	64	88	78	79
1988	47	88	81	80

Source: Ornstein, Mann, and Malbin (1990, pp. 198–99).

[a]Data show percentage of members voting with a majority of their party on party-unity votes. The percentages are normalized to eliminate the effects of absences, as follows: party unity = (unity)/(unity + opposition).

Democrats were still divided on a wide range of policy issues. Because of that, and because the Democratic leadership was disinclined to make strong use of its new powers, little change was visible. Within a few years, however, due in part to growing Democratic homogeneity and to changes in the party leadership, partisanship in the House grew progressively stronger.

In the chapters that follow, we will elaborate on the argument and present evidence to support it. Because the Democratic party was in the majority from 1955 to the present, and because it was the focus of most of the institutional reforms that are relevant to our discussion, chapters 2 through 4 will concentrate almost entirely on the Democrats. Chapter 2 will consider the motivation for, and the content of, the various reforms enacted from 1970 through 1977. It will also discuss why, if the purpose of the reforms was to strengthen partisanship and leadership, there was little visible evidence of an effect until 1983 and later. Chapter 3 will begin with some theoretical perspectives on the factors that shape members' roll-call vote decisions. Then we will examine in detail the changes in the makeup of the House Democratic party during and after the reform era, and document the growing cohesion within the party on a range of previously divisive issues. This chapter will also consider the revitalization of the Democratic Caucus as an institutional vehicle for influencing policy outcomes.

In chapter 4, we will discuss changes in the Democratic leadership—how each new Speaker from McCormack through Wright was more inclined to exert policy leadership and employ the powers granted through the reforms than was his predecessor. We will also detail the ways in which each of the new leadership powers was employed to advance the Democratic program, with particular emphasis on the speakership of Jim Wright. Chapter 5 will examine the impact of the Republicans—both in the House and in the White House—on the resurgence of partisanship. In particular, we will argue that a shift in the ideological balance among House Republicans toward the conservative end of the spectrum, and the vigorous support for a conservative policy agenda by President Reagan, worked to unite both parties in the House and pit them against one another. The impact of divided partisan control of government on congressional partisanship will also be assessed. The chapter will also discuss some legislative consequences of the combination of the reforms and the increase in partisanship. Finally, in chapter 6 we will summarize our discussion and consider the prospects for House partisanship in the 1990s, with particular attention to the likely impact of the transition in the presidency from Reagan to Bush, and in the speakership from Wright to Foley.

2

Reform and Its
Consequences:
A Closer Look

The development and passage of the reforms adopted by the House from 1970 through 1977 was a complex process. These institutional changes affected almost every facet of the House's operation, and touched a variety of political and personal interests of members. To understand the reform process, we need to look in some detail at the specific changes it made. First, however, we must consider the motives that launched the reform effort.

The Motivations for House Reform

As we noted in the previous chapter, the Democratic Study Group (DSG) was formed in 1959 by a group of liberal Democrats in the House. It was founded because liberals were frustrated at their inability to get legislation they favored passed by the House. The group attempted to provide research on legislative proposals and to coordinate action on bills through a whip system (Sheppard, 1985, pp. 11–12). It was an important base of support for presidential initiatives during the Kennedy-Johnson years, but after the election of Richard Nixon in 1968, the DSG leadership saw the need for new independent action.

After the 1968 election, the Executive Committee of the DSG held a series of meetings to determine the organization's strategy. The discussions were dominated by two considerations: "implementation of the DSG national Democratic program," and "how [to] prevent the entrenched conservative Democrats from acquiescing in the passage of the Nixon Administration's policy."[1] Various ideas were offered about how to accomplish these goals, with much disagreement about them.

Richard Bolling proposed stripping the seniority of Mendel Rivers (D, S.C.), the very conservative chairman of the House Armed Services Committee. The effect of this would have been to remove him as chairman. Others thought, however, that singling out one individual was unlikely to be effective and could result in a backlash. Some members favored a move to replace Speaker John McCormack, but little attention was given to this proposal at the time.[2]

These varied perspectives persisted over the course of a few meetings. Finally, Donald Fraser (D, Minn.) argued that the main problem of liberal Democrats was "that DSG must find some method to make the people who held positions of power—i.e. primarily the chairmen—responsible to rank and file Democrats" (Sheppard, 1985, p. 40). There was unanimity within the group on this view, and unanimous support for Fraser's proposed solution: an automatic secret ballot at the opening of each Congress for all committee chairmanships. In accepting this view, the Executive Committee rejected any radical notion of abolishing the seniority system. "Instead, Fraser simply wanted an instrument of control, an 'up or down' vote on the senior Democratic member of each committee" (Sheppard, 1985, p. 40).

Since the discussions had demonstrated the varied views within the Executive Committee, these DSG leaders decided to canvass the sentiments of the even more diverse membership. They discovered that there was a wide variety of sentiments about the reform proposals, and a remarkable lack of knowledge about current institutional arrangements like the seniority system. It became apparent that even the DSG membership was unprepared for any major changes in the role of the Democratic Caucus, and that any significant reforms would require a great effort to educate the rank and file. Therefore the DSG leadership proposed, and secured the adoption of, a limited first step: monthly meetings of the Democratic Caucus. This move not only provided a potential forum for the discussion of institutional change, but also shifted the focus of any reform effort to the Caucus and away from the House floor, where DSG strength would have been diluted by Republican participation.

Soon after the adoption of the Caucus-meetings proposal, the DSG leadership began its educational effort. In March of 1969 a DSG staff report on House voting on thirty "key votes" in the Ninetieth Congress (1967–68) was circulated to the members. It compared the voting patterns of DSG members, non-DSG Democrats, and Republicans, and concluded that non-DSG Democrats had more in common with the GOP than with their DSG colleagues.[3] The study argued that non-DSG Democrats were responsible for two-thirds of the seventeen Democratic defeats on the key votes, and showed that "one of every three Democratic committee or subcommittee chairmen—42 of 114—voted more often *against* than in support of Democratic programs" (DSG staff, 1969, p. H6749).

The following year, another staff study, which traced the history and operation of the seniority system, was completed and circulated.[4] The report discussed both the pros and cons of the seniority system, but was more forceful on the latter.

> The seniority system has fragmented and diffused power in the House, thereby crippling effective leadership and making it impossible to present and pursue a coherent legislative program. In 60 years' time, the pendulum has swung from one extreme where virtually all power was lodged in one man, the Speaker, to the other extreme where power is scattered among dozens of powerful committee and subcommittee chairmen. (DSG Staff, 1970, p. 5171)

The report also discussed a variety of proposals to alter the system, including the DSG leadership's automatic-vote idea. It is important to note the strong emphasis in both reports on how institutional arrangements worked to frustrate the passage of liberal/Democratic-party legislation. Furthermore, there was nothing secretive about this. Far from seeking to keep these reports as internal DSG documents, Richard Bolling and Donald Fraser inserted them in the *Congressional Record*.

The next step by the reformers was to get the Caucus to create a committee to examine the reform proposals. This move was a tactical device to avoid having reforms linked solely to the DSG. It was accomplished in March of 1970, with the creation of the eleven-member Committee on Organization, Study and Review (known as the Hansen Committee, after its chairman, Julia B. Hansen of Washington).[5] The Hansen Committee drafted proposals dealing with Caucus votes on committee chairmen and with the distribution of subcommittee chairmanships for consideration by the 1971 organizational Democratic Caucus. These proposals, which we will discuss below, launched the succession of Democratic Caucus reforms that transformed the House.

Thus we see that a major impetus for launching the reform effort in the House, as well as a basis on which the reforms were "sold" to members, was the potential to change policy outcomes.[6] The leadership of the DSG, which initiated or articulated the case for most of the changes the Democrats adopted, wanted to create a situation in which liberal policy proposals would win more often. What is more, they told everyone, allies and adversaries alike, that that was what they wanted to do. They believed that their policy preferences were shared by a substantial majority of House Democrats, but that institutional arrangements like the seniority system, which gave committee chairmen power indepen-dent of their party, worked against these common goals. Throughout the early 1970s, the DSG engineered the passage of a wide variety of rules changes, following a number of different reform "tracks," that sought to reverse this perceived institutional bias.

Before turning to a discussion of specific reforms, we should empha-size that the preceding discussion is not an argument for a unidi-mensional explanation of institutional change in the House. Policy mo-tivations were not the *only* reasons for supporting or opposing the re-forms. There was plenty of self-interest of other kinds involved. Some members feared that their electoral fortunes might be adversely af-fected, while others were moved by the ways particular proposals would have an impact on their individual power within the House.[7] Indeed the influence of these other types of self-interest was depended upon by the reformers in some instances to bolster support for particular pro-posals.[8] Rather the contention is only that policy goals were a primary motive among the DSG leaders who proposed, packaged, and mustered support for most reforms, and that these policy goals were an important common ground among rank-and-file members who supported the re-forms, in addition to (or sometimes in spite of) other motivations.

Three Tracks of Reform

Since the process of policy-making in the House is itself so multifaceted, it should not be surprising that institutional changes designed to affect the outcomes of that process are also multifaceted. In this section we will discuss specific reforms, organizing them into three categories: altera-tions in the distribution of committee power, efforts to strengthen the Democratic party, and moves to increase Democratic control of those to whom power is granted.[9] Of course we will see that many reforms over-lap more than one category.

The Powers of Committee Chairmen

The proposals in this category either removed powers from committee chairmen or provided ways for others to restrict the exercise of those that were retained. Most analyses of the reform effort have seen this as-pect as primary, in terms of both cause and effect. As we discussed in the last chapter, these changes were seen as causing the transition to "sub-committee government," leaving the parties even more incapable of pursuing any coherent policy agenda. Yet the DSG effort launched in late 1968, targeted primarily on the committee chairmen, sought to do the reverse—to advance the liberal policies they supported.

The first moves in this direction were not directed at the Democratic Caucus, but instead were part of the Legislative Reorganization Act of 1970.[10] Most of the provisions of the act dealt with efforts to streamline congressional procedures and had no direct policy implications. A few items, however, dealt with the powers of chairmen: the most senior majority member of a committee could preside if the chairman were absent;[11] a committee majority could move for floor consideration of a bill after it was cleared by the Rules Committee if the chairman chose not to do so; and roll-call votes in committee were to be publicly disclosed.[12] Most important for our purposes, however, was the provision dealing with the "recorded teller vote."

Most legislative activity on the House floor, particularly attempts to amend bills, occurs in the "Committee of the Whole" because of the relatively less stringent procedural rules in force (Oleszek, 1989, pp. 144–48, 163–69). But it was impossible to tell how individual members voted on these amendments because House rules barred roll-call votes in the Committee of the Whole. Liberals believed that this arrangement worked against their interests, partly because they had difficulty getting their adherents to the floor for votes, and partly because members were often compelled by committee leaders to support positions they did not really favor.[13] As DSG staff director Conlon said (1982, p. 243), behind the wall of secrecy members were forced "to vote against their districts because the only people who knew how they were voting were the autocratic committee chairmen and their allies who were . . . on the floor with them and who could use their powers to reward and punish accordingly." Liberal and moderate representatives sponsored a successful amendment to the Legislative Reorganization Act to provide for recorded votes on "teller votes" on amendments in the Committee of the Whole, in order to block this aspect of chairmen's influence.[14]

The Caucus-centered reforms began in 1971, when the Hansen Committee made its first set of recommendations, all of which were adopted. They permitted a separate Caucus vote on any committee chairman if requested by ten members.[15] Other provisions limited all Democrats to one subcommittee chairmanship (barring senior members from "stockpiling" them), and guaranteed to every subcommittee chairman the right to hire one staff member. The latter provision was a first step in breaking the chairmen's monopoly over committee resources. On many committees the members had no access to staff without the chairman's permission. This made it more difficult to formulate legislative alternatives to bill provisions favored by the chair. At least sixteen new subcommittee chairmen received their posts because of the limitation rule, many of them relatively junior liberals (Ornstein, 1975, pp. 100–105).

In January of 1973, a much larger step in the limitation of chairmen's power was taken with the adoption of the reform package that came to be known as the "Subcommittee Bill of Rights." Here again, legislative goals were the basis for the proposal, and for DSG support for it. A memo to the DSG from a staff aide to a Democratic member, which outlined the original idea, stated: "A substantial portion of the blame for Congresses' [*sic*] inability to legislate in the public interest is attributable to the fact that too much power rests in the hands of a few men, most notably the committee chairmen" (Sheppard, 1985, p. 99).

Under these rules, committee members would bid in order of seniority for vacant subcommittee slots and for subcommittee chairmanships, rather than leave them to appointment by the committee chairman. Each subcommittee would have a specified jurisdiction, and all bills referred to the committee generally would have to be sent to a specific subcommittee with jurisdiction over the matter. (On some committees, before the reform, subcommittees had only letters rather than names, and chairmen assigned bills anywhere they pleased.) In addition, every subcommittee was guaranteed an adequate budget, and the subcommittee chairman would select *all* of its staff.[16] Thus the ability of a committee chairman to use *arbitrarily* the chair's position to determine a legislative outcome was substantially reduced, as was his or her ability to reward or punish members for their behavior.

The Caucus also strengthened the procedures for voting on committee chairmen. The 1971 rule made a vote possible only if ten members requested. In 1973 the Hansen committee proposed to make votes automatic at the opening of each Congress, and the Caucus added the provision that the vote would be by secret ballot if 20 percent of the members requested. This new rule increased the chances for a successful challenge against a chairman, although the political conditions for such an event were not present until after the 1974 election, which resulted in the election of seventy-five mostly liberal freshman Democrats.

The 1974 freshmen organized their own caucus and invited prospective committee chairmen to address them. These encounters occurred in four closed meetings in early January, "with chairmen answering questions about specific legislative business or grievances about their conduct" (Sheppard, 1985, p. 200). Some made a good impression, while others did not. W. R. Poage (D, Tex.) of Agriculture was evasive in discussing issues like food stamps and school lunches (Sheppard, 1985, p. 200). These issues had long been a source of conflict between Poage and House liberals. He exhibited far less concern than they wished for the problems of the poor.[17] F. Edward Hebert (D, La.) of Armed Services was condescending, referring to the freshmen as "boys and girls"

(Lyons, 1975, p. A2). Hebert and Democratic liberals also had long-standing conflicts over the Vietnam War and defense policy. As Les Aspin (D, Wis.), one of Hebert's committee opponents, said, "It's very hard to object to anything Hebert does on procedural grounds. . . . He's very fair. Of course he can afford to be because he's got the votes. . . . [The] committee thinks its role is to find out what the military wants and then to get it for them" (*CQWR*, Jan. 18, 1975, p. 165).

In subsequent meetings of the Democratic Caucus, challenges were launched against these two chairmen as well as some others. Poage and Hebert were rejected (along with Wright Patman of Texas, chairman of Banking and Currency),[18] and new chairmen were installed in their place by the Caucus. House Democrats had taken the revolutionary step of overriding the seniority system, at least in part because of the divergence in policy views between the committee chairmen and the majority of Democrats.

This was the culmination of one track of the reform effort. The DSG and its supporters had sought to reduce the ability of chairmen to act as a roadblock against legislative outcomes favored by liberals. To accomplish this they attempted to restrict directly the powers of chairmen, and to put in place procedures which would end chairmen's independence from Caucus sentiment. Rules changes like the Subcommittee Bill of Rights accomplished the former, and the actions of 1975 made the latter a reality.[19]

Strengthening the Democratic Party and Its Leadership

A second category of reforms dealt with moves to increase the influence of the Democratic party and its leadership in the policy process. This trend has been recognized in the congressional literature, but until recently it has been perceived as relatively unimportant compared to the "decentralizing" trends of the committee-related reforms. For example, Collie and Brady (1985, p. 275) noted some changes in this category, but said that in "the literature on the institutional character of the recent House, few scholars have discussed the significance of party. Rather, attention has focused on the dispersal of power among an increasingly important but disjointed network of subcommittees."

When this strain of reform did receive attention, it was usually to note its contradictions with the committee changes, and thus the inconsistency or lack of a pattern to the reform effort. Sheppard (1985, p. 211), for example, said that "conflicting criticisms and contradictory goals produced reforms . . . rife with inconsistencies," and Rieselbach (1986, p. 70) termed the various reform trends "incompatible." Yet these changes were offered by the same people as the committee reforms, usually as part of a package. Moreover, the impetus for the two trends stemmed, as we shall see, from similar motives.

One initial move in this category was the creation of the House Democratic Steering and Policy Committee in 1973. DSG members worked on a proposal for such a committee in the summer of 1972, and they saw it potentially as "an Executive Committee of the Caucus" which would function like DSG's own Executive Committee (Sheppard, 1985, pp. 96–97). The leadership and representatives of the membership would meet and shape party positions on policy matters, and then bring them to the Caucus for consideration. In the words of a DSG internal memo on the subject, "We believe the proposed Committee would strengthen the leadership and the role of the Caucus" (Sheppard, 1985, p. 98).

The committee had twenty-four members. Half were elected by the members from geographically defined zones with approximately equal numbers of Democratic representatives. These elected members could serve a maximum of four years, and any zone's representation had to alternate between senior and junior (less than twelve years' service) members. The other twelve members included the three elected party leaders (Speaker, majority leader, and Caucus chairman), the majority whip and four deputy whips, and four others appointed by the Speaker.[20] The rules of the Caucus stated that the committee would "make recommendations regarding party policy, legislative priorities, scheduling of matters for House or Caucus action, and other matters as appropriate to further Democratic programs and policies."[21]

The same year, the Speaker, majority leader, and whip were added (as nonvoting members) to the Committee on Committees (who were the Democrats on Ways and Means), but in 1975 the committee assignment function was transferred to Steering and Policy. Some of the impetus for this shift came from the desire to replace the relatively conservative Ways and Means contingent with a more liberal group,[22] but more important was the desire to strengthen Steering and Policy. As Donald Fraser, sponsor of the move, said, "the whole exercise . . . was to enhance the steering committee's status. Now it amounts to something" (*CQWR*, Dec. 7, 1974, p. 3250). As a result of this change the distribution of perhaps the most valuable "commodity" in the House was moved from a group largely independent of the party leadership to one in which half the votes were controlled by the leadership and its appointees.

Another important move related to committee assignments involved the Rules Committee. In the previous chapter we noted that through the 1950s the conservative coalition often dominated the Rules Committee, and used it to block the passage of liberal-supported legislation.

At the outset of the Kennedy administration, Speaker Rayburn moved against the committee by supporting its enlargement. This permitted the Democrats to make the committee more representative, but the shift was only incremental and it still remained largely independent.[23] In 1975 a more radical change was imposed: the Speaker was given the authority to appoint (with Caucus approval) the chairman and the Democratic members of Rules. With this move, the party leadership was given direct control over what had been one of the most important independent power centers in the House.

In 1974 the House considered a plan for an extensive realignment of its committee system, which had been drawn up by a select committee headed by Richard Bolling.[24] After long conflict, the House adopted an alternative plan offering only modest changes in the system. One element of the adopted plan gave to the Speaker the power to refer bills to more than one committee, either sequentially or simultaneously. The previous rule of single referral had been one of the primary underpinnings of committee power (Collie and Cooper, 1989, pp. 245–46). Now this monopoly power was undermined, and the Speaker's hand was strengthened further in 1977, when he was given the authority to set time limits on each committee's consideration of a bill (Davidson, Oleszek, and Kephart, 1988, p. 5).

The Speaker's control over the flow of legislation was also enhanced by increases (in 1973 and 1977) in the number of days in which the House could consider bills under "suspension of the rules." Under the procedure, debate on a bill is limited to forty minutes, and no amendments are permitted (Sheppard, 1985, p. 102; Bach, 1986a, 1986b). Finally, other moves to strengthen the position of the majority party included Caucus rules which stated that party ratios should be established to create firm working majorities on each committee (suggesting that the *minimum* ratio should be no less than three Democrats for every two Republicans), and that party ratios on subcommittees had to be at least as favorable to Democrats as the ratio on the parent committee. The ability of the leadership to count and corral votes for party programs was also enhanced by an expansion of the whip system (Dodd, 1979).

Thus at the same time the reformers were breaking down the power of committee chairmen and enhancing the role of subcommittees, they were strengthening the hand of the majority party and its leadership. This does not necessarily indicate some schizophrenic impulse on their part, nor that there was one group moving in one direction and another group in the opposite. Rather, we have seen that both tracks of reform were related to the policy motivations of the proponents. The picture will become clearer when we consider the third category of reforms.

Collective Control of Power

The key to understanding the various elements of the reform effort we have been considering is to recall the view offered by Donald Fraser, discussed at the beginning of this chapter, regarding the liberals' main problem. He said that DSG had to find a way "to make the people who held positions of power . . . responsible to rank and file Democrats." Despite the reformers' disagreements regarding other proposals to achieve their policy goals, on this point they achieved unanimity. Action needed to be taken against the committee chairmen not because reformers wanted to undermine the committee system, nor because they wanted to so disperse power that the system was incapable of action. Rather, they wanted to remove the chairmen's capability to frustrate the wishes of a majority of the party. Similarly, only a few reformers like Bolling were willing to place overwhelming power in the hands of the Speaker. Instead most sought to strengthen the party as a collectivity, and to enhance the ability of the leadership to move legislation that had party support.

The underlying theme in both categories of reforms we have examined so far was the protection of the interests of the party majority. One significant way this was done was by adopting mechanisms which put the institutional bases of power in the House under collective party control. Votes on committee chairmen permitted the *Caucus* to judge whether a chairman should continue to serve or should be replaced. And note that this decision was by secret ballot, so that the judgment could be rendered free not only from the influence of the chairmen, but from that of colleagues as well.

Another manifestation of this theme relates to the Subcommittee Bill of Rights. Most discussions of the effects of this package of reforms fail to note that the enhancements of the status of subcommittees and their chairmen were not vested as "property rights," analogous to the pre-reform circumstances of full committees and their chairs. Instead a Democratic party caucus was established for each committee. While committee members could bid for subcommittee slots and chairmanships in order of seniority, the committee caucus could overturn those choices by secret ballot,[25] and they have done so on a number of occasions. Smith and Deering (1984, pp. 197–98) note instances of subcommittee chairmen being voted down, and many of those actions were influenced by contrasting policy views between potential subcommittee chairs and committee Democrats. For example, in 1979 there were three instances (on two committees) in which a more liberal member defeated a more senior colleague. One defeated candidate said, "Members were voting on whether one candidate's views are closer to their own than another's" (Smith and Deering, 1984, p. 198). More recently, Roman Mazzoli of Kentucky was removed from his subcommittee chairmanship on Judiciary in 1989, at least in part because he often voted with committee Republicans (Cohodas, 1989).

Committee caucuses are empowered to set the number, size, and jurisdictions of subcommittees. They can also ratify the selection of subcommittee staff, control the size of budgets granted to subcommittees, and determine whether specific pieces of legislation should be handled by the full committee or the subcommittee with jurisdiction.

Thus the Subcommittee Bill of Rights was not intended to create an atomistic subcommittee structure that merely duplicated on a larger scale the previous independence of party that committees and their chairmen had. Instead a wide range of potential restrictions on subcommittees was part of the original structure of these reforms. The rules changes affecting committees and subcommittees were designed to make both responsible to appropriate groups of Democratic members. As Richard Conlon, the DSG staff director (1982, p. 242), said,

> while the subcommittee bill of rights did enhance the power and prestige of subcommittees and their chairmen, they have far less power than did the prereform committee barons who held power by virtue of seniority alone, were answerable to no one, and for the most part did as they pleased. . . . Today, such arbitrary and obstructive behavior is curbed as a result of the various procedural reforms enacted over the past decade. . . . Committee chairmen and their committees, and subcommittee chairmen and their subcommittees, are given wide latitude, but if they obstruct the will of the majority of Democratic members, there are now means of dealing with such behavior.

Most of the committee-related reforms we have been discussing applied generally to all House committees. However, four committees—Appropriations, Budget, Rules, and Ways and Means—are recognized as more important than the others, and they were the focus of special actions by the reformers in the effort to enhance the collective control of power. For example, on Appropriations, subcommittees had long exercised independence within their areas of jurisdiction, with the full committee often just ratifying their decisions (Fenno, 1966). This made them the most important subcommittees in the House. In light of this, a rule was adopted under which the Democratic Caucus would vote to ratify Appropriations subcommittee chairmen in the same way they voted on full committee chairmen.[26] The chairman of the Budget Committee is elected by the Caucus, just like the holder of a leadership post.[27] We have already noted that the chairman and members of Rules are selected by the Speaker, and that Ways and Means Democrats were stripped of the committee assignment function. Ways and Means was also enlarged by half, to make it more representative of the Caucus, and it was forced to create subcommittees. Finally, Ways and Means and Rules were the targets of a reform in the use of "closed rules."

Most major bills that come to the House floor do so under the provisions of a *special rule,* granted by the Rules Committee, which sets the terms for debate. A closed rule is one that permits no amendments to the bill, and bills from Ways and Means had usually received such rules because committee leaders claimed Ways and Means dealt with policies too complex for legislating on the floor (Manley, 1970, pp. 220–34). Critics, on the other hand, argued that this was just a device to prevent liberals from offering alternatives to the conservative policies it produced. In 1973 the Caucus adopted a rule by which fifty members who wanted to offer a floor amendment could propose it to the Caucus. If a majority of the Caucus voted in favor, the Democrats on the Rules Committee were required to make the amendment in order during floor consideration.[28]

The reforms designed to strengthen the leadership also contained provisions to foster collective control. The Rules Committee nominations by the Speaker required Caucus ratification, as did the Steering and Policy nominations for other committees. In addition, members of the Caucus were permitted to make alternative nominations for Appropriations, Budget, and Ways and Means. Other rules were imposed that moved in the same direction. Caucus meetings could be called not just by the leadership, but also by a petition of fifty members. The closed-rule reform was a potential limit on the Speaker's use of the Rules Committee, and restrictions were imposed by the Caucus on the use of suspension of the rules by the leadership. Finally, the Caucus extended its control over leadership posts themselves by making the chairmanship of the Democratic Congressional Campaign Committee and the party whip elective offices.[29]

House Reform and Member Goals

So we have seen that a wide range of reforms in the House were linked together by a common goal, and by a common theme or approach.[30] The goal was to improve the chances for enacting into law policies favored by a majority of Democrats. The approach was to make people who held power through the party—leaders, committee and subcommittee chairs—responsible to the majority of that party, and to facilitate moving party-supported measures through the legislative process. All three tracks of these reforms were proposed by the same set of people—

the DSG leadership—and they made no secret of the policy motivations behind their actions.[31] The DSG staff studies discussed above made clear that the reformers' target was the opposition to party policies by conservative Democrats who had disproportionate power through seniority and the committee system. DSG leaders argued to their members in favor of the reforms on the basis of their policy effects, and these arguments were hardly secret from non-DSG House Democrats. It is also important to note, however, that the DSG reformers did not target the committee *system* or the seniority *system*, only the unacceptable consequences of each. (Indeed the abolition of the seniority system was explicitly rejected, and the range of its impact was reinforced—see Conlon, 1982, pp. 244–45.) The reformers had a stake in these institutional arrangements. The achievement of certain of their personal goals could be blocked if these systems were undermined.

Some theoretical conceptions of the motives of elective politicians see them as solely interested in the achievement and maintenance of office. Some examples are the spatial models of electoral competition, building on the work of Downs (1957), and the "electoral connection" analysis of Mayhew (1974a), which is explicitly focused on Congress. In some of these studies a single motive is employed for the sake of theoretical tractability (i.e., to make the problem sufficiently manageable that deductions predicting behavior can be arrived at), while in others the authors believe that the assumption is a close approximation of reality. To be sure, election or reelection is a powerful motive for American politicians—probably the most powerful— and it may make sense for theories to focus on it exclusively to see how far they can take us. However, there is a good deal of evidence that indicates that the actual goals of congressmen are more complex than this.

In his study of congressional committees, Fenno (1973) found that members had a variety of goals, including reelection, power in the House, good public policy, and higher office. The first three goals were differentially represented on different types of committees, and the goals that dominated each committee shaped their structure and decision making. Building on Fenno's work, Smith and Deering (1984) found that representatives had multiple motivations for seeking committee assignments (p. 85), and that the types of goals that were most prominent on committees had an important effect on changes in subcommittee orientation after reform (pp. 265–70).

John Kingdon's (1973, 1989) study of representatives' decision processes on roll-call votes offers another perspective on this matter. Kingdon examined the impact of various influences on a member's decision. These included interest groups, the constituency, the administration, party leadership, fellow congressmen, staff, and the member's own attitudes. He found that in about half the cases, representatives perceived no conflict among the influences they saw as relevant,[32] but when there was perceived conflict, the influence that would most often outweigh others pulling in the opposite direction was the member's own attitude (Kingdon, 1973, chap. 10).[33] From this we can infer that for representatives with both reelection and good policy as goals, the two will not often conflict, and that when there is conflict between them, policy commitments can sometimes overcome other influences.

The literature on congressional recruitment and on party activists also provides support for the view that policy preferences motivate some congressmen's behavior. Regarding the former, various studies indicate that policy commitments are one of the most important influences on a candidate's decision to run for office.[34] Other analyses argue that the incentives for members to act as "policy entrepreneurs," who seek to be the dominant spokespersons on an issue and to press legislative solutions related to it, have increased (Uslaner, 1978; Loomis, 1988). One prototypical example of this type of member is Henry Waxman (D, Cal.), who was one of the successful challengers to a subcommittee chairman in 1979 that we discussed earlier. That year Waxman was quoted as saying, "My commitment is not to Congress as an institution, but to the issues that this institution deals with."[35] It is worth noting that Waxman, like many other members, is perceived to be safe from electoral challenge, and is thus free to pursue his policy goals.

Studies of party activists are relevant to our discussion because these are the kinds of people from among whom congressional candidates are drawn. Analyses of activists have long shown that they tend to have stronger and more extreme policy views than rank-and-file party members.[36] Particularly interesting is the recent research on party switching among activists. Kweit (1986), Nesbit (1988), and Kessel, et al. (1989) all show that attitudes on issues are strongly related to party switching, with relatively conservative Democrats tending to switch to the Republicans, and the opposite occurring among liberal Republicans. If ideological motivations exert a powerful influence among party activists, should we not expect to find them operative among members of Congress, most of whom were also party activists before their candidacies were launched?

We should emphasize again that this is not an argument for the primacy or exclusivity of policy goals among representatives. Rather, we assert, with Fenno and others, that policy is one of a number of motivations for members' behavior, virtually absent in some congressmen and powerful in others. Assuming the accuracy of this perspective, and recalling the approach adopted by DSG reformers, it is not surprising that the reforms adopted by the House were not one-dimensional or simplistic. The liberals *had* to strike at the power of committee chairmen, to remove them as roadblocks to policy change. This was partly done by shifting power to subcommittees. There were, as we have noted, electoral and power benefits to the reformers from those changes, but that doesn't make them inconsistent with policy goals. Many DSG Democrats who became subcommittee chairmen used their new positions to try to advance policies they favored.[37] Remember also that subcommittees and their chairmen were constrained by the new rules imposing collective responsibility, just as committee chairmen were.

It is, moreover, difficult to see what plausible alternative there was to increased reliance on subcommittees. Centralizing all power in party leaders was simply inconsistent with the goals of the overwhelming majority of reformers, and would have been even less acceptable to opponents. Members were willing to enhance the leadership's influence over the agenda in order to facilitate moving legislation; they were not prepared to accept a dictatorship of the leadership that made decisions on legislative matters and then commanded the rank and file. The leadership (like the chairmen) was to be responsible to the members, *not* the other way around. The committee and leadership reforms were pursued because they advanced the policy goals of DSG members without significantly undermining their power and reelection interests.

An appropriate term for the goal and approach of the reformers might be *conditional party government.* Unlike in parliamentary systems, party would not be the dominant influence across all issues, and the leadership would not make policy decisions which would receive automatic support from the rank and file. Rather, the direction of influence would be reversed and there would be party responsibility *only if* there were widespread policy agreement among House Democrats. When agreement was present on a matter that was important to party members, the leadership would be expected to use the tools at their disposal (e.g., the Rules Committee, the whip system, etc.) to advance the cause. Chairmen and members on relevant committees would be expected not to be roadblocks to the passage of such legislation. Committee leaders who frequently violated these expectations risked the loss of their positions. Rank-and-file members who frequently opposed the party would be less likely to receive desired committee assignments because of the leader-dominated assignment system.[38]

Note that this characterization includes the expectation that it will not operate equally across issue areas. One obvious reason for this is that agreement among Democrats will vary from issue to issue because of variations in the personal views of members or in the sentiments in their districts. But another, partly related, reason is that there are systematic differences between types of issues and their relevance for intra- and interparty disagreement. Moreover, these different types of issues vary in the ways they tie into the committee system. Some legislation the House deals with is simply trivial. Bach (1988) shows that between the Ninety-seventh and Ninety-ninth Congresses, there was a substantial increase in the proportion of bills passing the House by unanimous consent. This was largely due to an increase in commemorative legislation (e.g., bills designating "National Milk Week" and other similar national observances), which grew from 16.9 percent to 34.8 percent of all measures enacted into law (p. 44, n. 50). Such measures serve to "stroke" certain constituency interests, and are unlikely to provoke disagreement. Members don't really care personally one way or the other, and these bills usually receive no committee attention.

Another category of measures deals with relatively low-cost distributive programs, which provide benefits to a limited number of districts (usually helping members of both parties) without being so expensive as to damage everyone else's interests. Many of the bills considered by a committee like Merchant Marine and Fisheries are of this type. The affected members care a lot (for electoral reasons), and others don't care much at all.[39] Bills from Merchant Marine that became law in the One Hundredth Congress included the approval of a fishery agreement between the U.S. and the Soviet Union and the extension of another with Korea, the authorization of appropriations for the San Francisco Bay Wildlife Refuge, and the delay of regulations relating to sea-turtle conservation. Every one of these bills passed the House by voice vote, indicating that there was little or no controversy about them.

A third category involves programs that affect large numbers of politically active constituents residing in all districts. Examples include veterans' legislation and Social Security benefits. Virtually all members care a lot about such bills, but they are not likely to involve partisan conflict. Indeed, there is likely to be little disagreement of any kind; within broad limits, these constituents will get whatever they want. Among the veterans' bills passed by the House in 1988 were cost-of-living increases for disabled veterans and dependents of deceased veterans covered by various programs; improvements in job-training, counseling, and employment programs for veterans; and improvements in Veterans Administration health-care programs. All three bills passed unanimously on roll-call votes, even though the last two were opposed by President Reagan.[40] Bills in the second and third categories are good candidates for passage by suspension of the rules (with two-thirds support required for passage and no amendments permitted), and Bach's data (1988, table 3) show that suspensions have accounted for an increasing proportion of bills not passed by unanimous consent. All of the bills from the Merchant Marine and Veterans' Affairs committees cited above passed under suspension of the rules.

A final category of issues comprises substantive matters of national import about which there is disagreement in the electorate.[41] Such issues are likely to provoke partisan disagreement in Congress because the partisan electoral system tends to channel conflicting opinion along partisan lines. The kinds of people who become candidates for the two parties are likely to hold different personal orientations regarding desirable governmental action on these issues (as do party activists), and the supporting constituencies of Democrats and Republicans are also likely to have divergent preferences. This type of issue will be an important part of the legislative business of some committees and will fall into the jurisdiction of others with comparative rarity. The prestige committees will frequently deal with these matters: Appropriations, deciding the levels of spending for most federal programs; Budget, setting spending limits that constrain authorizing committees; and Ways and Means, presiding over policy areas like taxation and welfare.[42] Constituency committees like Post Office and Merchant Marine, on the other hand, will seldom deal with bills of this type. Policy committees (e.g., Judiciary, Armed Services, Education, and Labor) will fall somewhere in between, with Commerce perhaps the most important because of its broad jurisdiction (Smith and Deering, 1984, pp. 99–100).

The relevance of this discussion of issues and committees to our analysis of partisanship and reform is twofold. First, it is clear that a significant proportion of the House's legislative business involves matters about which there is little disagreement. Bach's (1988) analysis indicates, moreover, that the proportion of bills involving such issues is growing. This will place a limit on the amount of partisanship we should expect to see, both generally and particularly in floor-voting statistics.[43] (It also suggests that we should approach gingerly the comparison of voting data from different historical eras.) Second, the variation in types of issues across committees implies that the interests of policy-oriented Democratic reformers should have been more focused on some committees than on others.[44] This was true, as we have seen, in the passage of the reforms, when the four prestige committees were singled out for special regulation.[45] The analysis in chapters 3 and 4 will show that it was also true in the application of the reforms and the pursuit of the goals that lay behind them.

In this section we have discussed the goals of representatives and how they were related to the reform effort.[46] We argued that liberal policy goals provided the major impetus for institutional change, but that reformers had other interests as well. They chose the particular approach to reform because it could advance their policy goals without impeding the achievement of their electoral and power goals. The result, which we have termed *conditional party government*, was intended to foster strong partisan action on behalf of policies on which there was Democratic consensus. Members who held power through the party were expected to advance these legislative goals, and those who failed to do so risked the imposition of sanctions through the collective control mechanisms created by the reforms. There is, however, an obvious question to raise in response to this discussion. If the reform effort had the motivation and approach we have outlined, then why was not the late 1970s a time of strong leadership and party voting among House Democrats?

The Gradual Impact of Reform

There are three main reasons for the apparent lack of stronger partisanship in the years after reform. They relate to the degree of Democratic homogeneity, a narrow conception of strong leadership among analysts, and the particular people in the Democratic leadership.

Democratic Party Homogeneity

Democratic homogeneity will be the main focus of the next chapter, so we will offer only a brief discussion here. During the reform years and for some time thereafter, House Democrats were deeply divided on many policy matters. The DSG may have represented a majority of Democrats, but it didn't speak for all of them, nor for a majority of the House on most issues. Divisions along seniority lines were precisely the impetus for the committee-oriented reforms. The seniority split was mainly due, as the research on declining party voting showed, to North-South divisions over policy. While regional disagreement on civil rights issues declined during the 1970s (Sinclair, 1982, chap. 7), conflict on other matters—for example, government management of the economy and foreign and defense policy—increased (Sinclair, 1981a, 1981b, 1982). Moreover, new issues arose which produced more than just sectional divisions. "Energy, environmental and consumer issues, and foreign and defense policy questions split not just North from South in the Democratic party; they also frequently divide northern Democrats" (Sinclair, 1981b, p. 184).[47]

These divisions meant that on most issues there would not be a party consensus, and so the basis for conditional party responsibility would often not be present. Consequently, when the Democratic Party leaders did try to exert policy leadership in such circumstances (e.g., in support of President Carter's programs), they frequently met failure (Rohde and

Shepsle, 1987, pp. 123–27). It was not until the 1980s that sufficient Democratic consensus emerged on a wide range of issues so that significant visible partisan effects resulted.

Conceptions of Strong Party Leadership

We have seen that many analysts had concluded that the effect of the reforms was to render effective party leadership difficult if not impossible. These conclusions seem, however, to be based on a narrow conception of strong leadership. Specifically, these analyses seem to employ what might be termed the "Boss" model of leadership, shaped by the Reed-Cannon years. In this view, strong leaders dominate their members and use their institutional powers to ride roughshod over opposition both within and outside their parties. Since this kind of dominant leadership was not produced by the reforms (even the ones that purportedly increased leadership powers), the conclusion was reached that reform maintained weak leadership or made things worse. And because researchers correctly concluded that today's individualistic members would never accept such domination, the implication followed that it was unlikely we would see strong leadership in the future. For example, Sheppard (1985, p. 234) said that the Steering and Policy Committee was almost unanimously pronounced a "flop," partly because the members who were elected by the Caucus were "not necessarily disposed to defer to the leadership." And Rieselbach (1982, p. 199) argued that "subcommittee autonomy . . . suggests that structural change has produced more fragmentation than centralization. Party leaders simply cannot impose their preferences on independent subcommittees."

But the "Boss" model is not the only possibility for strong leadership. To be sure, the reformers were not prepared "to defer to the leadership" or to have the leaders "impose their preferences," as may have been true under Reed and Cannon. But if a party has sufficient common ground on issues, it may create strong leaders to act as its agents in pursuing the party's legislative agenda.[48] Such leaders do not command or control the mass of the membership (although they may seek to do so to marginal individuals who can make the difference between winning and losing). Instead the leaders use powers granted to them by the members to accomplish goals they hold in common. The members sacrifice a *limited* amount of their independence to the leaders, because the commonality of preferences ensures that most members would only rarely be pressured to take an action they do not prefer.

This perspective grows out of a line of research which argued that context largely determines leadership powers. That is, instead of strong party leaders being the cause of high party cohesion, cohesive parties are the main precondition for strong leadership. Conversely, members will not accept powerful leaders acting against or in the absence of party homogeneity. For example, in his study of Speaker Cannon and Rules chairman Smith, Jones (1968) argued that the House took action against them because they had lost touch with their procedural (i.e., party) majorities in pursuing substantive ends. Such behavior "is contextually inappropriate because it violates the bargaining condition in the House" (p. 618). In a later discussion of leadership under reform, Jones (1982, p. 118) said, "The key to understanding legislative leadership lies in the membership, not in the leaders."

Cooper and Brady (1981) explicitly argued that "leadership style" was based on context, which they saw as including both member support and leaders' powers. Institutional context, rather than personal traits, primarily determines leadership style in the House. To be sure, style

> is affected by personal traits. Nonetheless, style is and must be responsive to and congruent with both the inducements available to leaders and member expectations regarding proper behavior. . . . Thus, if Rayburn was a more permissive and consensual leader than Cannon or Reed, this is not because he was inherently a less tough or more affective person, but rather because of his weaker sources of leverage and the heightened individualism of members. (p. 423)

Building on the Cooper-Brady analysis, Rohde and Shepsle (1987) discussed the interrelationship of institutional arrangements regarding leaders' powers, follower coherence or homogeneity, and the strategies leaders pursue.

> The degree of follower coherence is determined in large measure by outside forces. Within the context of a given set of preferences, leadership strategies and the structure of rules are adjusted. When there is a high degree of homogeneity of preferences, party leaders tend to be granted significant central control to pursue the common objectives (e.g., Reed and Cannon), and the leaders vigorously use the tools they have been granted. As preference homogeneity declines, institutional arrangements tend to be altered again to reduce the capacity of leadership for independent forceful action, and leaders tend to respond with caretaker, housekeeping strategies (e.g., Democratic leadership circa 1930–1970). [pp. 122–23]

Thus the mix of preferences in a party's membership is shaped by electoral forces. This mix largely determines the types of powers the party leaders are given, although there may well be a time lag between significant changes in the party's membership and correspondingly large changes in the rules. The rules changes may also occur over a period of time, as in the reform era we have been discussing. Member preferences can also, in turn, be affected by the character of the rules, albeit to a lesser degree. That is, if the leaders or some party institution have the ability to distribute rewards or punishments based on party loyalty, then members (especially those on the fringes of the party) may well exhibit more loyalty than would otherwise be the case. If, on the other hand, the party has no such mechanism, party loyalty will probably be lower. As Cooper and Brady (1981, p. 417) argued in their discussion of the transition in the House from hierarchy to bargaining, "If it is true that factionalism in the party system led to the decline in party control mechanisms, it is also true that the decline of these mechanisms had the further effect of allowing party factionalism greater expression." Member preferences and institutional rules then interact to shape leadership behavior.

Given the logic of this argument, and the mixed-goal membership we have posited, we would certainly not expect a recurrence of "Boss rule" in the House. It is, however, perfectly plausible for policy-oriented party members, given sufficient agreement on policy goals, to endow their leaders with significant powers that can be employed to achieve those goals.[49] Strong leaders are still possible in an era of individualistic members, but the collective membership becomes "the Boss."

Changing Leader Orientations

The analyses of leadership we have been discussing place little import on individual characteristics of leaders in explaining leadership style or power. The quotation from Cooper and Brady above indicates their view that Rayburn was more permissive and consensual than Cannon because he had weaker powers and a more individualistic membership, not because of personal traits. In turn, they make a parallel argument comparing O'Neill and Rayburn: "Thus, given his sources of leverage in the formal and party systems, O'Neill has little choice but to adopt a leadership style that in many key respects is similar to Rayburn's" (1981, p. 424). Indeed, they contend (p. 423) that "the personal traits of leaders are themselves shaped by the character of the House as a political institution at particular points in time through the impact of socialization and selection processes that enforce prevailing norms."

Yet it seems on further examination that this perspective, while basically correct, is not quite complete. We have already endorsed the view that membership homogeneity largely determines leader power, and that the two in turn largely determine leader style. However, the discussion of these forces in the House during the period from Cannon to O'Neill sees them largely as *constraints* on leader style. That is, a fractionalized membership and declining powers kept leaders from being as powerful as they might have wanted to be. But it seems possible that these forces would operate asymmetrically in an era when homogeneity and powers were expanding. Greater agreement and stronger powers may not be as effective a *positive* inducement to leader action, compared to the limiting effects of the reverse situation encouraging leader inaction.

It will be difficult to compel a leader to exercise powers he didn't want in the first place. Moreover, even if such powers are employed to some degree, lack of enthusiasm or vigor in their use will surely limit their impact. The membership's only recourse in such a case would be to depose the leader, a messy prospect to say the least. Such action would likely be taken only if the deviation from members' expectations were extreme. Thus a divided membership and weak powers may be sufficient conditions to produce a restrained and consensual leadership. On the other hand, a relatively homogeneous party membership and enhanced sources of institutional leverage may be *necessary* conditions to produce a strong leader, but they may not be *sufficient*. It is likely that an additional necessary condition is that the leader, at least to some degree, must *want* to exercise his powers and be influential. Therefore increases in homogeneity and leader powers may not produce any immediate effect on leader style. It may take time, either through replacement when old leaders step down or through the adjustment of the attitudes of continuing leaders.

Moreover, even the replacement of the top leader may have limited immediate effect. While we would agree with Cooper and Brady's assertion, cited above, that the character of the House shapes the personal traits of leaders through selection processes and norms, the pattern of leadership succession that operates in the House may delay the impact of the selection process. Each of the last twelve Speakers had previously served as his party's majority or minority leader.[50] So even if a new Speaker comes to power, it is likely that he was chosen into the leadership in response to a set of member expectations and goals that existed some time before, and which may be different from those that are operative at the time of the succession.

We will discuss changes in the orientations of Speakers from the reform era to the present in chapter 4, so we will only note at this point that there appears to be good reason to believe that circumstances were consistent with this discussion. As Roger Davidson said (1988, p. 357), regarding the reforms that were designed to strengthen the party and its leadership,

> Speaker John McCormack (1962–1971) resisted most of the changes; his successor, Carl Albert (1971–1977), who mediated between the barons and the reformers, was a transitional figure who hesitated to use the tools newly granted to him by the rules changes. Thomas P. O'Neill (1977–1986), a moderate reformer in his earlier years, moved cautiously into the brave new world.

Each successive Speaker was more positively disposed to the reforms, and more inclined to use the powers they granted. O'Neill's successor, James Wright, was selected into the leadership after the reform process was completed (1976), and became Speaker after the party's homogeneity had greatly increased (1987). He was, as we will see, quite familiar with the Speaker's expanded powers, and was prepared to employ them vigorously.

Summary

In this section we have offered three reasons for the gap between the passage of the reforms and any evidence of a substantial effect in terms of increased partisanship. In the process we have discussed some theoretical conceptions of the relationship between party members and their leaders that will structure the presentation in subsequent chapters. We have argued that one principal reason for the delayed effects was policy divisions within the Democratic party. As homogeneity of preferences increased, party leadership became more vigorous and party cohesion in voting increased. Second, we have contended that analysts' conceptions of strong leadership have often been too limited. In effect, parties and leaders were gradually getting stronger, but we weren't noticing because we were thinking of influential leaders in terms of the "Boss" mold. Finally, we have argued that limited powers and party homogeneity may be enough to prevent a leader from being powerful, but increases in both may not be sufficient to produce stronger leaders. That will also probably require some positive commitment on the part of the leader. Based on these perspectives, we can now turn to a discussion of evidence and events, beginning with a consideration of changes in the Democratic Caucus, both as a collection of members and as a part of the institutional structure.

3

The Democratic Caucus: Membership Change and Organizational Developments

The House Democratic Caucus may be thought of in two ways. First, it is the set of Democratic members of the House, and so we can consider it from the point of view of changing party membership and shifting policy preferences over time. Second, it is an institutional arrangement, a device for taking collective action by the party. In this context, we can discuss Caucus decision making, as in the analysis of reforms in previous chapters. In this chapter, we will consider the Caucus from both perspectives. Since, however, a good portion of the evidence presented will deal with roll-call data, some theoretical matters related to House voting must be considered first.

Some Perspectives on Roll-Call Voting

Goals and Preferences

We have argued that representatives have a variety of goals, and that the relative importance of them varies from member to member, and, for a single representative, from subject to subject.[1] Some congressmen will care personally about policy outcomes on a number of issues, while others will almost never have such concerns. Particular representatives may see all decisions in terms of how their chances of reelection are affected; others (either because they feel electorally safe or because other goals are more powerful) may rarely be influenced by worries about potential defeat. Variations in member goals will mean that the forces that influence their preferences regarding roll-call voting alternatives will also vary.[2]

40

Given this perspective, it is useful to make a distinction between *personal* preferences and *operative* preferences. By the former we mean the legislator's own views on the alternatives available for choice—what he or she would choose if no other influences were present. The latter term refers to the preferences that actually govern the voting choice, when all the other forces pressuring the member in one direction or the other are taken into account. Within this classification, the other influences on representatives' voting decisions (in addition to their own attitudes), such as the constituency, interest groups, or party leaders, can be thought of as potential inducements to a legislator to adopt operative preferences that are different from personal ones.

The inclination of a member to depart from his or her personal preferences will depend on the relative importance of various goals and on the circumstances involved in the particular decision. If reelection is the sole or primary goal for a member, then a conflict between personal preferences and strong constituency desires will likely result in constituency wishes being followed. If, on the other hand, a representative's chief goal is good policy, he or she will be less likely to adopt operative preferences that are different from personal ones. Finally, a member who wants power within the House may feel relatively little pressure from constituency demands, but may be more likely to comply with the wishes of party members or leaders. Viewing the matter across issues, matters on which the electorate has strong and well-articulated views will find any member paying more attention to reelection interests, while more obscure or technical decisions will place greater emphasis on policy and power goals.

The relative importance of different goals to a congressman is not fixed over time, but it is surely more stable than the variation across members.[3] Hence the replacement of one representative with another can often yield significant differences in voting behavior, particularly if it also involves a shift in party representation.[4] The nature and relevance of influences on members' preferences can also change. If, for example, party control of the presidency shifts, the ways in which the president's desires can affect voting decisions will also change for most members. Given a shift from Democratic to Republican control of the presidency, we would expect Republican congressmen to become more responsive to presidential preferences, and Democrats less so. To take another case, the reduction of the powers of committee chairmen would limit their ability to distribute rewards and to impose sanctions on other members, and thereby to influence the shape of legislation under their jurisdiction. We would expect, therefore, that the inclination of other representatives to defer to the preferences of those chairmen would decline.

Members' constituencies are particularly important influences on their preferences. Most of the research we discussed in chapter 1 saw constituencies as geographic entities, with their regional location being a particularly important consideration.[5] Here, however, we must take note of another focus (characterized by Fiorina, 1974, and Fenno, 1978) that viewed constituencies in more complex terms. Fiorina conceived of constituencies as either heterogeneous or homogeneous on issues, and argued that these types have different implications for members' behavior. In particular, his analysis showed that members from homogeneous districts are constrained to support the constituency position, while those in heterogeneous districts tend to have more options. Fenno argued that within a particular congressional district, there are different types of constituencies (termed *geographic, reelection, primary,* and *personal*), nested like concentric circles. He showed that members have differing relationships with the various types of constituencies, which in turn have differing effects on their behavior.

These analyses offer a number of insights relevant to our discussion. Using Fiorina's characterization, if district opinion moves from homogeneity to heterogeneity, then it may become less constraining to a member who holds personal preferences different from the majority view (especially if good policy is an important goal). Drawing on Fenno, we can see that two districts that appear similar from one perspective may be very different from another. Two members of the same party may both represent similar reelection constituencies, but one may have a homogeneous primary constituency while the other's may be heterogeneous. This may lead them to respond differently on the same issue. Moreover, one aspect of a constituency may change over time while another aspect remains undisturbed. For example, both parties' constituencies within a particular district may be heterogeneous at one point. However, voter sentiments may realign themselves over time, with the more conservative Democrats becoming Republican and the more liberal members of the GOP moving in the opposite direction. This could happen, moreover, without any change in the district-wide distribution of preferences. As a result, both partisan constituencies would be more homogeneous and more distinct from each other, while the geographic constituency retained its previous character. Each party within a district would tend to recruit congressional candidates who were representative of its homogeneous preferences, thus consistently offering the voters divergent alternatives in district elections.

So as representatives make voting choices, they will encounter various influences that pressure them to make decisions that are different from their own preferences, or that reinforce those preferences. How much impact each influence has will vary from member to member, depending on his or her goals. The impact of these influences will also vary over time, as the institutional bases of power are altered or as political circumstances change. The most important influence on a representative is his or her constituency, and the degree of consensus or conflict within each type of constituency within the district will have a profound effect on behavior.

Variable Agendas

Goals and preferences are not the only factors that influence voting patterns.[6] The nature of the agendas from which choices are made is also important. In the analysis of legislative voting, the term *agenda* has two meanings. One refers to the issues that are considered. Thus in her study of voting alignments in the House, Sinclair (1982, p. 3) said, "By the political agenda, we mean the set of problems and policy proposals being seriously debated." The other meaning of *agenda* refers to the kinds of votes taken and the determination of the specific alternatives for choice. It concerns things like whether a particular amendment may be offered, or the order in which votes will be taken, etc. For example, Ferejohn, Fiorina, and McKelvey (1987, p. 170) wrote, "We think of an *agenda* as a set of alternatives together with a rule that specifies the way in which votes are taken." While the two meanings are related, one might say that they deal respectively with the "substance" and the "mechanics" of voting.

For the purposes of analyzing and interpreting congressional voting patterns, one important consideration regarding the agenda (in both meanings) is that the alternatives are themselves endogenous. That is, the choices of what issues members will consider and what particular votes they will face are determined by the members themselves, although those choices are shaped by the same kinds of considerations that govern voting decisions. Not only do the operative preferences of members govern choices among alternatives on the floor; subsets of members and *their* operative preferences determine the nature of those alternatives. The subsets will include party leaders, committee and subcommittee members and their leaders, ideological factions, the proponents of individual amendments, etc. Because floor choices are dependent in part on the nature of the alternatives, changes in the processes by which alternatives are generated may lead to shifts in voting patterns (e.g., levels of partisanship) even if the distribution of operative preferences on the issue is unaltered. Thus decreases in the power of committee leaders or increases in the influence of party leaders, as targeted by the reforms of the 1970s, have a great potential to affect partisanship not only because they can shape the preferences of members on the floor, but because they can also have an impact on the alternatives from among which those members choose. The distinction between types of preferences and their relevance to shaping the agenda also implies that if members' personal and operative preferences might lead to different decisions in a particular instance, it would be in their interest to try to shape the agenda to avoid being faced with such a choice. We will return to this matter in the next chapter.

Another relevant point about the agenda is that not only will preferences and alternatives on an issue change over time, so also may the frequency with which votes are taken on that issue. The saliency of an issue to members, to voters, and to other outside forces is variable. In one Congress members may cast many votes on a "hot" issue, while in other years they will face few or none. An example of this is the drug issue, which gave rise to many votes in the One Hundredth Congress (1987–88), while there were comparatively few in previous ones. If the distribution of preferences and the character of alternatives all differ from issue to issue,[7] then variations in the number of votes on a given issue will have implications for the patterns of partisanship in voting over a number of Congresses. If, moreover, the number of votes on each issue fluctuates, then the set of all votes within a Congress has an even more variable character. In one Congress the voting agenda may be numerically dominated by one group of issues, and in a subsequent Congress another group may be predominant. These variations could lead to quite different levels of party voting.

This discussion should make it clear that because voting choices are the product of a member's own preferences, the influences that pressure the member to depart from those preferences, and the nature of the alternatives, interpretations of congressional voting over time must take into account all of these factors. For example, if partisanship in voting is low in one Congress and then higher in a later one, the change might be due to nothing more than votes on partisan issues being rare in the former and frequent in the latter. Alternatively, the mix of issues may not change, but the mix of types of votes may, as in the case of the rules change regarding recorded teller votes. If amendments provoke different voting patterns compared to, say, the passage of legislation, then aggregate levels of partisanship may vary simply because there are relatively more amendments voted on at one time than at another. Congressional voting, both individually and in the aggregate, is a response to an agenda. If agendas vary, it is likely that the character of voting coalitions will also. Therefore we cannot infer merely from changes in voting patterns that members' preferences (either personal or operative) have changed. Such conclusions can be justified only to the degree that the different aspects of the agenda have been controlled for.[8] With these ideas about preferences and agendas in mind, we can now turn to consider evidence regarding variations in the diversity of policy views among House Democrats.

Variations in Homogeneity among House Democrats

Changing Factionalism

As we noted earlier, in the years leading up to the House reforms Democrats faced factional divisions within their party, particularly between northerners and southerners. Indeed these divisions were a major cause of the reform effort. After reform, the party's factional divisions first became more complex, then declined in importance as the bases of divisions were worked out. In this section we will discuss a number of the most important factions, and then turn to evidence of increasing homogeneity within the party.

Southern Democrats and Boll Weevils. The sectional rift has been the most consequential source of intraparty division for Democrats since the Second World War. Disagreements became more pronounced with the increased prominence of issues like social-welfare policy, civil rights, and the Vietnam War during the 1960s (Sinclair, 1982), and these issues continued to be divisive into the reform era. During this period, fewer and fewer southern Democrats exhibited high levels of party loyalty, as figure 3.1 shows. Southerners were placed into two categories based on their party-unity scores:[9] Those who voted with the party less than half the time (scores from 0 to 49), and those with scores of 70 or higher. (Members with intermediate scores are not portrayed in the figure.) Figure 3.1 shows the proportion of all southern Democrats in each category from the Eighty-fourth through the One Hundredth Congress. The proportion of party opponents was low but rising until the Eighty-ninth Congress, when it took a large jump to 46 percent in response to the Johnson administration agenda. This percentage continued to increase through the Ninety-second Congress, the first reform Congress, and then began a steady decline. The proportion of loyalist southerners provides the mirror image of these figures. By the One Hundredth Congress, 70 percent of southern Democrats were loyalists and only 5 percent were party opponents, compared to 14 and 62 percent, respectively, in the Ninety-second Congress.[10]

These data show clearly that even before the Reagan era, and following the period of reform, the proportion of southern Democrats who were supportive of Democratic party positions was growing. The sectional division within the party was becoming muted. This was particu-

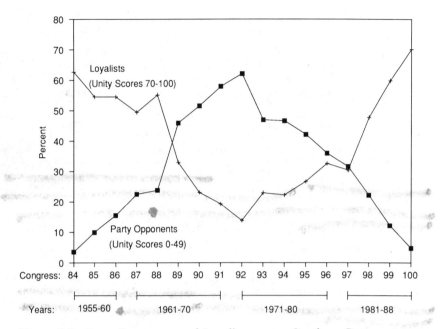

Figure 3.1 Party Opponents and Loyalists among Southern Democrats, 84th–100th Congresses

larly due to electoral changes which reduced the pressures on members from the South to oppose their northern colleagues. One involved passage of the Voting Rights Act of 1965, which enfranchised many black voters who consistently voted for Democratic candidates. Meanwhile the issue disagreements mentioned above drove a wedge between northern and southern Democratic voters, making the Republican party an increasingly attractive alternative for the more conservative southerners. As black voters came into the Democratic party in the South, and as conservative whites departed, the party became more liberal.

Employing the theoretical concepts of Fiorina and Fenno, we can say that southern Democratic constituencies became less homogeneously conservative. Then, over time, both primary and reelection constituencies of southern Democrats became more similar to the corresponding constituencies of their northern colleagues. More similar constituencies led to more similarity in voting behavior. Moreover, these changes, plus the party switching from Democrat to Republican of conservative activists and officeholders, affected the kinds of candidates who were recruited to run for the House under the Democratic banner in the South. Conservatives were more and more likely to choose to run in the Re-

North vs. South Dems

publican party. Relatively liberal candidates, on the other hand, found increasing success when they sought Democratic House nominations. Thus we would expect that not only the operative preferences but also the personal preferences of northern and southern Democratic representatives were becoming more similar.[1] These electoral developments facilitated greater sectional agreement on matters like civil rights, defense, and the budget, as we will see below.

As the numerical strength of conservative Democrats decreased, and as the electoral potency of the Republican party in the South grew, the remaining conservatives became more and more frustrated. They felt that their voice was being ignored within the party. After the 1980 election, thirty-three of these members (almost all southerners) formed the Conservative Democratic Forum (CDF). Their purpose was to pressure the Democratic leadership to consider their views and to provide conservatives with better committee assignments. Charles Stenholm (D, Tex.), the Forum's leader, said, "Conservatives among the House Democrats have been ignored for too long, and we now mean to moderate the liberal leanings of the House leadership" (*New York Times,* Nov. 21, 1980, p. A21). Stenholm even threatened to run against O'Neill for Speaker.

Realizing that the Democrats' reduced numbers (they lost 33 seats in 1980, down to 243) meant that every vote would be important if they wanted to counter Reagan's initiatives, the leadership tried to accommodate the CDF (which became popularly known as the "Boll Weevils"). O'Neill agreed to expand the Steering and Policy Committee, and appointed three CDF members to new slots. Forum members also received appointments to Budget, to Appropriations, and to Energy and Commerce (Cohen, 1981, p. 190). Some liberals were not pleased, but Stenholm and his supporters thought they got no more than their due. Unfortunately for the leadership, these moves did not "buy" sufficient loyalty from the Boll Weevils, and the conservative Democrats provided enough votes for the Republicans to achieve victory on tax and budget votes in 1981 and 1982. The party's response to these defections is discussed later in this chapter. After the 1982 and 1984 elections, when there were few southerners who fell to Republican challenges, some CDF members became more loyal to the party or left the group entirely. It is likely that they no longer felt the electoral threat that led them to join in the first place. *Threat from white constituencies?*

So changes in electoral influences permitted southern Democrats to find more common ground with northerners. (As we shall see, changes among northerners facilitated this too.) Many southern Democrats are now quite similar in outlook to their party colleagues (in terms of both personal and operative preferences), although there still remains a significant minority who are—due to electoral pressures and personal outlooks—a good deal more conservative.

New Breed Northerners. Another major division that emerged in the party after the reform years was within the northern wing. A loosely defined group of younger members—variously labeled "New Breed Democrats," "Neoliberals," "Atari Democrats," or "Watergate Babies"—argued for alternatives to traditional liberal positions. Most were elected between 1974 and 1978, but they quickly sought a larger voice in directing the party in the House.[12] "A sampling of their political catechism includes the stated intention to be fiscally responsible though compassionate toward those most in need of government aid. They express an eagerness to work with business as well as labor to reach broad national goals and a willingness to make political compromises in the spirit of participatory democracy" (Cohen, 1983, p. 1328). Led by members like Richard Gephardt (D, Mo.), Tony Coelho (D, Cal.), and Tim Wirth (D, Colo.), these Democrats sought innovations in economic policy, and were more accepting of stronger defense positions than most traditional liberals.

One view that caused friction with other (especially more senior) northerners was their disinclination to endorse traditional Democratic social-welfare programs, often on efficiency grounds. As James Blanchard (D, Mich.), a member of the class of 1974, said, "Clearly we don't think of ourselves as New Dealers—at all—or proponents of the Great Society either. The question is, how can we best deliver services, and limit our objectives to what we do best" (*New York Times*, Apr. 1, 1979, p. 50).

The discussion of budget policies below will illustrate how active these members were on the issue. They first organized opposition to the leadership's positions, then served as a catalyst for significant compromises within the party, providing the basis for a Democratic budget after the defeats of the first Reagan Congress. New Breed members were also ambitious. A number (like Blanchard and Wirth) successfully sought higher office,[13] while others, like Coelho, Gephardt, and Leon Panetta (D, Cal.), achieved House leadership posts.[14]

Traditional Liberals. This group of Democrats dominated outcomes in the House during the Eighty-ninth Congress, after the party's landslide victory in the 1964 elections, and they later provided most of the votes for the reform effort. Their numerical peak came with the election of the class of 1974. After that the developments described above reduced their share of Democratic seats, and economic and budget pressures prevented them from passing new initiatives that reflected their preference for a large, activist federal government. Ironically this occurred as the committee reforms were transferring power to liberals, especially by giving them access to subcommittee chairmanships (Ornstein, 1975). This frustrated liberals, and that feeling was compounded by Reagan-administration efforts to block new programs and to reverse many of their successes from earlier decades. "It's disappointing and frustrating. We're not doing what we ought to be doing," said Henry Waxman (D, Cal.). "The liberal agenda is fighting to keep what we have" (*CQWR*, Aug. 9, 1986, p. 1797).

Voters' concerns about the economy, antagonism toward bureaucracy, and vehement opposition to most tax increases helped to give the term *liberal* a pejorative connotation. Republicans used it as a bludgeon against opponents (recall George Bush's tarring Michael Dukakis with the "*L* word" in 1988), and most Democrats avoided it. Rep. Thomas Downey (D, N.Y.) said, "I don't know anyone who, like me, comes from a marginal district who calls himself a liberal. . . . Liberals have been associated with unpopular causes, like busing, and mushy thinking" (*CQWR*, Aug. 9, 1986, pp. 1797, 1800).

On the other hand, as frustrating as it may have been, being on the defensive provided liberals with an easier task than passing new programs would have. It was less difficult for them to persuade their moderate and conservative colleagues of the virtues of programs that were already operating and providing benefits to their constituents. Nor was it entirely impossible to pass new programs. For example, conservatives and moderate Democrats on the Budget Committee in 1986 supported liberal efforts to expand funding for some antipoverty programs focused on children.[15] Moreover, as preference homogeneity within the Caucus increased, liberals found the balance of party opinion tilting more in their direction on important issues like defense and foreign policy, albeit not as much as they would have liked.[16]

The Deficit-Conscious Class of '82. Strictly speaking, a "class" elected in a given year is not a faction, for the latter is defined by members voluntarily connected by shared attitudes or behavior. Yet the cohesion of Democrats who were first elected in 1982 on a single issue—reducing the budget deficit—and their size,[17] plus their importance for understanding increasing Democratic cohesion, justify discussion of them here.

The negative attitude of these members toward deficits did not imply a common conservative orientation on other issues. Indeed, many of them held liberal positions on other matters, and saw deficit reduction not as an end in itself, but as a prerequisite to launching new initiatives. "Our goal," said James Cooper (D, Tenn.), "is to reduce deficits *now* so we can afford the programs we need in the future" (Calmes, 1986b, p. 1269).

New Breed Democrats had already increased the saliency of the deficit in the party, but the class of '82 provided the numbers to do something about it, or at least to put some weight behind new approaches. For example, when the conference report containing the Gramm-Rudman-Hollings budget-reduction plan came to the floor in 1985, 65 percent of the class supported it while a majority of Democrats were voting nay. In 1984, class member Buddy MacKay (D, Fla.) sponsored a plan for a budget freeze. (MacKay chaired a budget study group comprised mostly of members of the class.) A leadership aide called the idea "unthinkable" at the time, and it was soundly defeated, but thirty-one of eighty Democratic aye votes were cast by members of the class (Calmes, 1986b, p. 1271).

Given their more liberal orientation on other issues, the members of the class of 1982 were important in another way: they were the block to further progress on Reagan's agenda and they shattered the pivotal role of the Boll Weevils. When Reagan first won election, the House contained 192 Republicans and 243 Democrats, of whom 47 were members of the CDF.[18] If the Republicans voted as a bloc,[19] slightly more than half of the Forum's members would guarantee a majority on the House floor. Every CDF vote over that would compensate for the defection of a moderate Republican. With the election of 1982, on the other hand, Republican strength declined to 166 seats while CDF membership fell. Even after the 1984 elections, with Republicans rebounding to 182 seats and with thirty-five Boll Weevils, *unanimous* agreement of the two groups alone would not produce the 218 votes needed for a House majority. As a consequence, more and more efforts to find a policy position that could win on the floor took place *within* the Democratic party.

Thus between the end of the reform years and the latter part of the Reagan presidency, factional change within the Democratic party in the House, coupled with variations in other relevant political circumstances, provided the basis for greater Democratic cohesion.[20] The balance of operative preferences among House Democrats shifted away from positions favored by southern conservatives and those desired by traditional liberals, and toward a common ground between.

The Resurgence of Democratic Cohesion

The data on Democratic party-unity scores presented in chapter 1 showed some evidence of the ebb and flow of agreement in the party. But party-unity votes encompass only a portion of the record votes taken in a Congress, and a varying portion at that. A more broadly based picture of the degree of homogeneity in voting responses among

Democrats can be had from the data in figure 3.2, which shows average party cohesion[21] on both party-unity and non–party-unity votes in the Eighty-fourth through the One Hundredth Congresses, with consensual votes excluded.[22]

Cohesion increased a bit with the transition from Eisenhower to Kennedy, then declined sharply during the Johnson presidency and Nixon's first term. It is striking to note that while cohesion was generally higher on party-unity votes until the Eighty-ninth Congress, from the Ninetieth through the Ninety-fifth it was lower on those votes. That means that the same votes that divided Democrats from Republicans were also most likely to divide Democrats from each other. After the Ninety-fifth Congress, cohesion began to increase, particularly on party-unity votes, and by the Ninety-seventh, cohesion on unity votes surpassed the level for other votes. The gap continued to widen in succeeding Congresses. In the Ninety-ninth Congress, Democratic cohesion on party-unity votes surpassed the highest level achieved in any previous Congress in the series (reaching 72 points), and it rose even higher in the One Hundredth.

So there is strong evidence of increasing homogeneity in voting responses among Democrats, but recalling the theoretical discussion ear-

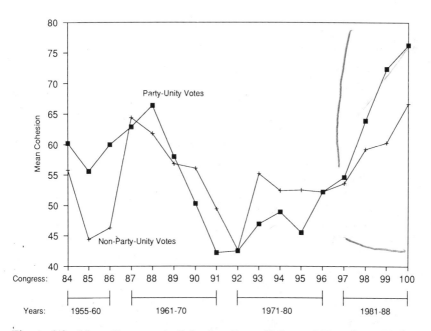

Figure 3.2   Mean Democratic Cohesion, Party-Unity and Non–Party-Unity Votes (Consensual Votes Excluded): 84th–100th Congresses

Table 3.1 Average Democratic Cohesion in the House, by Issue 84th–100th Congresses (Consensual Votes Excluded)

		Issues				
		Appropriations		Non-Appropriations		
Congress	Procedural Housekeeping	Foreign/ Defense	Domestic[a]	Foreign/ Defense	Domestic	All Votes
84	77 (8)[b]	59 (6)	65 (3)	48 (17)	59 (75)	58(109)
85	88 (4)	49 (9)	45 (28)	52 (27)	51 (88)	51(156)
86	78 (4)	25 (4)	59 (18)	53 (21)	55(100)	55(147)
87	88 (4)	55 (13)	51 (15)	68 (33)	64(110)	63(175)
88	72 (12)	64 (16)	74 (18)	62 (23)	63(100)	65(169)
89	56 (25)	63 (16)	67 (24)	62 (22)	55(177)	58(264)
90	52 (29)	43 (9)	54 (45)	51 (36)	54(189)	53(308)
91	43 (21)	28 (10)	40 (39)	32 (51)	54(150)	46(271)
92	55 (28)	31 (20)	39 (64)	31 (73)	46(244)	43(429)
93	61 (56)	40 (38)	48(100)	45(116)	53(440)	51(750)
94	61 (42)	32 (44)	50(110)	42(113)	53(603)	50(912)
95	70 (49)	37 (71)	42(121)	42(140)	51(593)	48(974)
96	68 (81)	40 (44)	44(124)	47(152)	54(479)	52(880)
97	83 (27)	37 (22)	58(122)	42(103)	56(261)	54(535)
98	88 (36)	42 (22)	63(143)	47(164)	70(268)	63(633)
99	91(124)	51 (13)	64(144)	60(184)	69(245)	69(710)
100	94(115)	73 (17)	70(118)	66(189)	73(240)	74(679)

[a]Includes omnibus and aggregate continuing and supplemental appropriations.
[b]The numbers in parentheses are the number of votes of that type.

lier in the chapter, one must wonder whether these changes could be merely the consequence of shifts in the mix of issues or types of votes, rather than a real change in the pattern of members' responses. While any full-scale analysis of this matter would require far more space than is available here, it is both possible and necessary to present a brief consideration.[23]

Table 3.1 presents average Democratic cohesion scores by Congress, with the votes broken down into a set of broad issue areas. Issues were divided into legislative and procedural/"housekeeping" categories.[24] Within the former group, votes were categorized as either foreign affairs/defense or domestic issues, and then each of those was broken down into appropriations and nonappropriations subsets. This yields five issue categories.

The first thing to note is the substantial variation over time in the number of votes in each category, as well as overall. The total number of record votes in each Congress varied from a low of 147 in the Eighty-fourth Congress to a high of 1,540 in the Ninety-fifth. The largest part of this increase came after the adoption of recorded teller voting (1971) and electronic voting (1973), which are discussed below. Before 1981, substantive (i.e., nonappropriations) domestic matters accounted for between 54 and 69 percent of the record votes (consensual votes excluded). In the Reagan years this declined to 35 percent by the One Hundredth Congress. Thus there is a significant potential for this changing mix to produce a differential impact on the overall cohesion scores. However, while there are notable differences in the Democratic cohesion level across categories that persist from Congress to Congress, examination of each category over time leaves the same basic picture that we have already noted.[25] Cohesion tends to be comparatively high in the earlier Congresses, drops substantially in the Johnson-Nixon-Ford years, is fairly stable under Carter, then increases substantially under Reagan.

Another perspective on the agenda is afforded by table 3.2, which presents the cohesion data broken down by the type of vote to which members are asked to respond. Four categories are used: passage by suspension of the rules (requiring a two-thirds vote), regular passage

Table 3.2 Average Democratic Cohesion in the House, by Type of Vote, 84th–100th Congresses (Consensual Votes Excluded)

	Type of Vote				
Congress	Regular Passage	Suspensions	Amendments	Procedural	All Votes
84	61 (45)[a]	63 (8)	58 (14)	55 (42)	58(109)
85	54 (55)	66 (8)	42 (29)	52 (64)	51(156)
86	58 (65)	76 (5)	47 (19)	53 (58)	55(147)
87	65 (92)	63 (11)	47 (16)	65 (56)	63(175)
88	65 (83)	53 (8)	45 (10)	70 (68)	65(169)
89	62(117)	56 (4)	36 (28)	59(115)	58(264)
90	58(134)	34 (3)	38 (37)	53(134)	53(308)
91	52(119)	49 (17)	39 (26)	41(109)	46(271)
92	52(133)	46 (29)	36(187)	41 (80)	43(429)
93	64(197)	54 (48)	42(348)	54(157)	51(750)
94	61(255)	52 (58)	42(407)	54(192)	50(912)
95	60(228)	58 (88)	39(473)	54(185)	48(974)
96	64(222)	58 (50)	42(421)	61(187)	52(880)
97	60(128)	68 (47)	43(236)	64(124)	54(535)
98	69(135)	73 (45)	51(291)	75(162)	63(633)
99	73(125)	69 (29)	56(307)	83(249)	69(710)
100	77(113)	70 (35)	61(288)	88(243)	74(679)

[a]The numbers in parentheses are the number of votes of that type.

(all final passage actions other than suspensions), votes on amendments, and procedural votes. Again there is considerable variation over time in the number of votes in each category, but the largest change is the enormous increase in votes on amendments between the Ninety-first and the Ninety-third Congresses (from 26 to 348). This was due to the change to recorded teller voting (permitting record votes on amendments in the Committee of the Whole), and to electronic voting, which made it feasible to increase substantially the number of record votes taken on the House floor. Before electronic voting, a roll call would take forty-five minutes or even more, while the new system usually took fifteen minutes, and when there was a series of votes to be taken together the limit could be reduced to five minutes.

Until the change in voting procedures, the lion's share of votes tended to be either passage or procedural, and Democratic cohesion in those categories tended to be similar. By the Ninety-third Congress, cohesion jumped sharply for procedural and passage votes, but the large increase in the number of amendment votes (where cohesion was consistently lower) made the overall increase smaller than might otherwise have been the case. Cohesion levels were then fairly stable until the Carter-Reagan years, when there was a deliberate attempt to reduce the amount of time spent voting, and so the total number of votes taken was reduced significantly.[26] In the Ninety-eighth through the One Hundredth Congresses, we again see the sharp increases in cohesion previously noted exhibited across all categories. The size of the increase does vary somewhat, but perhaps most striking is the fact that the overall increase of 20 points between the Ninety-seventh and One Hundredth Congresses is virtually matched by the increase on amendments, always the most divisive set.

So in looking at cohesion and variations in the agenda from two points of view, we do see in the data that at any point in time there are significant variations in the cohesion level across issues and across types of votes. These are worth exploring further in future research. The important point for the purpose of this analysis is that within the limits of the data presented, it is clear that the increase in Democratic cohesion since the reform era is not solely due to changes in the types of votes taken. We find growing cohesion exhibited across issue areas and across vote types. The operative preferences of House Democrats have become more homogeneous, leading to greater similarity of voting responses.[27]

Frequent reference has been made to previous research that indicated the sectional basis of policy divisions within the Democratic party. The discussion of factions in the preceding section argued that the electoral base of southern Democrats had changed, becoming more similar to that of their northern colleagues. Has this led to greater similarity in voting responses? Is the increasing Democratic homogeneity in voting due in significant part to a decline in sectional differences? One would expect so from the data on southern party opponents and loyalists presented in figure 3.1, and this expectation is confirmed by the sectional comparison of Democratic party-unity scores in figure 3.3.

The party-unity data show that while there is some variation over time in the scores of northern Democrats, that variation is dwarfed by the changes among southerners. Average unity among northern Democrats peaked at 94 percent in the Eighty-eighth Congress (during which the Kennedy-Johnson transition took place), declined to a low of 81 percent in the Ninety-fifth, and then climbed back to 91 percent in the One Hundredth Congress. Thus the range of variation was only 12 points. Party unity among southerners was around 70 percent until the Eighty-ninth Congress (after Johnson's landslide election), then dropped precipitously to the Ninety-second Congress low of 46 percent. Thus in 1971–72, the *average* southern Democrat supported his or her party less than half the time on those votes that divided party majorities. From that point on, southern unity began a gradual increase until it peaked at 76 percent in the One Hundredth Congress. The difference

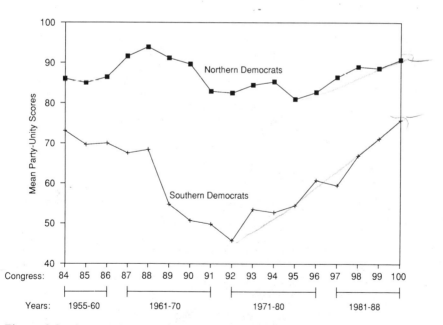

Figure 3.3 Average Party-Unity Scores, Northern and Southern Democrats: 84th–100th Congresses

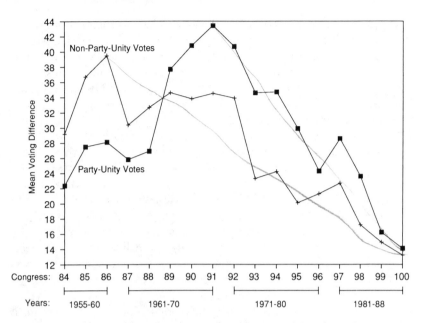

Figure 3.4   Mean Differences between Northern and Southern Democrats, Party-Unity and Non–Party-Unity Votes (Consensual Votes Excluded): 84th–100th Congresses

in average party unity between northern and southern Democrats was as great as 39 points (in the Ninetieth Congress); by 1987–88 it was down to only 15 points.

A broader picture of changing sectional disagreement can be had by considering it from a vote-by-vote point of view. Figure 3.4 shows the average absolute difference in the percentage of northern and southern Democrats voting aye on both party-unity and nonunity votes in each Congress. Through the Eighty-eighth Congress, the mean difference was stable on party-unity votes, then it increased sharply through Nixon's first term. On nonunity votes there was an increase under Eisenhower, a decrease under Kennedy, and then little variation through the Ninety-second Congress. From the "Great Society" years until recently, sectional intraparty disagreement was markedly *higher* on party-unity votes than on others. Beginning with the Ninety-third Congress (1973–74), sectional differences on votes of both kinds began a steady decline. By the Ninety-ninth Congress the mean difference had fallen to 16 points on party-unity votes (a decline of 25 points since the Ninety-first), and there was only 1 percentage point separating the two types of votes. Thus during the period from the mid-1960s through the 1970s, when the Congress confronted the issues of civil rights, the Vietnam War, and growing federal deficits, Democratic sectional divisions were high, and were greater on votes that divided the parties. From the mid-1970s the average sectional difference declined to low levels in both categories. The sectional split within the Democratic party, while not entirely gone, has diminished considerably in importance, and this is primarily due to changes in the responses of southerners.

The interplay between electoral and nonelectoral factors underlying the resurgence of partisanship among southern Democrats can be seen in table 3.3. It shows the average party-unity scores for southerners who were members of the One Hundredth Congress in each Congress they served in from the Ninety-fourth on, controlling for the class with which they were first elected.[28] From this we can trace changes in average party unity for the same people over time, and also detect differences among groups entering Congress at different times. The data reveal that there are clear and persistent differences among entering classes. In particular, the classes of 1976 and 1980 exhibit average scores considerably lower than those of the classes around them, and these differences are present in each Congress of which the classes were a part. The variations among classes spring at least in part from contrasts among the districts represented, and they may also be due to differences in the personal preferences of members. One can also see that, with the exception of the most senior cohort, the later classes tend to be somewhat more loyal than the earlier ones.

Looking at each class over time, on the other hand, we again see in every case the pattern of increasing loyalty. From the Ninety-fifth Congress through the One Hundredth, in every cohort the average unity in consecutive Congresses is equal or greater in the later one. (The data

Table 3.3 Average Party Unity of Southern Democrats, Who Were Members of the 100th Congress, in the 94th–100th Congresses, by Entering Class

Congress	1986 (N=9)	1984 (N=5)	1982 (N=18)	1980 (N=6)	1978 (N=10)	1976 (N=6)	1974 (N=7)	1972 and before (N=23)
94	—	—	—	—	—	—	56	57
95	—	—	—	—	—	42	55	59
96	—	—	—	—	62	51	63	65
97	—	—	—	48	64	51	64	66
98	—	—	71	54	65	59	67	73
99	—	76	72	57	69	64	68	76
100	79	80	77	60	74	65	74	81

also show that the increase in loyalty is not just a Reagan-administration phenomenon. The increase in the pre-Reagan years is substantial, although the later increase is somewhat larger.) This clearly demonstrates that the growth of loyalty among southerners is not due only to changes in membership. One partial explanation for this pattern is the change in preferences among Democratic constituents in southern districts described above, which would operate similarly across districts, leading members to change their responses on particular issues over time. Other explanations would include agenda change in the sense of variations in the substance of the alternatives put forward by the two parties on particular issues, and changes in the incentive structure which would have encouraged southerners to exhibit greater loyalty. Variations in responses to issues and shifts in the incentive structure will be dealt with later in this chapter; consideration of changes in the nature of alternatives will be found in succeeding chapters.

The analysis in this section has demonstrated that there has been a considerable increase in Democratic unity and cohesion since the reform years, that this increase is not merely an artifact of variations in the types of votes taken, and that most of the increase stems from a substantial decline in the sectional divisions among Democrats.[29] One should not conclude from this that House Democrats have become united on everything. In the Ninety-ninth and One Hundredth Congresses, Democratic cohesion was below 10 points on between 3 and 4 percent of the nonconsensual votes.[30] On most of those votes, northern and southern Democrats were divided. Still, Democratic representatives have shown greater homogeneity on a wider range of issues than most analysts would have believed possible a decade ago.

Some Specific Issue Perspectives

The discussion of changes in the behavior of Democrats has, to this point, dealt largely with aggregate voting statistics. We will now seek to enrich that description and get a better understanding of the changes through a brief look at the substance of policy-making in three important issue areas.[31]

Racial Issues

Probably the most striking change in responses to issues among Democrats has involved racial matters. The civil rights revolution drove a sharp wedge into the Democratic party. During the 1960s, legislative efforts to support school desegregation in the South or to guarantee civil rights for blacks tended to receive strong support from northern

Democrats and strong opposition from southerners. Republicans, virtually all of whom were northerners, tended to support these initiatives (Carmines and Stimson, 1989, pp. 163–64). During the 1970s, racial issues (except for busing) became less prominent legislatively, but on those that did occur, behavioral patterns began to shift. In both the House and the Senate, Republican support for the liberal position on race-related votes declined, and Democratic support increased (Carmines and Stimson, 1989). The North-South Democratic split decreased as southerners who were more supportive of civil rights replaced conservative predecessors. These new Democrats, along with their remaining senior colleagues, were responding to the more liberalized constituencies produced by the Voting Rights Act and partisan realignment.[32]

During the 1980s there were comparatively few race-related matters on the floor, but when they did arise they exhibited the new alignments. One example was the extension of the Voting Rights Act in 1981. When the bill came to the House floor, five weakening amendments were offered—all by Republicans. All five were defeated. Three received majority support from Republican members, but not one received a majority of southern Democrats' votes. Indeed, the largest number of southern Democrats to vote for any amendment was 26 (with 49 against), and their average support for the five amendments was 15 votes. On final passage the vote among southern Democrats was 71 to 6 in favor.[33]

A more recent issue, which mixed racial politics and foreign policy, involved attempts to impose economic sanctions on South Africa because of its system of apartheid. In 1985 the House passed, over President Reagan's strong objections, a sanctions bill. It received a strong negative vote from Republicans, but southern Democrats voted aye 73 to 6. In 1986, the House overrode the president's veto of a sanctions bill (with southern Democrats supporting the effort 69 to 4). Then in 1988 the House approved an even stronger set of sanctions with Democrats united in favor 220 to 10 (southerners voted aye 66 to 7).[34] Republicans charged, regarding the 1988 bill, that it sought to exploit the issue for domestic political advantage (CQWR, Aug. 13, 1988, p. 2294). This was unquestionably true, but what was remarkable was that southern as well as northern Democrats saw it as working to their political advantage.

A final and particularly vivid example involved the congressional effort to overturn the 1984 Supreme Court decision in *Grove City v. Bell.* In that case, the Court ruled that the application of a set of four civil rights laws which were linked to federal aid programs was limited only to the specific programs receiving aid and did not extend to the entire institution (such as a whole school). This was a drastic reversal of what was previously thought to be the reach of the laws, and liberals very much wanted to alter the interpretation. These efforts were blocked by President Reagan's opposition while the Senate was still in Republican hands, but in the One Hundredth Congress a bill was passed. The bill was vigorously opposed by the Moral Majority, and Reagan decided to veto it. In his veto message, the president said that the proposed law "would vastly and unjustifiably expand the power of the federal government over the decisions and affairs of private organizations . . ." (*CQWR*, Mar. 28, 1988, p. 774). The House overrode the veto with only eight votes to spare. Despite the racial issue, despite the continued popularity of the president in the South, and despite his couching his opposition in terms of increased federal power, Reagan was unable to persuade many southern Democrats. They opposed him 73 to 9. Clearly southern Democrats had come to believe that, even in extreme cases, supporting the liberal side on civil rights matters was the position favored by their constituencies. The issue that had once been the most divisive between northern and southern Democrats produced division no longer.

The Budget and Deficits

The support of Boll Weevil Democrats permitted President Reagan to win his stunning budget victories in 1981, but Democratic divisions over budget issues predated the Reagan presidency, and they were not only sectional in nature. The discussion of Democratic factions above noted that New Breed Democrats shared a concern about fiscal responsibility. In 1980 five of their number who were members of the Budget Committee refused to sign the conference report on the budget resolution, and then helped to lead a successful effort to defeat it on the House floor (*CQWR*, May 31, 1980, pp. 1459–60). Then in 1981, the initial Reagan successes occurred. A majority of southern Democrats supported the Republican substitute on the budget resolution offered by Delbert Latta (R, Ohio), and twenty-six southern defectors provided the victory margin on Latta's amendments to the reconciliation bill, which provided for reductions in appropriations for a wide range of domestic programs. (The details of these votes are included in table 3.4, which lists all "key votes" on the budget from 1981 through 1988.)[35] The following year Reagan's support began to waver, as House members exhibited concern about the size of the deficit. House Republicans repudiated the president's budget and passed their own alternative, with members of the Conservative Democratic Forum giving them enough votes to win.

The arrival of the class of 1982 provided the shift in votes the Democratic party needed to gain control in the budget conflict. Thirty south-

Table 3.4 Key Votes on Budget Issues, 1981–1988

Key Votes	Vote	Rep.	All Dem.	North. Dem.	South. Dem.
1981					
Latta substitute on budget targets	273-176	190-0	63-176	17-144	46-32
Latta amendments on reconciliation	217-211	188-2	29-209	3-157	26-52
1982					
Latta substitute for the president's budget	220-207	174-15	46-192	9-151	37-41
1983					
Adoption of first concurrent resolution	229-196	4-160	225-36	168-6	57-30
1984					
Adoption of the first concurrent resolution	250-168	21-139	229-29	159-13	70-16
1985					
Latta amendment on reconciliation	209-219	166-15	43-204	15-151	28-53
House version of Gramm-Rudman-Hollings	249-180	1-178	248-2	167-2	81-0
1986					
Latta substitute on budget resolution	145-280	145-32	0-248	0-166	0-82
Adoption of budget resolution	245-179	17-160	228-19	154-11	74-8
1987					
Democratic budget plan	230-192	0-173	230-19	159-10	71-9
Budget reconciliation	206-205	1-164	205-41	143-21	62-20
1988					
Budget resolution	319-102	92-78	227-24	152-17	75-7

ern Democrats defected in 1983 in the vote on the budget resolution, about the same number as in previous years, but with most northern Democrats and new moderate southerners supporting the party, this wasn't enough to give the Republicans another success. That resolution, which restored many of the domestic-programs cuts made in the last Congress, received the support of fifty-two of the fifty-seven freshmen Democrats (Calmes, 1986b, p. 1271). Despite this level of support, members of the class were not automatic votes for the leadership, and their commitment to reducing the deficit was real and determined. In November of 1983, twenty-four freshmen joined the Republicans and some of their senior colleagues in sending down to defeat (203 to 206) a continuing appropriations resolution intended to provide funds for government agencies whose regular appropriations hadn't cleared. Majority Leader Wright was livid and Speaker O'Neill referred to the freshmen as "kind of ridiculous," but the freshmen believed their symbolic gesture was useful. One of them, Jim Moody (D, Wis.), said, "We were elected on economic issues, and the deficit is both the symptom and symbol of the perilous economic drift this administration and Congress finds itself in" (*CQWR*, Nov. 12, 1983, p. 2348).

In subsequent years, Democratic agreement on budget issues continued to build. In 1984 the southern margin in favor of the party's budget resolution grew to 70 to 16. Despite the president's landslide re-election and Republican House gains in the 1984 election, the Republicans' version of reconciliation in 1985 (to bring appropriations in line with the budget) failed narrowly, and southerners unanimously supported the House Democrats' version of the Gramm-Rudman-Hollings deficit-reduction plan. Then in 1986, not a single Democrat supported Latta's substitute on the budget resolution, and southerners voted for the Democratic alternative on final passage 74 to 8.

The growing Democratic cohesion on the budget had a number of sources. The shift in the numerical balance in the House was important, as was the reduction of disagreement on defense issues, which will be discussed in the next section. President Reagan had marshaled significant support from moderate and conservative Democrats for cuts in domestic programs, but by this time many of them had indicated that those cuts had gone far enough. For example, even G. V. "Sonny" Montgomery (D, Miss.), the prodefense chairman of the Veterans' Affairs Committee, said of Reagan's budget proposals, "You can't raise military spending as much as he wants and cut these other [domestic] programs" (*CQWR*, Apr. 26, 1986, p. 910). Most important of all, however, was the widespread agreement among more junior Democrats that deficit reduction had to be a top priority.

These factors came together in 1986 as the budget resolution was shaped.[36] Junior members of the budget committee (almost all elected in 1978 or later) devised a plan to reduce spending by dividing cuts equally between defense and domestic programs, shielding some social programs from any cuts, and increasing revenues for the sole purpose of cutting the deficit more than the amount required by Gramm-Rudman-Hollings. The initiative to use additional revenues to cut the deficit came from Marvin Leath (D, Tex.), a CDF member in his first term on the committee, and two members of the class of 1982, MacKay of Florida and Jim Slattery (D, Kan.). The plan was first opposed by the party leadership, but was endorsed by William Gray (D, Pa.), the Budget chairman who was first elected to the House in 1978. Even though he was a hawkish member of the Armed Services Committee, Leath supported the defense cuts as the price for reining in the deficit, and sold the plan to other southerners on that basis. This in turn secured liberal agreement for the domestic-program reductions. As Budget member Mike Lowery (D, Wash.) said, "The reason I'm for this budget is that it's got this defense number down. . . . To do that, I'm willing to take some real tough votes on the domestic side." Thus the various party factions had common ground on which to stand, producing the overwhelming margin on the final vote.

This widespread Democratic agreement persisted into the One Hundredth Congress. In 1987 only nineteen Democratic members dissented on the budget resolution, and the Democrats' intraparty compromise on reconciliation survived the defection of a number of their colleagues at both ends of the spectrum.[37] The Democrats' cohesion led President Reagan to agree to a budget summit with representatives of Congress in November of 1986 to resolve that year's conflict, and their agreement served as the basis for the 1988 budget resolution, the first such measure with bipartisan support in the decade.

Defense Policy

Since the Vietnam War, defense matters were a source of division within the Democratic party. The war split northerners from southerners, and northerners among themselves. After American withdrawal from Vietnam, those divisions persisted in disagreements over the amount of defense spending, the desirability of various weapons systems, and efforts to control the arms race with the Soviet Union. During the postreform period, the conservative-dominated Armed Services Committee generally proposed more defense spending than liberals wanted, but their efforts to make changes on the floor usually failed. From 1975 through 1981 (the first Reagan defense budget), the vote on passage of the House version of the defense procurement bill was overwhelmingly positive, as it ratified the committee's judgments. There were never more than sixty-seven negative votes, and virtually all of these came from northern Democrats.[38]

Over the next four years, committee and floor sentiments on defense began to change. As the discussion of budget politics indicated, the pressure of the deficit compelled the Congress to choose between defense and domestic programs, and more Democrats were favoring restriction of the former to avoid further cuts in the latter. Furthermore, members were more and more willing to use the amendment process (Smith, 1989) to modify the committee's judgments on the floor. During the debate on the defense authorization bill in 1985 (for fiscal 1986), the House adopted 165 amendments, although few of them made major changes (*CQWR*, June 29, 1985, p. 1262). Between 1982 and 1985, the floor coalitions on the passage of the defense bill showed a change from previous years; liberals who thought there was too much for defense and voted nay were joined by growing numbers of conservative Republicans who thought there was too little. In 1985, for example, sixty-four Republicans and forty-two Democrats opposed passage.

Then in 1986 the balance tipped further. Not only did the House adopt a significant reduction in budget authority for defense in the fiscal 1987 authorization bill (11 percent below Reagan's request), but it also passed five amendments that opposed important elements of the president's program.[39] They barred nuclear tests above one kiloton, cut funding for the Strategic Defense Initiative (SDI) by 40 percent, continued a moratorium on the testing of antisatellite missiles, prohibited deployment of any weapons that would violate certain limits in the unratified SALT II treaty, and banned production of binary chemical weapons for a year. On four of the five amendments (all except chemical weapons), a majority of southern Democrats voted with their northern colleagues. A substantial majority of them (56 to 19) also supported the cut in budget authority. Indeed, on twenty-five proposed amendments on which a majority of Republicans voted in opposition to a majority of northern Democrats, a majority of southern Democrats supported the northerners fourteen times. Contrast this with voting on the fiscal 1982 bill, when on the twelve similarly contested amendments, southern and northern Democrats did not vote together even once. On final passage, while a heavy majority of Republicans opposed the bill, only seven Democrats voted nay.

Defense policy had become a partisan issue, and no longer was a majority of southern Democrats ready to side automatically with the president on specific defense questions. The 1986 debate showed that southerners were not only interested in the amount of defense spending and its implications for other parts of the budget. A majority of them were also concerned about particular arms-control issues, and were willing to restrict the president's freedom of action regarding them. Similar conflicts like those in 1986 occurred during the defense debates of the One Hundredth Congress. A number of amendments backed by the Democrats passed on the floor, and defense spending was held well below the level desired by Reagan and Republican conservatives. In 1987 and 1988, the House majority leadership took a more active and aggressive role in the defense debate,[40] and on final passage in both years Democrats voted strongly in favor and Republicans were strongly opposed.[41] Upon passage of the bill in 1987, Armed Services chairman Les Aspin made a comment that could have applied equally to the year before or the year after: "It's becoming a much more Democratic defense bill" (*CQWR*, May 23, 1987, p. 1066).

Thus on three important and previously divisive issues, House Democrats had found positions that a wide range of members could support. The basis for the old sectional conflict on racial issues disappeared as the constituencies of southern Democrats changed. This change also permitted or facilitated the shifts among southerners on budget and defense questions. It is important to note that on these two latter issues, the proposals that secured majority support from both northern and southern Democrats tended to be ones that were not 100 percent satisfactory to either liberal or conservative proponents. Rather, they tended to be middle-ground proposals that a less divided Caucus found sufficiently attractive to support. In the rest of the chapter, we will discuss how the growing homogeneity on policy affected the institutional role of the Democratic Caucus.

The Changing Role of the Democratic Caucus

As the description of the reforms of the 1970s showed, the Democratic Caucus is not only the set of all House Democrats. It is also an institutional structure capable of taking collective action, and it has existed since 1796. When the Democrats took control of the House after the revolt against Speaker Cannon, the Caucus (which for decades has done little more than select party leaders) became the principal device for party rule. It was the domination of the Speaker that was the target of the revolt, not party responsibility.

During this period (dubbed the era of "King Caucus" by Republicans), the core of Caucus influence was its ability to impose a common position on all Democrats in floor voting. With a few exceptions, a two-thirds vote in the Caucus in favor of a position required all party members to support it.[42] The Caucus also dominated the committee system. It was at this time that the committee assignment function was vested in the Democratic members of Ways and Means, subject to Caucus approval. "The caucus often controlled the committees by forbidding reports on other than specified subjects, or by other than specified committees, without its express consent; by issuing instructions to the Rules Committee as to the terms of special rules under which bills could be taken up in the House; and even by developing legislation in the caucus itself and bringing it to the floor after formal committee reference" (Galloway and Wise, 1976, p. 173).

Another centralizing force was the decision to make the chairman of Ways and Means the majority floor leader (Cooper and Brady, 1981, p. 416). The floor leader thus combined the resources of a major committee chair and influence over colleagues' committee assignments with his right to be recognized at any time. He used this right to control the conduct of business in the House (Galloway and Wise, 1976, p. 173). The dominance of the Democratic Caucus, however, lasted for only about a decade. By 1920, policy conflicts had so divided the Democrats that the use of the Caucus for policy purposes began to decline. They had, moreover, lost control of the House, and the Republicans did not employ their caucus in that role. By the time the Democrats won back control, the Caucus had again been relegated solely to the task of selecting party leaders.

The stage was set for a resurgence of the Caucus when (in 1968) DSG leaders saw it as a potential vehicle for institutional reform, and sought more frequent meetings in order to prepare the way. Speaker McCormack and Majority Leader Albert were initially opposed to the idea (Sheppard, 1985, p. 42). However, a delegation from DSG persuaded them, and the party leaders agreed to support the proposal (regular monthly meetings, plus additional meetings that could be called by petition of fifty members) if it could be presented as their plan.

Until 1975, the Caucus largely confined its activities to matters of procedural reform. But with the large influx of new activist members in the Watergate landslide, and after the rejection of the three committee chairmen, more members began to see it as a place for considering policy matters.[43] In March of 1975 junior liberals petitioned for a special meeting of the Caucus, and on a 189 to 49 vote the group adopted a resolution proposed by freshman Bob Carr (D, Mich.) that opposed new military aid to South Vietnam and Cambodia. Earlier the Caucus had employed the reform permitting it to block closed rules by voting to instruct the Rules Committee to allow floor votes on two amendments dealing with the oil depletion allowance.

These ventures into policy matters bothered a number of members, particularly senior ones. Some liberals supported the idea of Caucus involvement with policy, but worried about it going too far. Thomas Foley (D, Wash.), then chairman of the Agriculture Committee, said that the Caucus could "function properly as a gun behind the door to ensure that committees let members consider issues they want considered."[44] But Henry Reuss (D, Wis.), chairman of Banking and Currency, said if the Caucus "started pronouncing on all substantive matters, especially before the committees considered the matters, the caucus would then be intruding on the jurisdictions of committees." Some liberals were particularly concerned that events like these would further strain party unity. Not surprisingly, conservatives were more negative, and they sought to rein in the group by proposing that Caucus meetings be opened to the press and public. Joe Waggoner (D, La.), a leader of the conservative faction, said, "We don't really like sunshine for the caucus, but we've got to stop this damn caucus from legislating" (*CQWR*, May 3, 1975, p. 911). Republicans were also critical, charging that "King Caucus" had returned, and that Democrats were riding roughshod over minority rights.

In September of 1975 the open-meetings proposal was adopted by the Caucus, supported by a coalition of conservatives and liberals who supported open meetings as a matter of principle. At the same meeting, the Caucus rule that permitted a two-thirds majority to bind all party members was repealed. The device had been used only once in recent memory, on a 1971 vote repealing a House rule that gave Republicans one-third of all committee staff (*CQWR*, Sept. 13, 1975, p. 1956).

Because of the open-meetings rule and the disagreements about the desirability of involvement with policy matters, the Caucus again began to fall into disuse. In April of 1978 the Caucus (over leadership and Carter-administration opposition) passed a resolution urging Ways and Means to report legislation that would roll back a scheduled increase in Social Security taxes, the first legislative stand in three years (*CQWR*, Apr. 15, 1978, p. 868). Speaker O'Neill and Majority Leader Wright also were negative about Caucus policy involvement. Barbara Sinclair summarized their views as follows (1983, p. 94): "During the Carter administration the leaders preferred not to use the caucus because they believed it to be unpredictable, because they feared it might limit their flexibility on important matters, and because they believed superior instruments [e.g., the Steering and Policy Committee] were available to them." For all these reasons, the Caucus became inactive, and members generally didn't attend. There were thirty-nine meetings called during the Ninety-fifth and Ninety-sixth Congresses (1977–81), and only five achieved a quorum (Malbin, 1981, p. 1642).

Caucus activity began another turnaround after the election of Ronald Reagan. The principal reason was the selection of Gillis Long (D, La.) as Caucus chairman late in 1980. A moderate Democrat who was a member of the Rules Committee and was close to Speaker O'Neill, Long had run on a platform of reviving the Caucus. "Long said his goals were three-fold: to unify the party, make the caucus an active forum for setting Democratic policies and strategies on major questions, and make House Democrats a more important force in the Democratic national party" (Granat, 1983, p. 2115). One of Long's first moves was to return to closed meetings of the Caucus, an idea that was accepted without opposition. Long said (*NJ*, Dec. 4, 1982, p. 2076), "I think closing the Caucus meetings and letting us argue our problems in private has kept the situation from becoming strained. I'm very proud of the progress we've made in trying to develop the Caucus as a policy-making body. We're also giving younger Members who are not committee chairmen an opportunity to develop and show leadership potential." The effort at revitalization worked. Caucus attendance increased, and seven of the first eleven meetings in 1981 achieved a quorum (Malbin, 1981, p. 1642).

In early 1981, Long organized an "issues conference" to discuss Democratic policy proposals. From that beginning he created the Committee on Party Effectiveness, a group of about forty House Democrats who met once or twice a week to develop a party agenda and discuss political strategy. The committee was an ideological cross-section of the Caucus, although the membership was weighted toward representatives in their second to fourth terms. In particular, care was taken to include moderate to conservative Democrats, for the goal was to find common ground among the party's factions. "We began to use those meetings for strategy sessions for the floor on controversial issues that were anticipated, or to talk about the overall direction of the party, or to bring in pollsters that would discuss with us the current state of affairs, or to bring in experts on policy matters."[45]

The meetings were remarkably successful, and shortly before the 1982 elections, the committee produced a 135-page statement on a number of issues, particularly economic policy.

> We felt a desperate need to give definition and focus to the Democratic agenda and message. We surprised ourselves. Initially I had some skepticism, given the ideological and regional diversity, that we would come up with anything more than pabulum. But we ended up with a series of papers that gave definition to the Democratic party point of view that really had some bite to it, and clearly provided a series of points of differentiation vis-à-vis the Republican caucus and presidency. That material then became very helpful to Democrats, especially candidates, both incumbents and challengers, in helping define and articulate a position. . . . Also that whole process did more to generate a new sense of cohesiveness in the Caucus—it was just remarkable, because we all found out we had common denominators that we could identify.[46]

After the elections, the Caucus directed the Democratic caucuses on each committee to report about those proposals in the statement that fell within their jurisdictions. In 1983, Long and Speaker O'Neill worked with Budget Committee chairman James Jones to produce a Democratic budget resolution that reflected some of the proposals in the report of the Committee on Party Effectiveness (Price, 1984, p. 281). Many observers attribute a significant portion of the increased party cohesion we discussed above to Long's efforts. Richard Gephardt, a leader of the New Breed Democrats, said of Long, "He's a believer in cohesion and consensus between the disparate elements of the party." And Buddy Roemer (D, La.), a Boll Weevil, said, "I always felt my views were welcome. . . . Always I felt the caucus was searching for alternatives" (*CQWR*, Oct. 15, 1983, pp. 2118, 2119).

The successes of the Caucus led the party to increase scheduled meetings to twice a month, beginning in 1985. Gephardt (then Caucus chairman) said, "The focus of those meetings will be to talk about strategy and substance. . . . It will allow the leadership to talk to us and us to talk to the leadership, and it will be a time for the campaign committee to talk about politics" (*CQWR*, Dec. 8, 1984, p. 3054). Gephardt also organized annual weekend retreats for House Democrats, at which they could discuss politics and issues, and hear from outside experts.[47]

The Democratic Caucus and Collective Control

Thus in the 1980s the Caucus was a focus of efforts to increase party consensus. Building on this consensus, it also employed the mechanisms of collective control at its disposal to enhance the chances of getting Democratic policy proposals through the House.

The Caucus and the Leadership

One consequence of increased Democratic cohesion was that there was increased pressure on party leaders to reflect personally positions that were widely shared by members, and the Caucus was frequently the device used to apply the pressure. For example, in June of 1982 freshman congressman Jim Bates (D, Cal.) collected 112 signatures to call a Caucus meeting. The purpose was to find out why a number of members of the leadership had voted for funds to flight-test the MX missile. "Bates said he felt that neither the House floor nor Committees provided an adequate forum for debate on the subject" (Granat, 1983, p. 2117). Under intense pressure, nineteen Democrats (including Majority Leader Wright, Caucus chair Long, and Richard Gephardt) switched to opposition on the vote in July on procurement of the missile. "Relatively senior members who either hold leadership posts or are widely believed to aspire to them accounted for more than a third of the Democrats who voted 'pro' MX in May and 'against' MX in July" (Towell, 1983, p. 1483).

In September of 1983 another Caucus meeting was called by petition, this one to discuss the continued presence of U.S. Marines in a peacekeeping role in Lebanon. The Reagan administration wanted the ability to maintain the Marines indefinitely. Speaker O'Neill was willing to support the president, but engineered a resolution that would authorize the Marine presence for only eighteen more months. In an unusually strong move, O'Neill organized support for the resolution and got the Rules Committee to draft a favorable rule for floor consideration. But many liberals opposed the eighteen-month extension, and freshman Barbara Boxer (D, Cal.) organized the petition drive for the Caucus meeting. She said, "We were faced with the 18 months and no other alternative. This was such an important issue that I thought we should discuss it among ourselves and develop other options" (Granat, 1983, p. 2117). The meeting took place the day before the floor vote on the leadership-sponsored resolution. "As members later told it, the closed-door meeting was filled with passionate words, the kind most lawmakers would be unwilling to express in public" (Granat, 1983, p. 2115).

Despite the debate, O'Neill persisted and the resolution passed, but primarily because of overwhelming Republican support. Democrats opposed it 130 to 134, and they supported a much more restrictive substitute (which failed) 146 to 118. During the next few months, however, 241 Marines were killed in Lebanon in a suicide bombing, and O'Neill charged that Reagan had abandoned the diplomacy-centered approach that had formed the basis for the 1983 resolution. The Democratic leadership drafted another resolution calling for the "prompt and orderly withdrawal" of the 1,600 remaining Marines. The resolution was overwhelmingly endorsed by the Caucus (*CQWR*, Feb. 4, 1984, pp. 227–28).

The Caucus's discussion of issues was not limited to attempts to pressure its leaders. Along the lines planned by Long and Gephardt, it was also used to discuss options and take positions. In 1983, the Caucus also met to consider the budget and Central American policy. In April of 1985, the Caucus unanimously endorsed economic sanctions against South Africa (*CQWR*, Apr. 6, 1985, p. 637). At the opening of the One Hundredth Congress, the Caucus endorsed legislation to call for Reagan-administration compliance with the SALT II treaty, and in February 1987 it called for a halt to virtually all U.S. nuclear weapons tests if the Soviets also continued their moratorium (*CQWR*, Feb. 7, 1987, p. 246).

In addition to the desire to see specific issue positions supported by the leadership, in 1984 another kind of pressure was exerted by factions in the Caucus: pressure to expand the leadership circle in order to ensure that the various positions within the party were adequately represented. The impetus for the expansion came from a group of relatively junior members led by Tony Coelho (D, Cal., then chairman of the Democratic Congressional Campaign Committee) and Richard Gephardt, as well as from the Boll Weevils. O'Neill responded positively to these requests, telling the Caucus, "We must find some new themes and some new directions for our party," and that he wanted to employ the "talent in the Caucus" (Granat, 1984b, p. 3054). One aspect of the leadership response was a plan to employ more actively the Steering and Policy Committee. "Several members said Steering and Policy is a good organ to use for consensus-building because of the diversity of its membership" (Granat, 1984b, p. 3055). O'Neill also appointed in 1985 a new six-member group, called the "Speaker's Cabinet," to provide advice on policy matters. They represented a variety of ideological perspectives and met regularly with the leadership and major committee chairmen.

A final example of Caucus efforts to influence the leadership was the adoption, early in 1985, of a rule providing for the election of future party whips, instead of continuing appointment by the Speaker. (Recall that a similar move had been rejected twice during the reform era because of leadership opposition.) The intent was to give the Caucus control over the choice of a leader who might well rise to be a future Speaker, and who would be an influential party spokesman in the meantime. "This is just another wave coming out of the November election," said Leon Panetta (D, Cal.), "with the Caucus wanting to have more say in where we're going from here" (*CQWR*, Feb. 2, 1985, p. 176).

The Caucus and Committee Chairmen

We saw in chapter 2 that in 1975 the Caucus used the new procedures for secret-ballot votes on nominees for committee chairmen to reject three southern chairmen. In two of the cases, their conservatism and frequent opposition to party positions were part of the reason for their ouster. In succeeding Congresses, there were a number of challenges against other nominees. In particular, in 1979 there was a challenge against Jamie Whitten, who was in line, by seniority, to become chair of Appropriations. Whitten, one of the more conservative southerners, was opposed by a group of junior members and by a coalition of civil rights, environmental, and consumer groups. He was supported, however, by Speaker O'Neill, who noted in a speech to the Caucus that the opposition had focused on Whitten's voting record. In a remarkable indication of his disinclination to use party control mechanisms to stimulate loyalty, "O'Neill said a party support record was 'no reason to turn a man down'" (*CQWR*, Jan. 27, 1979, p. 153). Whitten was approved for the chairmanship 157 to 88 (although this was more than twice as many negative votes as were cast against any other chairman). Indeed no other committee chairman was rejected by the Caucus until a decade after the 1975 insurgency.

At the opening of the Ninety-ninth Congress in 1985, a cross-section of House Democrats sought to depose Melvin Price (D, Ill.) as chairman of the Armed Services Committee. Price, who was eighty and infirm, had succeeded to the chairmanship ten years earlier, when the Caucus rejected Hebert of Louisiana. The prime movers behind the challenge were Les Aspin (D, Wis.), a critic of the military who was seventh-ranking in seniority on the committee and wanted to replace Price, and Dave McCurdy (D, Okla.), who was more supportive of the Pentagon. Some people wanted a new chairman because they doubted Price's ability to provide needed leadership. McCurdy said, "I want this committee to be the powerful committee it should be," and a junior member stated, "We need a more forceful and more physically able person to lead us" (*CQWR*, Dec. 22, 1984, p. 3143). Others disagreed with Price's strong prodefense stand.

When it became apparent that the challenge to Price might succeed, Speaker O'Neill and other senior members intervened to support him, vigorously lobbying other Democrats.[48] Under pressure from O'Neill, the Steering and Policy Committee unanimously proposed Price as chairman, and the Speaker made a forceful speech to the Caucus on his behalf which was credited with switching a number of votes. When the vote was taken, however, Price was narrowly rejected, 118 to 121. "Democrats who opposed Price said their objections were based on concern about Price's ability to effectively lead the committee, and discomfort with his support for Reagan's military buildup" (Cohodas and Granat, 1985, p. 9). Immediately after the vote, Steering and Policy nominated the next-ranking Democrat, Charles Bennett of Florida, by a 17 to 5 vote. Bennett was also prodefense, but, though seventy-four, was more vigorous than Price. Aspin was nominated in the Caucus to oppose Bennett, and won by 125 to 103. Some Aspin supporters believed he would be more effective in the media, while others "said Aspin could present alternatives to the Reagan administration's defense buildup" (Cohodas and Granat, 1985, p. 9).

Failure to represent policy positions supported by the Caucus was only a partial cause of Price's ouster. Policy opposition was a clearer motivation two years later when Aspin himself was the target of an attack in the Caucus. During his time in the chair, Aspin had angered many of the liberals who had originally supported him. "The core of some liberals' discontent with Aspin is their sense that he lied to them on MX. They say he promised to oppose the MX in return for their support of his insurgency against Price. Instead, in 1985 he engineered a compromise with the Reagan administration that provided for limited production and deployment of the missile" (Calmes, 1987b, p. 83). Aspin denied making any promises about MX, but liberal anger was renewed later in 1985 because many of them believed that he had sold out a number of the House's positions in arriving at compromises with the Senate on the fiscal 1986 Defense conference report. Les Au Coin (D, Ore.) said, "People were angry because no one can tell where Reaganism ends and a distinctive Democratic doctrine begins" (*Washington Post,* July 31, 1985, p. A4). A Caucus meeting was called by petition at which many members attacked Aspin, causing the leadership to delay a floor vote on the conference report. The final straw for many was Aspin's vote in June of 1986 in support of an administration proposal for additional aid to the "Contras" in Nicaragua. George Miller (D, Cal.) said, "There is a great sense of betrayal" (*CQWR,* July 12, 1986, p. 1565).

As a result of these events, a challenge developed against Aspin's chairmanship at the beginning of the One Hundredth Congress, with a rather unlikely principal challenger: Marvin Leath of Texas. Leath, a conservative Boll Weevil Democrat, ranked fourteenth in committee seniority. He had, moreover, taken many of the same prodefense positions that had undermined Aspin, including support for MX and Contra aid. But he had taken those positions straightforwardly, reflecting his district and his convictions, while many thought that Aspin had led them to expect one thing and then had done something else. More important, as we saw in the discussion of budget politics, Leath had been a catalyst for the compromise in 1985 that permitted Democrats to agree on a reduction of both defense and domestic spending, and he had accrued a great deal of goodwill for it. Liberals disenchanted with Aspin hoped that Leath could continue on that course, building a common defense position for Democrats. As Russo of Illinois, a Leath supporter, said, "Philosophically, he and I are totally different. . . . But he is a consensus ball-player. He believes that spending all this money on defense programs doesn't necessarily get you a strong defense, just as spending a lot of money on social programs doesn't solve all your problems there. . . . The only one who can take on Ronald Reagan on defense is a conservative Democrat like Marvin Leath" (Calmes, 1987b, p. 84).

Leath pressed this theme of consensus building in his campaign against Aspin. He said, "I can get liberals to think more in terms of defending the country adequately, and conservatives to realize the nuclear arms threat" (Calmes, 1987c, p. 104). On this basis he was able to build a coalition of disaffected liberals, Boll Weevils, members of the Black Caucus (including Budget Committee chairman William Gray of Pennsylvania, with whom he had worked closely), and Texans. The coalition achieved initial success; on January 7 the Caucus voted 124 to 130 against continuing Aspin as chairman.

A second Caucus meeting was scheduled for twelve days later to choose a new chair. The Steering and Policy Committee endorsed Charles Bennett, whom Aspin had defeated two years earlier. In addition to Bennett, Aspin, and Leath, Nicholas Mavroules (a liberal from Massachusetts, eleventh in seniority) also announced his candidacy. Most observers and participants, however, thought that it would come down to a choice between Aspin and Leath. The Leath supporters emphasized his consensus-building capabilities, his honesty, and the breadth of his support. A group of pro-Leath members (including five subcommittee chairmen from Armed Services) published a letter that said, "We need someone to lead that committee who can forge a consensus among the diverse members of our party," and termed Leath "an honest broker to all concerned" (*Washington Post,* Jan. 6, 1987, p. A1). It claimed that eighteen of the twenty-seven Democrats on Armed Services opposed Aspin, and that thirteen were for Leath. Aspin's people counterattacked with an analysis of 135 votes cast by Leath during his eight years in the House, covering both defense and other issues. It claimed that the Texan had "made a career of voting against his party" (Calmes, 1987a, p. 140). Many people thought that the analysis and the issue it raised became the key to the outcome. First Mavroules and then Bennett were eliminated on successive ballots. On the third ballot, Aspin won over Leath by a 133 to 116 vote.

Democrats who favored defense cuts and restrictions on weapons systems claimed before the vote that they had already won, regardless of the outcome, because they had made Aspin chairman and then had sent him a message by voting him down, and because all the candidates were appealing for votes on their issues. As Barney Frank (D, Mass.), who voted for Aspin on the final vote, said, "You never heard such a chorus of commitments to arms reduction, procurement reform and no [defense] spending increases" (Calmes, 1987a, p. 142). Rep. Pat Williams of Montana, a Leath supporter, emphasized a lesson for Aspin: that it was the Caucus, and not just the Armed Services Committee, that would determine the House's defense positions. "That was always in our minds. The chairman has to be made to know that promises should be kept, and that the caucus is watching" (*Washington Post,* Jan. 18, 1987, p. A5).

The two contests over the Armed Services chairmanship provide good evidence for our characterization of the use of the vote on chairmen as a control mechanism for protecting shared policy positions within the Caucus. Price was deposed because members thought he couldn't provide adequate leadership on behalf of House positions, and because he was too prodefense for many Democrats. Aspin was selected to replace him because he was a defense critic who could be an effective spokesman. When Aspin strayed too far from Democratic positions in compromising with Reagan and the Senate, and when he voted in opposition to the party majority, the Caucus demonstrated that it could remove him. Then, in the final choice, they retained as chairman the candidate who was more representative of their views. Aspin appeared to get the message (or wanted members to believe he had). Describing Aspin's campaign, Barney Frank said, "I know one of the things [Aspin] said was, 'Look, I understand what you're saying when you said I did not sufficiently represent the [Democratic] caucus's position. I will be much more firm in sticking to those positions'" (*Insight*, Feb. 16, 1987, p. 19). And after the vote, observers said Aspin stood before the Caucus and said that the assault on him had struck a "responsive chord," and promised not to repeat past mistakes (*Washington Post,* Jan. 23, 1987, p. A6).

Beyond the effect of this particular challenge on Les Aspin, there is evidence that the existence and use of the rules for voting on chairmen has had a more general impact on party loyalty among senior Democrats. Crook and Hibbing's (1985) analysis showed that members who occupied or were close in seniority to committee chairs dramatically increased their levels of party support during the period 1971–1982. Moreover, this result was not merely due to a regional shift in control of chairmanships, because the result held for both northern and southern Democrats.

To conclude this section, we can present data on a particularly striking example, Jamie Whitten of Mississippi. Recall that liberals had launched a challenge against Whitten when he was nominated to succeed to the chair of Appropriations in 1979 because of his low support for party positions. Evidence of this low support can be seen in table 3.5. During the Eisenhower years, Whitten's party support began to drop and did so more quickly than that of the average southerner. It stabilized at around 35 percent between 1961 and 1976, and then rose a bit after the reforms were in place. By the Ninety-fifth Congress, before becoming chairman, he was more loyal (relative to both other southerners and all Democrats) than he had been. After he was challenged for the chairmanship, his party support continued to increase until, in the One Hundredth Congress, he was not only noticeably more loyal than

Table 3.5 Jamie Whitten's Party Loyalty Compared to that of Other Democrats, 84th–100th Congresses

| Congress (Years) | Whitten's Party-Unity Score | Difference between Whitten's Score and Average for:[a] | |
		Southern Democrats	All Democrats
84 (1955–56)	75	+ 2	− 5
85 (1957–58)	55	−15	−23
86 (1959–60)	47	−23	−33
87 (1961–62)	35	−33	−46
88 (1963–64)	34	−34	−41
89 (1965–66)	22	−33	−57
90 (1967–68)	33	−18	−42
91 (1969–70)	36	−14	−35
92 (1971–72)	34	−12	−36
93 (1973–74)	36	−18	−38
94 (1975–76)	36	−17	−39
95 (1977–78)	45	−10	−28
96 (1979–80)	52	− 9	−24
97 (1981–82)	68	+ 8	− 9
98 (1983–84)	78	+11	− 4
99 (1985–86)	79	+ 8	− 4
100 (1987–88)	88	+12	+ 2

[a]A positive number here means Whitten was more loyal than average; a negative number means less loyal.

other southerners, but also a bit more loyal than the average Democrat. Apparently the combined effect of the Caucus's new power over chairmen's positions and electoral change in Mississippi persuaded Jamie Whitten that his party's policies had become more acceptable.

The adoption of the automatic vote on chairmen, and the demonstration on five occasions that a chairman could be voted down, had altered the relationship between committee leaders and their party. As Polsby, Gallaher, and Rundquist (1968, p. 790) said,

> The extent of a seniority rule's application may be said to constitute a measure of the allocation of discretion and hence of power as between party leaders and committee chairmen. . . . Thus, like pregnancy, seniority is for most purposes a dichotomous variable. When seniority operates as a partial influence upon decision-making rather than as an automatic determinant of committee rank, political influence flows to those

empowered to vary the application of the diverse criteria of choice. . . .

Committee Assignments

Caucus control over chairmanships has the potential to affect directly only the most senior members. The process of committee assignments can have a much more widespread impact. Remember that during the reform era, the responsibility for the assignment function was switched from members of Ways and Means to the Steering and Policy Committee. This was done to enhance Steering and Policy's status and put these rewards more in control of the leadership. Ironically, the Speaker at the time, Carl Albert, opposed the switch, but this did not dissuade the reform leaders or the Caucus. Rep. David Obey of DSG said, "It ought to be a function of the leadership, and if the leadership doesn't want it, I want them to have it anyway. I want members to owe their committee assignments to the leadership, not to the Ways and Means Committee" (Sheppard, 1985, p. 198).

There is little evidence that Speakers Albert and O'Neill tried to dominate assignment decisions. O'Neill, for example, occasionally backed individual candidates from the northeast, but otherwise usually let other members make their deals (Cohen, 1981). But there is good evidence that the committee collectively, as the agent for the Caucus, does take into account loyalty to the party in making assignments. For example, Smith and Ray (1983) showed that party loyalty is one of the few factors that significantly affected whether nonfreshman assignment requests were granted in the Ninety-fifth through Ninety-seventh Congresses. Smith and Deering (1984, p. 242) reported that O'Neill provided "leadership support scores" for members who were seeking assignment transfers, and in some cases when they were not provided, committee members asked for them.

Furthermore, as we would expect from our theoretical discussion of variations among committees, loyalty is much more important for assignments to the three prestige or control committees filled by Steering and Policy. Sinclair (1981b, p. 187) quotes a comment by one of the party leaders. "We tried to put reasonable people on the [important] committees. Some members who wanted new assignments didn't get what they wanted. Members who never go with the leadership—never help out. It's not only [the other leadership figures] and I who did this. The other Steering and Policy members—the elected ones—feel the same way." Smith and Deering (1984, pp. 242–43) also stated that evidence showed party loyalty was especially important for assignments to the prestige committees. More recently, a member of Steering and Policy, when asked if members' votes on party-supported legislation were important when making assignments to the top committees, responded: "Oh yes, absolutely. We take that into consideration. We don't put people on those major committees if we don't think they will at least give us some strong consideration."[49] Moreover, the Caucus wasn't always just a rubber stamp for Steering and Policy. On occasion, the reform rules permitting nominations from the Caucus floor were used to fill vacancies differently than the Committee proposed. For example, in 1979 the Caucus voted to put Wyche Fowler (D, Ga.) on Ways and Means instead of Steering and Policy choice Sam Hall (D, Tex.), even though the latter was strongly pushed by Majority Leader Wright. Hall was significantly less supportive of the party than Fowler.[50]

The Case of the Boll Weevils

A more general example of the Caucus's use of mechanisms of collective control comes from the treatment of the Boll Weevils who provided the margin of victory for many of President Reagan's major policy initiatives in 1987.[51] As we noted earlier, the Conservative Democratic Forum (CDF) was formed to pressure the Democratic leadership and to support conservative positions, and the organization was successful in securing good committee assignments for its members at the opening of the Ninety-seventh Congress. When the Forum's members then supported Reagan on important votes, many party loyalists were angry. On June 26, 1981, Peter Peyser (D, N.Y.) took the House floor to complain about the previous day's Democratic defections on a vote to block consideration of a Republican-drafted rule to govern floor debate on the reconciliation bill. These defections facilitated the passage of the Reagan budget cuts. Peyser said, "We certainly in the Democratic caucus can decide who sits with us and who does not. Rank and file Democrats in the House have had it. We have been abused and betrayed by those who have accepted and benefitted by this party's support. We are really mad as hell, Mr. Speaker, and we are not going to roll over and play dead any more" (*Congressional Record*, June 26, 1981, p. H14352).

Talk began among House Democrats about punishing the defectors, but throughout the first half of 1987 the leadership was opposed. Majority Leader Wright went to a meeting of the CDF in June to tell them "he would protect their right to vote as they chose, even though he might disagree with their position." Speaker O'Neill had said, on a public-television show the previous month, that "there is no way, when you have a party like I have with so many different philosophies, that you punish a person" (Arieff, 1981a, p. 1025). After the Democrats' defeat on the tax bill in July, sentiment for sanctions against the conservatives grew stronger, but the leadership was able to persuade the liberals to put off a Caucus meeting on the matter until after the summer recess.

When Congress reconvened in September, a meeting of the Caucus was called by a petition of a group of liberals. In preparation for the meeting Democratic leaders tried to convince members that any actual punishment of disloyalty should be delayed until the next Congress convened. O'Neill told the Caucus that the proper time to exert discipline was when the Caucus would select committee chairmen and members of the four "leadership committees" (Broder, 1981b, p. A8). Instead of immediate action, Wright presented the Caucus with a future-oriented policy, which he later outlined for reporters.[52] It included the following:

1. Amnesty for past votes, and an invitation to the defectors to return to the fold
2. An explicit statement that committee chairmanships and appointments to prestige committees were rewards from the Caucus, and that "we expect some responsibility to the party and their colleagues" from members holding those positions
3. Notice that the Steering and Policy Committee would designate a few important policy issues each session as "litmus-test" votes, and "those who hope to be rewarded by the caucus can expect to have their votes scrutinized"
4. Even on these key votes, a distinction to be drawn between "occasional aberrations on the basis of conscience, conviction or constituency and a pattern of consistent conniving with the opposition"

Wright emphasized that the party wasn't seeking to punish anyone. "But there are rewards. You don't take a thing away, but you don't necessarily renew it, either" (*New York Times*, Sept. 17, 1981, p. A21). This was apparently a reference to the potential for replacement of committee chairmen, but it wasn't completely clear. More pointed was O'Neill's noting that Rep. "Sonny" Montgomery (D, Miss.), one of the leading Boll Weevils and chairman of the Veterans' Affairs Committee, had "only six votes cast against him" for chairman the previous December (Broder, 1981, p. A8).

There was, however, no immediate evidence that the new policy had any effect on the defectors. Gramm of Texas announced his intent to continue on his previous course, and he met with Reagan-administration budget director David Stockman to work on the new Republican budget initiatives. Again in 1982, the Boll Weevils provided the vote margin for the Republicans to pass their budget proposal.

The CDF felt the consequences of the new policy regarding party loyalty when committee assignments for the Ninety-eighth Congress were made early in 1983. The most extreme action was the actual re-moval of Phil Gramm from his seat on the Budget Committee. Gramm complained that he was being punished for voting the positions he had taken at home, but Wright disagreed. "Denying a person a reward is not a punishment," he said. An assignment to Budget "is a prize, a plum, it is a leadership assignment" (*CQWR*, Jan. 8, 1983, p. 5). Moreover, as Ross Baker (1985) has pointed out, Gramm did much more than simply vote against the party, and he was personally disliked by many Demo-crats. What incensed many of his colleagues, and particularly Wright, was that he sat in on Democratic budget strategy sessions and then re-ported the details of them to the Republicans (Barry, 1989).

Montgomery of Mississippi was also the target of action, although he didn't lose his position. When Steering and Policy renominated com-mittee chairmen, Montgomery was endorsed to remain head of Vet-erans' Affairs by only a 16 to 11 vote. He was surprised by the level of opposition. The full Caucus was more supportive (179 to 53), but Montgomery felt the pressure. "'I got the message, loud and clear,' Montgomery said, promising he would support the leadership where he could" (Plattner, 1983, p. 4).

Party loyalty was also taken into account in making new committee assignments. John Breaux of Louisiana, a Boll Weevil, sought appoint-ment to Gramm's vacancy on Budget, but was defeated by Martin Frost of Texas, a leadership loyalist. A Democratic leader said of Frost, "He's proven himself to be a national Democrat," and a member of Steering and Policy said, "On Budget, we were looking for political philosophy" (Roberts, 1983a, p. A25). On Appropriations, Doug Barnard of Geor-gia was denied his request for a seat vacated by another Georgian. Barnard was a member of CDF; Bill Boner, the moderate from Ten-nessee who got the seat, was not (Roberts, 1983b, p. 1). The only CDF member who won assignment to one of the choice committees was Ronnie Flippo of Alabama. Flippo had defected on the 1981 budget vote, but opposed the Reagan tax plan and voted with his party on the 1982 budget.

Another instructive example involved Buddy Roemer (D, La.). Roemer, a member of CDF, had sought assignment to a medium-level committee (Banking and Currency), and received it. However, shortly after Steering and Policy made the assignment (and before Caucus ratification), members discovered through a story in the *Washington Post* that Roemer had indicated that he would switch parties if he didn't get what he wanted. The leadership of the DSG then decided to fight the assignment in the Caucus, but Caucus chairman Gillis Long got them to agree to refrain in exchange for an apology. "Roemer addressed the caucus on January 6. He delivered a statement apologizing for his comments to *The Post* and pledging his loyalty to the party" (Baker, 1985, p. 333).

Thus in the actions regarding the Boll Weevils in 1981–83, we see a precise reversal of the "Boss" model of leadership. Instead of leaders initiating retaliation against defecting party members, we find a relatively cohesive membership pressuring reluctant party leaders to threaten and impose a range of sanctions on deviating Democrats.[53]

Summary

In this chapter we presented some theoretical perspectives on floor voting, and then described the decreasing factionalism and increasing homogeneity of responses among House Democrats since the reform era. This was followed by a description of the ebb and flow of Democrats' inclination to employ their Caucus for various purposes. Finally, we offered an account of the ways the Caucus has been used as a mechanism for collective control of those to whom the party has given power. Barbara Sinclair (1983, p. 97) put the results succinctly: "Both the party leadership and the committees are aware that if they were regularly to thwart the wishes of a majority of their party colleagues, the caucus would provide a mechanism through which they could be brought to heel."

4

The Democratic
Leadership:
Party Agents and
Agenda Management

The increasing homogeneity on policy matters within the Democratic Caucus made it more frequently possible to create a party position on various issues. The mechanisms of collective control developed in the reform era reinforced this homogeneity, and provided ways to encourage party and committee leaders to pursue legislative outcomes that reflected a party consensus, if one existed. In this chapter we will be primarily concerned with the ways leadership activity to advance the party's policy goals has increased over time. In particular we will examine growing leadership use of the tools granted through the reforms to shape the agenda in order to improve the chances for victory. First, however, we will briefly discuss the evolution of leadership activity in general, and the elaboration of the means of communication between leaders and members.

The Evolution of Leadership Activities

Before the reform era, the system of committee government placed constraints on the activities of the Democratic leadership. Most of their task was to find ways to facilitate the passage of legislation produced by committees, and (if a Democrat was in the White House) to pursue the priorities of the president as well. Even in the 1970s, for example, Speaker Albert would frequently say, "I never do anything without the consent of my committee chairmen" (Rhodes, 1976, p. 30). As the influence of chairmen in committee and on the floor was weakened, as the electoral independence of members grew, and as the leaders changed and the opportunities for them to have an impact on the process increased, the activities performed by leaders grew more elaborate. Some of the changes involved improving the two-way flow of information between the leadership and the rank and file. Others involved an expansion of ways to help members achieve their goals.

Communications, Coalition Building, and the Whip System

If the Democratic leadership is to be the agent of its party's membership on behalf of policy positions that have widespread support, then it is important that good two-way lines of communication be maintained. That way the leadership can discern members' views and mobilize effective support for desired legislative actions. During the postreform years, a number of developments occurred within the House Democratic party's organization to further those ends. One was the renewal of frequent meetings of the Democratic Caucus under Gillis Long. Since Caucus meetings potentially include the entire Democratic membership, this is obviously the most representative group available. However, many members did not always attend Caucus meetings. Sometimes a quorum would not be present, and even if one were, the number of absentees could be large. Thus representativeness was not assured. More important, as the number of attendees grew, the Caucus became more unwieldy. Only a limited number of members could speak in the usual amount of time available, and many Democrats might be reluctant to be outspoken in such a large group on a sensitive issue. The Caucus was valuable as an occasional outlet on important issues, as in the instances discussed in chapter 3, but it was not as useful for regular exchanges between leaders and members.

Another avenue for communication was the Steering and Policy Committee. Recall that the Democratic Study Group leaders who proposed the committee thought of it as an executive committee for the Caucus, which would give junior members a voice in leadership and policy decisions. Since its original twenty-four members included the top leadership, others appointed by the Speaker, and a dozen members elected regionally, it had the potential for useful communications within a relatively small group. Moreover, the subsequent expansion of the committee to thirty-one members included the addition of the chairmen of the four "leadership" committees, thus tying in the parts of the committee system whose activities would be of most concern to the party. The committee's activities grew more diverse, particularly after Tip O'Neill became Speaker; it served "as a forum for wide-ranging discussion and as a 'consultative body'" (Sinclair, 1983, p. 73). Its members often would be briefed by committee chairmen on important legislation, and the chairmen would receive feedback on potential problems.

Thus Steering and Policy became another useful communications device for the leadership.[1] During the late 1970s and the 1980s, however, another structure became even more important for this purpose: the Democratic whip system.

The Development of the Whip System. The party whip organizations developed out of the partisan conflicts of the late nineteenth century (Ripley, 1964). By the 1930s, when factional divisions began to show up in the large Democratic majorities of the New Deal period, the Democrats had a whip and fifteen assistants, each of whom was responsible for a specific geographic zone. In subsequent Congresses, the number of zones grew a bit, numbering eighteen in 1963 (Ripley, 1964), and twenty in 1975.[2]

Under Speaker Sam Rayburn, the activities of the whip system were relatively limited. Rayburn preferred to deal with the House through personal allies, so he rarely used the system. Carl Albert, who served as whip from 1955 to 1961, had so little to do that he employed his principal aide for congressional business rather than whip business (Ripley, 1964). Rayburn created the position of deputy whip in 1955 as a consolation to Hale Boggs (D, La.), who had wanted to be whip. But, as a senior aide commented, "Albert didn't have anything to do, so Boggs had double nothing to do" (Sinclair, 1983, p. 55). Partly in response to the inactivity of the whip organization, the Democratic Study Group set up its own whip operation, which persisted into the 1970s (Stevens, Miller, and Mann, 1974). Speaker McCormack employed the whip organization more frequently than Rayburn, particularly for discovering members' vote intentions, but the organization remained the same. The whip and his deputy were appointed by the Speaker and majority leader, but the assistant whips were selected by their zones. The method of selection varied. Sometimes assistants were just appointed by the senior Democrat in the zone; in other cases they were elected. Thus assistant whips were not necessarily loyal to the leadership or supportive of party policy. The empirical analysis dealing with the whip system at this time involves the Kennedy administration in 1962 and 1963 (Ripley, 1964; Froman and Ripley, 1965). This was before the deep sectional divisions of the Great Society years occurred. That research shows that whip counts were relatively infrequent (seventeen in those two years, involving issues on which the leadership was strongly committed), that they were fairly accurate, and that the leadership won most of the time.

During the 1960s, with Democratic presidents, the whip system was primarily used for informing members of leadership positions, ascertaining members' intentions, and stimulating attendance. Efforts at persuasion were usually left to the top leaders or to congressional liaison staff from the administration. During Democratic administrations, the congressional liaison staff also served as an additional means of vote counting. When the Nixon administration came to power, however, the executive branch assets were lost. In addition, the move to recorded teller voting and electronic voting substantially increased the number of decision points for which the leadership had to prepare. These changes induced the Democratic leadership to expand the number of appointed whips. The first step was the creation in 1970 of the post of chief deputy whip, supported by three deputy whips. Then in 1975, three at-large whip positions were created, to provide representation in the system for representatives from the Black Caucus, the Women's Caucus, and the freshman class organization (Dodd, 1979, p. 31). These new posts permitted a division of labor within the whip organization: the zone whips continued to act primarily as information gatherers, while the appointive whips took on the additional task of persuading members to support the party program.

The prestige of the whips was enhanced when the whip and his deputies were put on the Steering and Policy Committee at its creation,[3] and the effectiveness of the organization was increased by an expansion of its staff and budget. Membership on Steering and Policy was particularly important, because it was the center of efforts to create a party program during the Nixon years. Whip John McFall (D, Cal.) was an important adviser to the Speaker, and participated in leadership meetings with the president. Moreover, since appointive whips were members of virtually all of the major committees in the Ninety-third and Ninety-fourth Congresses (Dodd, 1979, p. 33), they could represent leadership interests to their committees and keep the leaders informed of committee activity. This elaboration of the whip system permitted an expansion of the scope of its activities relative to the Kennedy years (Dodd, 1979).[4]

Despite the growth of the whip organization, members were not entirely happy with its operation. Waldman (1977, p. 40) reported, "Many of those [House Democrats] I interviewed were dissatisfied because of the lack of vigor in these efforts [by the leadership to mobilize and change votes], although some conservative Democrats seemed content with the 'light hand' of leadership. Many members seemed to resent that they had rarely if ever been contacted by the Speaker or the Majority Leader in an effort to affect their vote. . . ."[5] Particularly critical were liberals who were very loyal to the party. They made comments like "The whip system doesn't amount to a hell of a lot; it's a tally operation rather than bringing people along," and "The whip system is lousy. All they do is count. They don't put an arm on you."

The limited scope of persuasion activities was partly due to the heterogeneity of preferences among the factions in the Caucus at this time, as well as to the number of appointive whips available for the task. As the divisions among Democrats abated, the leadership moved to further expand these resources.

The Whip Organization in the Carter and Reagan Years. When Tip O'Neill became Speaker in 1977, and John Brademas (D, Ind.) was appointed whip, the number of at-large whips was increased to ten. Brademas was defeated for reelection to the House in 1980, and O'Neill appointed Tom Foley (D, Wash.) to be his replacement. In anticipation of the greater demands on the whip system with the presidency and the Senate in Republican hands, a fourth deputy whip was added, and the at-large whips grew to fifteen. As figure 4.1 shows, before O'Neill was Speaker the whip organization included around 10 percent of the Democrats in the House; by 1981 it included 18 percent.

During this time, the whips would meet every Thursday morning when Congress was in session.[6] "For both leaders and whips, information exchange is the single most important function served by the meetings" (Sinclair, 1983, p. 58). O'Neill and Majority Leader Wright always attended. The leadership would announce the schedule for the coming week, convey other information, and answer questions. Upcoming major legislation would often be discussed, with the leaders or a whip from the committee of jurisdiction explaining the issues involved.

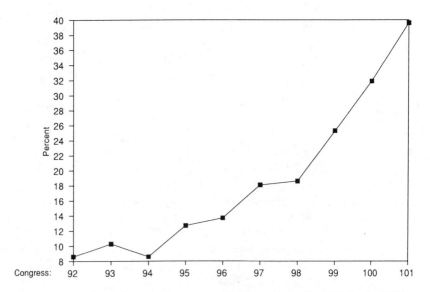

Figure 4.1 Proportion of the Democratic House Membership in the Whip Organization, 92d–101st Congresses

In addition, the meetings offered members of the organization the opportunity to voice opinions or complaints on behalf of themselves or the members they represented. For example, Sinclair (1983, pp. 59–61) reported that members complained about the leadership's failure to keep to the schedule, and about problems with the Carter administration. In 1981, when the votes of the Boll Weevils were giving victories to the Reagan administration, criticism was voiced against the leadership for permitting these defections without imposing sanctions. The leadership, in turn, used the meetings to enhance morale and build support for party positions.

The primary purposes of the whip organization continued to be polling and persuasion. The number of whip polls had increased further, to about eighty in the Ninety-fifth and Ninety-sixth Congresses (Sinclair, 1983, p. 56). Accurate information was the main goal, so under Brademas the members were assured that whip poll information would be kept confidential (this was not true in the past), and an effort was made to avoid slanting the questions put to the members. Still, there was no doubt about where the leadership stood. As an aide to Brademas said, "A whip check is a declaration of party policy. These are not Gallup polls. . . . The question is always phrased so the right answer is yes" (Cooper, 1978, p. 1302). On especially important bills, O'Neill developed an innovation to reinforce the regular whip operation: the task force. This was a group of members who would work together to pass that particular bill. The Speaker would appoint the task-force chair, who was usually a junior member on the committee of jurisdiction. This was done because junior members had more time for these tasks. It also helped to build links to the leadership. Junior members also disproportionately made up the membership of these task forces, for the same reasons (Sinclair, 1983, pp. 142, 145–46).

As in earlier years, the zone whips only did polling. Persuasion tasks fell to appointive whips (plus task-force members, if there was one). The track record of the organization was very good. On sixty votes on bills or amendments checked by the whips in the Ninety-fifth Congress (through May of 1978), the leadership position won fifty-five times, and only one defeat came as a surprise (Cooper, 1978, p. 1304). When necessary on close votes, the persuasion of the whips was reinforced by the top leaders. For example, on a 1979 amendment to cut funds from the budget resolution, which the leadership opposed, the ayes were leading when the votes ran out. O'Neill, Wright, and Brademas worked with the whips, persuading sixteen Democrats to change their votes to defeat the amendment (Cooper, 1978, p. 1301).

Under Whip Foley, the whip organization continued to expand. In 1985, the number of deputy whips increased to seven, and at-large whips to thirty-two. The whole organization included sixty-three members, one-fourth of the House Democrats (see figure 4.1). Then in 1987, when O'Neill retired, Wright and Foley moved up to Speaker and majority leader respectively. Tony Coelho (D, Cal.) became the first elected whip, and under him the organization grew even further. There were ten deputy and forty-four at-large whips in the 100th Congress, and then fifteen and sixty-five respectively in the 101st (1989–1991). The system of task forces had become regularized, and in 1987 four task-force chairmen were recognized as part of the whip system with the same status as deputy whips. (Task forces were organized around continuing issues as well as particular bills. The Contra-aid task force, for example, had the largest number of members—about seventy-five—and had had the same chairman for six years, David Bonior of Michigan, the chief deputy whip since 1987). Thus by 1989, the whip organization had grown to 103 members, 40 percent of the Caucus. With this many members, plus task-force participation, the task of contacting and persuading others in the party could be accomplished with great efficiency.

Task forces have become central to the whip system's operation. One member of the leadership said, "Every bill that goes to the floor that's of any major consequence at all has a whip task force, made up of people in the whip organization and members on the committee. . . . Then we meet two or three times a day, usually, when that bill is on the floor, whipping certain votes."[7] When a task force is formed, a notice will go out to the whip organization, inviting participation, and anyone who wishes to join can do so. This will sometimes cause problems on a troublesome bill. For example, at the first meeting of the task force formed for the continuing appropriations resolution in 1987, only four members showed up (Barry, 1989, p. 569). The task-force participants will include from as few as ten members to as many as sixty or seventy on a defense or Contra-aid bill. When a task force begins work, the options will be discussed and the leadership's position will be explained. Once details are worked out, members will begin taking names, count votes, and report back. That process will continue until the result is determined.

There continue to be regular weekly whip meetings, which are attended by a large number of the members, usually between forty and seventy. Given the size of the organization, this tends to be a fairly representative group. The leader quoted above said that it is "almost like a mini-Caucus, a sounding board for what's going on out there." He continued,

> They are the best meeting of the week, they're the most
> interesting, you learn the most. They're the most vocal, they're the

most contentious, often. People just get up and start to spout off about why the leadership isn't doing this, what the leadership should be doing, what strategies we should be taking. They're very political in nature. . . . Each of the leaders says something, then we turn it over to them, and they jump all over us.

An example of the kinds of exchanges that occur in the whip meetings comes from July 1989. The conflict between Les Aspin, chairman of the Armed Services Committee, and Democrats with liberal views on defense (which led to the 1987 attempt to oust Aspin that was discussed in chapter 3) continued beyond that event. Many liberals still thought that Aspin was too accommodating to administration views on defense. At the whip meeting,

> Marty Russo stood up and launched a massive attack on Les Aspin, about how [he] was going his own way with the Republican minority leader and ignoring the majority of Democrats on the Armed Services Committee. Therefore he shouldn't even be managing the [defense] bill when it came to the floor, and there was going to be a huge brouhaha unless we got a rule [governing floor debate] that would protect the Democratic majority on the committee.[8]

According to interviews with party leaders and members of the whip system, the bases for selection of appointive whips include geographic considerations and the ability to get the work done. Deputy whips represented geographic or group-based interests. In the One Hundredth Congress, for example, Charles Rangel (D, N.Y.) was selected to be deputy whip from the Black Caucus, and Pat Williams (D, Mont.) was chosen to be the liaison with organized labor (Barry, 1989, p. 189). Appointive whips also appear to be selected partly on the basis of party loyalty, which would be consistent with their responsibilities for selling the party's position on legislation. Figure 4.2 shows the mean party-unity scores for appointive whips, zone whips, and other members among southern Democrats for the Ninety-fifth through the One Hundredth Congresses.[9] The unity scores for appointive whips are consistently higher than those for other members, except in the Ninety-ninth Congress.[10] These data also show that zone whips' scores were also higher than other members', from the Ninety-eighth Congress on. This was when the class of '82 entered the House, adding many loyalist southerners to the Democratic party.

The expansion of the whip organization is a reflection of what Barbara Sinclair has aptly referred to as the "strategy of inclusion," one element of a three-pronged leadership strategy begun under O'Neill

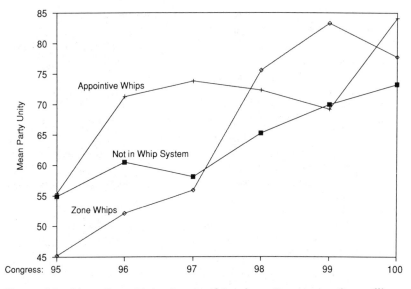

Figure 4.2   Mean Party-Unity Scores of Southern Democrats, Controlling for Membership in the Whip System

and continued under Wright (Sinclair, 1983, pp. 134–47; 1989b).[11] Members are brought in to participate in the process. This expands leadership resources, and gives independent members a sense of playing a significant part in shaping legislation. As one leader said, "I have always believed in the principle that the more people you involve in the decision-making process and the leadership process, the better off you are going to be as an entity in achieving the goals you want to achieve."[12] The larger whip system is also a direct response to demands among members for broader participation and input into party decisions. In the words of one at-large whip, "more members of the Caucus now feel a much broader sense of participation as a consequence of having this mechanism that allows everyone in."[13]

The Service Orientation of Party Leadership

The expanded communications network just described permitted the Democratic leadership to discover the degree of policy agreement that existed within the Caucus on various issues. It also provided a way to assess member satisfaction or dissatisfaction with the leadership or with other aspects of their situation. The former task was crucial if the leaders were to act successfully as the members' agents on policy matters. The latter effort was also important to maintain support for the leadership among the rank and file—support that could be drawn on to advance party interests. Since members' goals were not solely legislative, but involved electoral, power, and personal interests as well, part of the leaders' role as agents included activities which served those other interests.

Some services the leadership can perform for members, such as influencing committee assignments, are very consequential but can be done only occasionally. Given the number of leadership seats and Speaker's appointees on the Steering and Policy committee, the potential impact of the leadership on assignments is great, and it is likely to be especially consequential on the most-desired prestige committees. As we have seen, during the Carter-Reagan years support for party leadership positions became a progressively more important consideration in the allocation of assignments to major committees. Members knew that if they wanted leadership help, they had to help the leadership.

Other services performed by leaders are more routine, but can still be important to members. Speaker O'Neill referred to these powers as "little odds and ends":

> The power to recognize on the floor; . . . like men get pride out of handling the Committee of the Whole, being named the Speaker for the day; those little trips that came along—like those trips to China, trips to Russia, things of that nature; or other ad hoc committees or special committees, which I have assignments to. . . . And often times they have problems from their area and they need aid or assistance, either legislative wise or administrative wise. We're happy to try to open the door for them . . . (Malbin, 1977, p. 942)

Another leadership activity that has an important impact on members is scheduling. The scheduling of individual bills for floor action can affect the bills' chances for success, and so this can be very consequential to committee leaders. Bills with doubtful prospects can be delayed until greater support can be marshaled. Regarding the interests of rank-and-file members, particularly controversial issues can be kept from the floor until the Senate acts on parallel legislation, in order to avoid putting the members on the spot unnecessarily.. Members "want the leadership to provide protection from the casting of votes that are politically unpopular if there's no payoff."[14] Leaders can also help by scheduling votes so that they don't conflict with members' previously scheduled obligations. Scheduling is also important in a more general sense. As the workload of Congress has increased over the years, members have found it more and more difficult to meet their obligations and maintain some semblance of orderly family life. In response to the question "What do members want from the leadership?" one leader said, "They want to know how their lives are going to be run for the next six months or the next three months. In fact that's probably the number one thing they want, . . . because our lives are so hectic as it is. They want to know with some certainty when we're going to meet, when we're going to have votes so that we can plan our personal lives and our lives back in the districts."[15]

Leaders also serve members' reelection interests directly by helping them raise funds or speaking on their behalf. O'Neill often appeared at fund-raisers or events honoring his colleagues (Malbin, 1977, p. 942), and Barbara Sinclair (1989b, p. 317) reported that in 1987 Speaker Wright traveled to twenty-five different cities for events sponsored by the Democratic Congressional Campaign Committee.

A final aspect of leadership service that has become more important in recent years, especially under Speaker Wright, is influencing the media or helping members to do so. Of course House leaders have always had to deal with the media, but in earlier years the relationship was haphazard, depending more on the press's initiatives. Beginning in the mid-1980s, the Democratic leadership's strategy became more deliberate, seeking to shape public opinion and media interpretations. Leadership interest in appearing on the television news and on talk shows has increased. The party leaders have held more frequent press conferences targeted on particular legislative priorities, and have sought to place more "op-ed" pieces in major newspapers. These efforts were buttressed by the activities of a group of House Democrats led by Don Edwards of California (Malbin, 1986, p. 2134). During 1986 these members met twice a week to discuss ways to use the media to help them win on the floor. They regularly called talk-show producers to suggest Democratic representatives as potential guests, and sought to improve coverage of the Democratic response to Reagan's Saturday radio addresses.

Under Speaker Wright these media-oriented activities became more extensive. He substantially expanded the number of the Speaker's staffers with press responsibilities, and increased the number of appearances on talk shows. A working group under Majority Leader Foley was charged with defining a "message of the week," and then with getting that message out to the media (Barry, 1989, pp. 251–52). In late 1987, Whip Tony Coelho drafted a formal "year-end communications strategy" for the leadership, designed to influence the wrap-up stories that would be done on the first session of the One Hundredth Congress (Barry, 1989, pp. 525–26). In addition, efforts were made at whip meetings to discuss ways members could defend themselves in the media if they supported the party position on controversial matters. "When I was [in the House] the first couple of terms, I was struck how frequently we would lose votes or amendments simply because members were gun-shy, and didn't know how they could articulate the responses and so on. Well, this gives us more opportunity for dialogue and the comfort level of people is raised."[16] The whip meetings were also used to announce and disseminate results from public opinion polls conducted by the Democratic leadership, when they would be advantageous for the party (Barry, 1989, pp. 173, 541). The leadership also tried to improve the media exposure of members who supported them, particularly south-erners. "We try to include them in task forces; we try to make them chairmen of task forces; we try to give them a visible role in the me-dia. . . . We try to see that they get their fair share of exposure."[17]

Thus during the postreform period the Democratic leaders in the House sought to enhance their two-way communications with mem-bers, to increase their efforts to assist Democrats in achieving their goals, and to improve interactions between House Democrats and the media. Each of these efforts helped to make the leadership more effec-tive in advancing the Democratic program in the House. Perhaps most important of all, however, was the leadership's use of the expanded powers granted by the reforms of the 1970s.

Employing the Fruits of Reform: The Leadership and Agenda Management

During the reform era, the Speaker's ability to shape the agenda on the House floor was enhanced by the power to refer bills to more than one committee, by expanded opportunities to bring up bills under suspen-sion of the rules, and by the authority to appoint Democrats to the Rules Committee. In subsequent years, each of these powers played a role in fostering the resurgence of partisanship in the House and in advancing the Democrats' legislative interests.

The Multiple Referral of Bills

The power to refer bills to more than one committee was included in the limited committee reorganization passed in 1974 (Davidson and Oleszek, 1977).[18] This was an important step for the House, because it was a departure from the system of fixed and specialized committee ju-risdictions and of single referral of bills, which was the bedrock of the period of committee government (Collie and Cooper, 1989, p. 245). Multiple referrals are generally of two types. A joint referral means that a bill is sent to two or more committees simultaneously. A sequential referral means that a bill reported by one committee is then assigned to one or more other committees.[19] In 1977, the Speaker was granted the further authority to impose time limits on the first committee in a sequential referral (Davidson, Oleszek, and Kephart, 1988, p. 5).

Early research on multiple referrals concluded that it had been an inconsequential or even a counterproductive change. Smith and Deering (1984, p. 253) argued that "multiple referral has institutionalized the fragmented consideration of legislation in many policy areas and made expeditious House action even more difficult to achieve in some cases." They cited evidence, compiled by a House committee considering further reorganization, that in the Ninety-fifth Congress multiply referred bills were less likely to be reported and less likely to pass than single referrals.[20] Sheppard (1985, p. 320) cited more specific data from the Ninety-fifth and Ninety-sixth Congresses: single referrals were twice as likely to be reported and three times as likely to pass as multiple referrals. Sheppard argued that these statistics showed that multiple referrals did the opposite of what was intended, leading to delay instead of expediting legislation.

As Collie and Cooper (1989, pp. 248–49) point out, however, the difference in passage success is likely due to systematic differences in the kinds of bills in the two categories. Single referrals include a large proportion of trivial matters (like "commemorative" bills, honoring an individual or group) which are easy to pass. Multiple referrals, on the other hand, tend to involve more complex and conflictual issues. We would expect that a smaller proportion of such bills would pass, regardless of how they were referred. Furthermore, the patterns relating to the different types of bills have been changing since the 1970s. While it remains true that a greater proportion of singly referred bills are passed, the proportion of multiple referrals that were reported exceeded the proportion for single referrals in each Congress from the Ninety-seventh through the One Hundredth, and the share of bills that was multiply referred has grown as well (Collie and Cooper, 1989, p. 249). It is worth recalling, moreover, that the earlier conclusions on the impact of multiple referral are based on the Carter years, when party divisions were still relatively deep. These divisions would, of course, cause trouble for complex controversial legislation. Increased homogeneity should have eased those problems, however, and the data from the Reagan years are consistent with that expectation.

The growth in the use of multiple referrals, coupled with the Speaker's power to set deadlines for committee consideration of such bills, has increased leadership influence over the content and scheduling of legislation, and those powers can be used to advance the party's agenda.[21] Davidson, Oleszek, and Kephart (1988, p. 21) make note of O'Neill's actions in connection with the 1986 trade bill, a major Democratic initiative. It was referred to six committees, and Majority Leader Wright was assigned to coordinate their activities and to promote a united front in support of the bill. Five of the committees reported the bill, and it received all but four Democratic votes on the floor. Wright was also charged with coordinating action on the omnibus antidrug bill, another important element of the party's agenda, portions of which were considered by twelve committees.

Suspension of the Rules

Another expansion of the leadership's influence over the agenda involved the DSG-supported increase (in 1973, and again in 1977) in the number of days available for consideration of bills under suspension of the rules. Suspensions require a two-thirds vote for passage and permit no amendments, so traditionally the procedure had been used for truly noncontroversial bills.[22] With the expansion of the number of days it could be used, however, everyone (particularly the Republicans) recognized that the procedure could be applied to bills which involved less consensus.

In 1973, many Republicans spoke in opposition to the rules change. They claimed that, contrary to the historical justification for suspensions, the procedure was being used for major bills involving substantial amounts of money. Barber Conable (R, N.Y.) charged that the Democrats were "increasing the hold of party over the will of the majority, and at the same time doubling the opportunity to bring bills to the floor under what amounts to a closed rule" (*Congressional Record,* Jan. 3, 1973, p. 21). Richard Bolling (D, Mo.) responded to the Republicans, noting that if majority control were switched, then they would probably be proposing the rules change and he would be objecting. However, he said that he had experienced Congress controlled by the Republicans, and "they believe in majority rule, and they exercise it with great skill, and some ruthlessness" (*Congressional Record,* Jan. 3, 1973, pp. 22–23).[23] In the 1977 debate, Henson Moore (R, La.) claimed that "legislative steamrollering of substantive legislation under this procedure . . . will become even more frequent," and Bill Frenzel (R, Minn.) said that by doubling the days for suspensions, "twice as many amendments can be suppressed. Twice as much debate can be limited" (*Congressional Record,* Jan. 4, 1977, pp. 60, 61). However, Majority Leader Jim Wright responded to Republican complaints by saying, "Since time immemorial, it has been the responsibility of the majority party in Congress to organize the Congress. With that responsibility has gone the obligation of establishing the rules under which the Congress would operate" (*Congressional Record,* Jan. 4, 1977, p. 66).

As table 3.2 showed, with the change in the rules and the adoption of electronic voting, the number of roll calls on suspensions jumped sharply. If these were supposed to be noncontroversial, why should there be so many record votes? One possibility, of course, is that increasingly these were bills that involved some significant disagreement. Another is that members increasingly wanted to be on the record in favor of popular programs that virtually everyone supported, an exercise in "credit claiming" (Mayhew, 1974). The data in figure 4.3 on suspensions in the Ninety-first to the One Hundredth Congresses indicate that both possibilities may apply. At the bottom of the figure is the total number of suspensions in each Congress, and the number with consensual votes excluded. In both 1973 and 1977, the number of suspensions jumped sharply, and there was a slight increase each time in the proportion of votes that were consensual.[24] This could reflect the credit-claiming motivation. On the other hand, the data show that the relative increase in partisan disagreement was much greater on nonconsensual votes, particularly after the Ninety-fourth Congress. Between the Ninety-fourth and the Ninety-ninth Congresses, the mean party differences increased only 8 points overall, but it increased 25

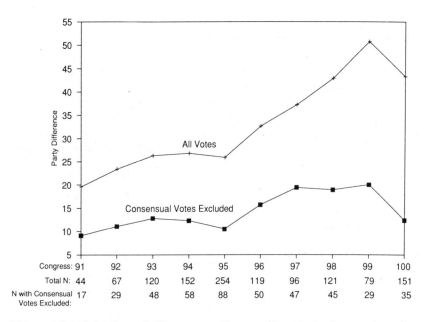

Figure 4.3   Mean Party Difference on Votes on Passage by Suspension of the Rules (All Votes and Consensual Votes Excluded), 91st–100th Congresses

points on nonconsensual votes to a level of 51 points. That may indicate many things, but lack of controversy isn't one of them.

Thus as procedural changes expanded the opportunities for consideration of bills under suspension of the rules, that device was employed more frequently for legislation on which there was significant partisan disagreement. It might be argued that this would not be very consequential, since a two-thirds vote was still needed for passage. That is, except in rare circumstances the Democrats, even if completely united, couldn't pass the bill without some Republican support. But the ability to garner two-thirds support on passage doesn't imply that all of the supporters were in agreement with the specific provisions in the bill. The suspension procedure is an ideal device for the Democrats to use to advance their agenda when the *existence* of a program has substantial public support, but the parties disagree about the particulars. The Democrats can shape the bill to their satisfaction in committee, and then bring it up under suspension. The Republicans are then put in the position of providing sufficient votes for passage, or explaining to their constituents why they opposed a popular program.

Not surprisingly, the attempted use of the suspension procedure on more controversial items led to an increase in the number of such bills that failed to pass.[25] In the Ninety-third Congress (1973–75), only one suspension attempt was defeated, but twenty-five lost in the Ninety-fourth, and thirty-three in the Ninety-fifth (*CQWR*, Sept. 30, 1978, p. 2694). The causes of these defeats varied, as examples from 1977 show. On a move to upgrade the status and salaries of the Office of Management and Budget, there was no strong sectional or partisan pattern: 48 percent of Republicans, 35 percent of northern Democrats, and 29 percent of southern Democrats voted nay. On a proposal to conduct a study of the desirability of adding certain Montana lands to the National Wilderness Preservation System, most of the opposition came from Republicans (75 percent voting against), but the margin of defeat came from fifty-two Democratic defections—only 19 percent of the members voting, but enough to kill the bill. Finally, on a bill to increase staff funds for former presidents, most of the opposition came from Democrats: 79 percent of Republicans voted for the bill, while 64 percent of the Democrats were against.

As the last two examples illustrate, sometimes attempts to suspend the rules failed because Democratic cohesion was insufficient. The Speaker's support is necessary to use the procedure, so the interests of the Democratic majority couldn't be overridden by a runaway committee. However, in some cases the Speaker was unaware of disagreements within the party, while in others he was aware of conflict but underestimated its magnitude. In late 1978, a number of Democrats proposed limits on the use of suspensions to guarantee that *their* interests would be protected. At the meeting of the Democratic Caucus to organize for the Ninety-sixth Congress, the party adopted a proposal negotiated with Speaker O'Neill (*CQWR*, Dec. 9, 1978, p. 3405). The new rule prohibited using the suspension procedure for any bill with an estimated cost of more than $100 million in one fiscal year. The restriction was waived for certain emergency situations and in the closing days of a congressional session. In addition, the Speaker could ask the Steering and Policy Committee for a waiver for any bill; if granted, members would receive four days' advance notice before the bill could be voted on. These procedures could protect a majority of Democrats from being faced with suspension votes on bills where they did not desire it; the rules, of course, did nothing to protect the interests of Republicans.

The Rules Committee and Special Rules

The third, and most important, expansion of the Democratic leadership's power over the agenda involved the change in the relationship between the Speaker and the Rules Committee. As we saw in chapter 2, up to the 1960s Rules had been dominated by a coalition of conservative southern Democrats and Republicans.[26] Most major legislation needed a resolution (called a "special rule") from the committee to be considered on the House floor. The special rule would set the amount of time for debate, and specify who would control the time and the circumstances under which amendments would be permitted. The conservative majority on Rules frequently used this power to completely block legislation they opposed, or to compel compromises in their favor as the price for letting bills go to the floor. This pattern of behavior led Speaker Rayburn to seek expansion of the committee's membership from twelve to fifteen in 1961. This increased the number of Democrats to ten, and the two new Democratic appointments gave the leadership a narrow eight to seven majority. However, the link to the leadership was limited and uncertain, and on a number of occasions Rules was still a roadblock to Democratic legislation (Oppenheimer, 1977, pp. 98–101; Rules Committee, 1983, pp. 184–212).

The more profound change in the Rules Committee–leadership relationship occurred in 1975 when the Speaker was given the power to appoint the members of Rules, subject to ratification by the Caucus. Under this arrangement, the committee was quickly transformed "into an arm of the leadership. It can now be relied on to be a traffic cop that serves the leadership instead of one that serves the chairman of the committee" (Oppenheimer, 1977, p. 114).[27] Beginning in 1975, three new roles for the Rules Committee began to take shape (Oppenheimer,

1981, pp. 216–18). As the "new traffic cop," Rules sought to expedite the passage of major legislation, rather than delay it. Under the "dress rehearsal" role, the committee's hearings offered bill managers the opportunity to preview their legislation before bringing it to the House floor. Finally, the "field commander" role was played by certain committee members. They served as the "eyes and ears" of the leadership, offering information and advice on legislation. Particularly important in this role was Richard Bolling, long a personal ally and friend of Tip O'Neill. Bolling's importance as an agent of the leadership was further enhanced when he became chairman of Rules in 1979.

Reflecting the new traffic-cop role, the Rules Committee began to use its authority to write special rules to facilitate the passage of important bills produced by the substantive committees. Until this time most rules were "open" (with no restrictions on germane amendments), while a few were "closed" (with all amendments barred). Closed rules were mostly used for tax bills from the Ways and Means Committee. But the Rules Committee began moving beyond this simple distinction by crafting "complex rules" (Oppenheimer, 1981, pp. 218–22), which would place limits on amendments without closing them off entirely, or would make complex allocations of debate time. An early example of this was the rule for the energy bill of 1977 (containing the Carter administration's energy program). The rule permitted a dozen amendments, reflecting major policy alternatives, including a Republican substitute. "Because of the rule, the House was able to complete action on this controversial bill in five legislative days and to prevent it from being loaded down with last-minute amendments" (Oppenheimer, 1981, p. 221).

As Bach and Smith (1988) pointed out in their detailed study of the politics of special rules, the use of complex rules was not merely a device for gaining partisan advantage, especially in the 1970s. These rules were also designed to counter the growing uncertainty of the floor environment. Bach and Smith argued (1988, pp. 12–33) that four developments helped to create this new uncertainty: (1) the change to recorded teller voting on amendments and electronic voting, (2) the Speaker's new power of multiple referral, (3) the shift of power from committee chairmen to subcommittees, and (4) the great increase in the number of floor amendments proposed and adopted.[28] In this new environment, committee bills could be beset by a wide range of attacks proposing alternative policies. Restrictive rules, as with the energy bill of 1977, could limit the alternatives to a manageable few, constraining the chances of delay or defeat. Indeed, part of the impetus for the use of restrictive rules came from rank-and-file members. In August 1979, John LaFalce (D, N.Y.) sent a letter to the Speaker, signed by forty Democrats, complaining that the growth in the number of floor amend-

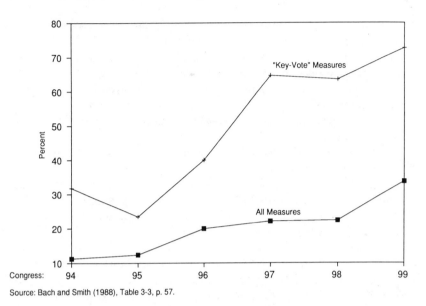

Source: Bach and Smith (1988), Table 3-3, p. 57.

Figure 4.4 Restrictive Rules as a Proportion of All Rules, for All Measures and "Key-Vote" Measures, 94th–99th Congresses.

ments was preventing members from meeting their other respon-sibilities, and urging increased reliance on restrictive rules (Bach and Smith, 1988, pp. 31, 33; Smith, 1989, pp. 40–42).

Partly for their own reasons and partly in response to members' wish-es, the leadership supported more frequent resort to restrictive rules. As data presented by Bach and Smith show (see figure 4.4), between the Ninety-fourth and Ninety-ninth Congresses, restrictive rules accounted for an increasing proportion of the rules adopted. Moreover, the growth was particularly great for more important bills, as shown by the data for "key-vote" measures (i.e., bills that involved key votes) as classified by *Congressional Quarterly*. By the Ninety-ninth Congress, almost three-fourths of key-vote measures involved restrictive rules, and another 13 percent used closed rules (Bach and Smith, 1988, p. 57).

The leadership was not always involved in shaping the actions of the Rules Committee. Sinclair (1983, p. 130) stated, "The party leadership involves itself in the designing of rules only on particularly important and problematical legislation." However, the "leaders are always in-formed of the intentions of Rules on legislation of consequence, and sometimes the committee clears its plans with them." Indeed, Anthony Bielenson (D, Cal.), a member of Rules, said, "The Speaker does not ask

much of us, partly because we mostly do what we think he wants"
(Plattner, 1985c, p. 1674). The increase in the use of restrictive rules was
greatest on legislation that was most important to the leadership. The
data on key-vote measures cited above reflect this. Another reflection is
that restrictive rules were much more likely to be used on legislation
from the four prestige committees (Bach and Smith, 1988, pp. 116–17).
In each of the Ninety-fifth through the Ninety-ninth Congresses, over
80 percent of the rules granted to bills from those committees were restricted or closed. The proportion for policy or constituency committees was much lower, but in the Ninety-ninth Congress it exceeded 40
percent for both groups.

Another reflection of the use of restrictive rules on bills that are
important to the leadership is presented in the data on multiply referred bills in figure 4.5 (Bach and Smith, 1988, p. 60). They show that,
except for the Ninety-seventh Congress, restrictive or closed rules were
more likely to be used when multiple referrals came to the floor. In the
Ninety-ninth Congress, almost two-thirds of the rules for multiply referred bills were restricted or closed, as compared to 39 percent for
single referrals. In the case of multiple referrals, the Rules Committee
potentially has another important role. If the various committees con-

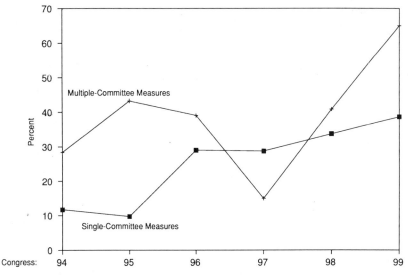

Source: Bach and Smith (1988), Table 3-4, p. 60.

Figure 4.5 Closed or Restrictive Rules as a Percentage of All Rules, for
Single-Committee and Multiple-Committee Measures, 94th–99th Congresses.

sidering a measure report different versions, Rules determines which provisions of the bill will go to the floor (Bach and Smith, 1988, p. 22).

While restrictive rules were not initially developed solely to seek partisan advantage for the majority, we will see from examples below that they were employed for that purpose more often in the 1980s. This strategy provoked conflict with House Republicans. As James Quillen of Tennessee, the ranking Republican on Rules, said in 1985, "We used to have a [bipartisan] coalition on the Rules Committee until the speaker packed it with an unreasonable amount of Democrats" (Plattner, 1985, p. 1672). This growing conflict is reflected in the increasing partisanship of roll-call votes on the adoption of special rules (see table 4.1).[29] Until the shift to electronic voting, roll-call votes on rules were relatively infrequent. They usually involved closed rules, or rules on bills the Republicans opposed. With the new voting rules, the number of votes on rules increased sharply from the Ninety-third to the Ninety-fifth Congresses, as did the proportion of such votes that were consensual. Electronic voting permitted the House to vote on many things that had previously been handled by voice votes. However, the number of nonconsensual votes increased as well, and on those the partisan split

Table 4.1 Some Characteristics of Votes on Special Rules in the House, 84th–100th Congressses

Congress	Number of Roll Calls on Rules	Percent Consensual[a]	Mean Party Difference, Excluding Consensual Votes (N)
84	14	21	34 (11)
85	16	13	44 (14)
86	12	17	26 (10)
87	10	20	47 (8)
88	20	40	50 (12)
89	23	17	47 (19)
90	22	23	28 (17)
91	29	21	23 (23)
92	43	51	32 (21)
93	89	44	38 (50)
94	118	60	45 (47)
95	134	56	41 (59)
96	112	52	59 (54)
97	60	30	49 (42)
98	80	21	62 (63)
99	113	26	60 (84)
100	91	13	67 (79)

[a]A majority of 90% or more.

grew a great deal. In the Ninety-first Congress, the average party difference was 23 points; by the One Hundredth Congress it was more than three times as large. Meanwhile, the proportion of consensual votes on rules roll calls declined sharply during the 1980s. Chapter 5 will consider in detail the Republican reaction to the Democrats' new strategies.

The Rules Committee, in addition to increasing the use of restrictive rules, developed other innovations (Bach and Smith, 1988, pp. 74–86). One was the "king of the mountain" rule, whereby a series of amendments would be taken on one subject and, if more than one passed, only the last successful amendment would become part of the legislation. Another was the "self-executing" rule, under which certain amendments would be considered to be automatically adopted when the rule was passed, without a separate vote. Each of these tactics has the potential to be turned to partisan advantage for specific legislative purposes, as well as to facilitate the Democratic leadership's management of the agenda. Restrictive rules can bar Republican amendments which would cause some Democrats political embarrassment if they were forced to go on the record. The self-executing provision can work analogously for positive actions: Democrats can support the inclusion of controversial provisions in bills without specifically voting for them. With king-of-the-mountain provisions, Democrats can vote for politically popular Republican initiatives *and* for Democratic alternatives, with the knowledge that only the latter will become part of a bill. Of course, as Bach and Smith (1988, p. 70) noted, there is not always a clear Democratic position, and then Rules members try to remain as neutral as possible.

A few examples will illustrate the use of special rules to secure advantages for the Democratic agenda. An early effort was the attempt, in 1981, to devise a rule that would prevent President Reagan from securing the cuts in domestic programs he desired in the budget reconciliation bill. The Republicans wanted a single up or down vote on the entire package, but the Democrats sought to put the GOP members on the spot by requiring in the rule that the various program cuts be voted on individually. Unfortunately for the Democrats, defecting Boll Weevils prevented them from passing their rule and permitted adoption of the Republican substitute (*CQWR*, June 27, 1981, pp. 1127–28). The Democratic leadership was more successful on budget matters in later years. For the 1984 budget resolution, the Democratic leadership devised a king-of-the-mountain procedure under which a number of alternatives would be permitted, but the leadership-supported plan would go last. The Rules Committee held hearings on the rule, but "the outcome was a foregone conclusion. House Democratic leaders had already instructed Rules Democrats on the precise rule to issue controlling floor debate . . ." (Tate, 1984, p. 751). The effort succeeded and the Democratic plan was adopted.

Agenda management was not confined to budget issues. The rule for the fiscal 1987 defense bill established a series of king-of-the-mountain provisions on arms-control proposals supported by the Democratic leadership and a coalition of centrist Democrats. In each case the Republicans had a chance to offer substitute provisions, but the leadership-sponsored alternatives were listed last. Those Democratic proposals were, moreover, themselves made unamendable by the rule. This prevented the opponents from trying to shift the result in their direction. Finally, the arms-control proposals were scheduled at three separate points during the two-week debate on the bill. "This allowed members who voted against Reagan on important amendments to follow those with 'pro-Reagan' votes on other amendments, in order to assuage conservative sentiment in their districts" (Towell, 1986, p. 1870). Thus the Speaker's new control over the agenda, and particularly his changed relationship with the Rules Committee, gave Democrats new opportunities to advance their shared policy goals.

The changed relationship between Rules Democrats and the Speaker did not develop entirely without conflict, however. For example, Oppenheimer (1981, p. 225) reported that during the Ninety-fifth Congress, Speaker O'Neill was having difficulty getting the support of one committee member for a rule. The Speaker indicated to the member that if he couldn't go along, he might find himself serving on the District of Columbia Committee instead. Given the Speaker's control over appointments, the leadership is usually able to get what it wants. In June of 1985, the committee wrote a rule on a Contra-aid bill in accord with the leadership's wishes, even though Chairman Claude Pepper sided with President Reagan on the issue. In 1984, O'Neill had to pressure Rules members to grant a closed rule on a tax bill, because some of them opposed its provisions. After three meetings, he finally got what he wanted. Chairman Pepper said, "The third time, the Speaker called us down and told us why he felt like he did. We went back and I said to the committee, 'In the final analysis, the way it's set up now, we are an arm of the leadership.'"[30] Perhaps nothing better illustrates the leadership's dominant relationship with Rules than the fact that O'Neill reluctantly reduced the committee's size in 1983 (from sixteen to thirteen) because he was unable to persuade any senior Democrats to take vacant seats (Ernhalt, 1983).

Bach and Smith (1988, p. 112) stated, "It would be a mistake to infer from the trends reported in the previous two chapters that the sole or even primary effect of restrictive rules has been to centralize power in the House." Certainly, as their evidence shows, it has not been the sole effect. Whether it has been the primary effect is open to judgment. It does seem clear, however, that their evidence and the research of others, as well as what has been presented here and what we will see further below, show that centralization of power in the leadership with respect to agenda control has been an *important* effect of the changing patterns of special rules, and an increasing one. And this centralization was not generally contrary to the wishes of Democrats on committees and in the Caucus. Smith (1989, pp. 188–95), and examples described below, show that the leadership and members of major committees frequently worked in partnership to shape the floor environment for their bills. (We will return to this point at the end of the chapter.) Moreover, the growing tendency to seek advantage from this power was dependent on the changes in the distribution of preferences in the Democratic Caucus. As Smith (1989, p. 43) says, the "declining internal polarization [among House Democrats] made it considerably easier for the Democratic leadership and the Rules Committee to adopt a strategy that would often require party cohesiveness on the floor."

Leadership at Full Tide: The Wright Speakership

The combined effects of increased Democratic consensus, new institutional powers for the party leadership, and a greater willingness by leaders to use the tools at their disposal reached their maximum when Jim Wright became Speaker in the One Hundredth Congress. In this section we will examine the interplay of those factors, concentrating on events in 1987, to show how far the House had moved away from committee and subcommittee government toward what we have termed "conditional party government."

Articulating an Agenda

The new Speaker startled many outside observers when, in his acceptance speech to the Caucus, he began outlining an agenda of legislative priorities for the House in 1987. As Barbara Sinclair (1989a, pp. 6–7) has demonstrated, the Democratic leadership had begun playing a developing role in agenda setting during the 1980s. Indeed, the attempt went back at least as far as Carl Albert in 1975, and O'Neill sought to articulate Democratic alternatives to Reagan's programs in 1983 and 1985. What made Wright's effort so surprising was the scope and specificity of the proposals, and the extensive efforts to keep its elements in the public eye and press them to completion.[31]

Wright said he wanted a "limited agenda that could be achieved" (Sinclair, 1989b, p. 313), and he elaborated it through discussions with

Majority Leader Tom Foley and the Steering and Policy Committee, announcing a schedule to House Democrats at a weekend retreat in January.[32] This was not, however, an agenda imposed from the top down. Wright indicated (Walsh, 1986, p. A4) that he had no intention of "trying to be the ayatollah, sending edicts down from on high." As Matthew McHugh (D, N.Y.) said, "Even if the Speaker wanted to impose an agenda, he doesn't have the tools to do it" (Hook, 1987, p. 1483). Rather, "for the most part, Wright has used the power of the speakership to propel issues about which there is wide consensus among Democrats" (Hook, 1987, p. 1483). Indeed, as he indicated in his speech at the Democratic retreat, he clearly saw his list of priorities as their common agenda: "I know I speak for all of you when I say we will brook no interference [with] the agenda we have promised the American people. We're not going to be combative. We are going to be firm. We're going to act and we're going to achieve" (Barry, 1989, pp. 114–15). Even on the issue that caused his colleagues the most nervousness, a tax increase, there are indications that there was significant (albeit not universal) support in the Caucus for the substance of his position.[33] Most of the disagreement involved whether it was good politics to press the matter.

Wright believed that the House should produce a program, not just individual bills, and saw it as his task to coordinate that program. He said, "The House should develop a program of action . . . rather than leaving the making of policy to a fragmented group of 21 standing committees without any cohesion. . . . There has to be a sense of coordinated policy, a cohesive pattern to what the institution does" (Hook, 1987, p. 1487). That statement could easily have appeared as a DSG policy position in the early 1970s.

While not every Democrat in the Caucus supported all of Wright's list of priorities, especially on taxes, there was considerable support for the effort to articulate an agenda for the party. It appears that this has become one of the legitimate and expected roles of the leadership. When a number of representatives were asked in interviews, "What do members want leaders to do?" establishing legislative priorities was usually one of the items mentioned. For example, one congressman's first response was, "They want to have an agenda set, so that there is a clear direction and purpose and set of goals."[34] One of the members of the party leadership, when asked how House Democrats responded to Wright's announcing and pushing an agenda, said,

> Very well. . . . Members liked it basically. They liked the certainty
> of the schedule. They liked the fact that he was moving ahead and
> was tough. Even though we ran over some of our own members a
> little bit, they liked that; they liked the type of leadership. And

we're starting to hear a little bit more from our Caucus about how we've got to take the bull by the horns now that we've got our leadership together, and we've got to start moving again.[35]

Employing the Leadership's Powers

The Whip System. Wright also moved aggressively on the organizational front. The sharp expansion of the whip system has already been noted. Wright appointed David Bonior as chief deputy whip immediately after being elected Speaker, establishing ties to House liberals, especially with regard to foreign policy. (Bonior was a leading opponent of Contra aid, and chairman of the Caucus task force on the subject.) During the One Hundredth Congress, Wright made extensive and aggressive use of the whip organization to count heads and marshal support for the agenda, and many participants believe that it made a difference in the outcomes. As one moderate southern whip said, "I think you'd have a lot of trouble getting a lot of this legislation through if it wasn't for the whips. The whip system is a big deal, and it really works. I spend a lot of time on it, and I know that others do too."[36] Whip meetings were used to plan strategy and build morale. Dan Rostenkowski, the chairman of Ways and Means, said, "Now the whip meetings are a tool for total control" (Barry, 1989, p. 99).

The Steering and Policy Committee. Wright indicated to members of the Steering and Policy Committee that he wanted to "use that panel more as a tool for developing Democratic policy" (Hook, 1986a, p. 3070). However, he moved quickly to strengthen his influence over the committee by replacing most of the staff and by making his own choices of members to represent groups in the Caucus (like blacks, women, and freshmen) who traditionally received Speaker's appointments. (O'Neill had permitted each of the groups to select its own representatives.) He picked fellow Texan Jim Chapman to represent the freshmen, even though Chapman had actually been first elected in a special election to the previous Congress (*CQWR*, Dec. 13, 1986, p. 3070). Wright even asked Jack Brooks, the most senior member of the Texas delegation, to run for election as a regional representative (Barry, 1989, p. 83).

The Speaker used this enhanced influence on Steering and Policy to affect committee assignments. He had the committee fill the vacancies on Public Works and Foreign Affairs early, in December, so that those committees could organize before Congress convened. He wanted the former to be able to report quickly two of the party's agenda items, and the latter to begin to deal with the burgeoning Iran-Contra scandal

(*CQWR*, Dec. 6, 1986, p. 3094). Before appointments were made to one of the prestige committees, Wright talked to candidates to make sure they understood their obligation to support the party position (Sinclair, 1989a, p. 4). When an Appropriations Committee vacancy occurred during 1987, Wright approached the appointment with care, and examined the records of potential candidates on fourteen "leadership votes" during the year. He said, "I can't afford to have any more members on these key committees who aren't leadership people" (Barry, 1989, p. 393). Jim Chapman of Texas was given an Appropriations assignment late in 1988, partly as a reward for providing the leadership with a crucial vote on the 1987 reconciliation bill (discussed below). As Sinclair (1989a, p. 4) said, the leadership was "sending a clear message to the Democratic membership that a willingness to take risks for the party would be rewarded."

One of the most remarkable examples of Wright's willingness to expand and to use his institutional powers, and of the fact that such behavior received support and encouragement among the membership, occurred when Butler Derrick, a party loyalist from South Carolina, came to see the Speaker during 1987 with a proposal.[37] Derrick was angry because a recent appointee to Appropriations was refusing to support the party position on welfare reform. Derrick argued that all committee assignments should be made temporary for the first term; only after that would renewal be automatic. Wright proposed the idea to the Steering and Policy Committee, and appointed a task force to study it. The task force never reported, but word got around to the membership. Just the possibility of such a change could do wonders to encourage loyalty.

Multiple Referrals. Wright never made any secret of his intention to use his institutional powers to advance the agenda he had proposed. He indicated that "the goal of leadership" was to press for passage of the majority party's programs (Cohen, 1987, p. 238). "House rules," he said, "if you know how to use them, are tilted toward allowing the majority to get its will done" (Hook, 1987, p. 1486).

The Speaker recognized that multiple referral of complex bills could be a roadblock to passage, so he intervened in the legislative process on behalf of such bills that were on his agenda. One example was the catastrophic health insurance bill, considered by the Energy and Commerce and the Ways and Means committees. Wright pressed strongly for the inclusion in the bill of a provision making Medicare pay outpatient prescription-drug costs. The committees produced bills that differed in some details. Demonstrating that leadership participation in such circumstances is not always regarded as an invasion of committee "turf,"

Wright was urged to get personally involved. Faced with strong administration opposition, proponents on both committees wanted to work out their differences before the bill went to the floor. "'A single bill with all the important players on board is necessary,' a committee leader said. 'And to get it, you, Mr. Speaker, need to be involved.' 'You need to take a major role,' the Speaker was told" (Sinclair, 1989b, p. 314). Wright called a meeting of the committee and subcommittee chairmen (*CQWR*, July 4, 1987, p. 1437). With the Speaker acting as broker, the Democratic leaders eliminated a number of conflicting provisions in coming to an agreement on a single bill. One, however, was retained: the Wright-supported provision on prescription drugs.

In 1988, a bill to impose new economic sanctions on South Africa because of its apartheid policy fell under the jurisdiction of eight committees. The bill was a leadership priority, so the committees were asked to act quickly, and later Speaker Wright set an informal deadline of June 9 for action. The deadline was not met, partly because Ways and Means had delayed action until they completed work on the bill making technical corrections to the 1986 tax reform. The leadership kept pressing the committee, however, and committee action was completed August 3. Wright scheduled it for floor consideration on August 11; on the day before, the Rules Committee stripped from the bill a Republican-sponsored amendment included by the Banking Committee and imposed a restrictive rule. The bill passed by a very partisan 244 to 132 vote (only twenty-four Republicans voted aye).[38]

Special Rules. During 1987, the Democratic leadership was particularly aggressive in using the Rules Committee to shape floor circumstances to favor Democratic legislative initiatives. Table 4.2 lists the ten bills that were Wright legislative priorities, with notes on the characteristics of the rules that were passed to govern their floor consideration.[39] A number of things are apparent. First, all are, not surprisingly, major pieces of legislation.[40] Second, virtually all involved conflict between House Democrats and the president. Reagan formally opposed passage of all but one of the bills (aid to the homeless), and there was much public administration criticism of even that one. Third, almost all of the bills received rules that restricted debate, and most provided blanket waivers against points of order (see Bach and Smith, 1988, pp. 105–6). The data in table 4.3 show that the bills that were priority items for the leadership were much more likely to receive restrictive rules or blanket waivers than other legislation. Only one of the Speaker's priority bills came to the floor under an open rule for amendments, while three-fourths of other bills did so. Where at least some amendments were per-

Table 4.2 Speaker Wright's Legislative Priorities in 1987, and Selected Bills with Simple Rules

	Wright Priorities
H.R.1	Clean Water Act Amendments. (Same bill vetoed by Reagan in 1986.) Closed rule; bill passed 406-8 (president opposed).
H.R.2	Omnibus Highway Reauthorization. (Almost identical bill passed in 1986.) Closed rule, waived all points of order; bill passed 401-20 (president opposed).
H.R.3	Omnibus Trade Bill. Rule waived all points of order; only amendments in Rule Committee report were permitted; bill passed 290-137 (D:247-6; R:42-131; president opposed).
H.R.27	F.S.L.I.C. Rescue. Only listed (unamendable) amendments permitted to one section of bill (Rule accepted by voice vote); bill passed 402-6 (president opposed).
H.R.558	Urgent Relief for the Homeless. Rule waived Budget Act; otherwise simple rule (rule adopted unanimously); bill adopted 274-126 (D:236-0; R:38-126).
H.R.1720	Welfare Reform. Rule waived all points of order; only two unamendable amendments permitted; bill passed 230-194 (D:217-31; R:13-163, president opposed).
H.R.2470	Catastrophic Health Insurance. Rule waived all points of order; only two unamendable amendments permitted; bill passed 302-127 (D:241-14; R:61-113; president opposed).
H.R.3030	Assistance to Farm Credit System. Rule waived all points of order; only amendments printed in Rules Committee report permitted (all unamendable); bill passed 365-49 (president opposed).
H.R.3545	Budget Reconciliation. Rule waived all points of order; included self-executing amendments; only listed en bloc amendments (unamendable) permitted; bill passed 206-205 (D:205-41; R:1-164; president opposed).
H. Con. Res. 93	Budget Resolution. Only four unamendable substitutes permitted; Democratic substitute adopted 230-192 (D:230-19; R:0-173; president opposed). (Final action by voice vote.)
	Selected Bills with Simple Rules.
H.R.157	Constitution Day Declaration. Passed by voice.
H.R.953	Maritime Programs in Transportation Department. Passed by voice.
H.R.1212	Restrictions on Private Sector Use of Polygraph Test. Passed 254-158 (D:208-33; R:46-125, president opposed).
H.R.1315	Nuclear Regulatory Commission Authorization. Passed 389-20.
H.R.1934	Write "Fairness Doctrine" into Law. Passed 302-102 (D:223-16; R:79-86; president opposed).
H.R.2897	Federal Trade Commission Reauthorization. Passed 404-10. (president opposed.)
H.R.2939	Independent Counsel Law. Passed 322-87 (D:238-3; R:84-84, president opposed).
H.R.3025	Approve Appalachian Radioactive Waste Compact. Passed by voice.

Table 4.3 Characteristics of Special Rules for Speaker's Priority Bills and Other Bills, 1987

	% Speaker's Priority Bills ($N=10$)	% All Other Bills ($N=45$)
Blanket Waiver of Points of Order	60	9
Open Rule for Amendments	10	76
Amendments Made Un-amendable (Closed Rules Excluded)	63 ($N=8$)	10 ($N=42$)
Bills Received "Simple" Rules	0	42

mitted, those to priority bills were likely to be ruled unamendable. This was true for only 10 percent of the other bills.

If we define a "simple" rule as one which is open to any germane amendment, provides no waivers against points of order, and has none of the rules "innovations," like self-executing amendments, described by Bach and Smith (1988, pp. 76–86), then *none* of the rules for priority bills qualifies. However, fully 42 percent of other rules are simple by this definition. Table 4.2 also presents a selected list of the bills that received simple rules in 1987. Many of the bills granted simple rules were non-controversial; eleven of nineteen passed by voice vote or with 90 percent or larger roll-call majorities. In other cases, there was a clear partisan position, but there were apparently no Republican alternatives that could undermine it. (On H.R.2939, providing for independent counsels to investigate executive wrongdoing, there were four roll calls on amendments. All were offered by Republicans; all lost; none received more than eighteen Democratic votes; and only three Democrats voted nay on passage.) In still other instances, like the bill to regulate the use of polygraphs, Democrats were divided on the details. Overall, however, it seems fair to say that most of the bills that received simple rules got them because there was no controversy,[41] or because there was nothing to gain from restrictions.

As noted, Speaker Wright's priority items all involved conflict between House Democrats and the White House, and usually with House Republicans as well. The Rules Committee crafted the rules for those bills in ways that would facilitate achievement of Democratic goals, and this was done in response to the Speaker's directions. As one member of Rules put it, "Wright had his fingers in just about everything that came through the Rules Committee. He had his opinions, and he sent word down to the Rules Committee that he wanted things handled this way or that way."[42] Another Rules Democrat said, "Wright would tell Pepper what he wanted, and Pepper would tell us, and we generally would do it."[43] Every priority bill passed the House. On the roll calls for adoption the largest number of Democratic defections was forty-one (on the reconciliation bill, which passed by only one vote), and the average was fourteen.[44]

The use of the Rules Committee to protect Democratic interests continued into 1988. With the elections approaching, one leadership concern was to prevent the Republicans from bringing up policy alternatives that could pose politically unattractive choices for Democrats with relatively conservative constituencies. For example, a compromise omnibus AIDS bill was put together, which was sufficiently satisfactory to the various segments of the Democratic party (although not completely satisfactory to any one). The Rules Committee then drafted a rule that permitted only twelve (unamendable) amendments, and barred thirty others (most of them proposed by Republicans), including one which would have required the notification of the spouse of any person diagnosed as having AIDS. Debate on the rule was closed off (barring a Republican substitute that would have permitted more amendments) by a highly partisan 198 to 182 vote (90 percent of Democrats and 3 percent of Republicans voted aye). The Democrats then beat back four conservative Republican amendments (with ten or fewer Democratic defections on each), and passed the bill easily.

Thus the crafting of special rules was an important tool for the Democratic leadership. As one member of the Rules Committee said, "Under Wright's Speakership, many of the rules were closed or restricted. That's why, frankly, we had such a very good record in the One Hundredth Congress in terms of accomplishment. We were able to put things through and get things done."[45] The increased use of restricted rules had come with encouragement from the rank and file, and Democrats' support for such tactics under Wright was generally strong (although, as noted, there were a few revolts).[46] During the debate on a closed rule in 1987, Robert Gregg (R, N.H.) plaintively said, "I can understand that the majority will once again want to use their power to undercut and essentially destroy the participatory process for those of us who are in the minority, but I cannot understand why they are doing this to their own party members . . ." (*Congressional Record,* July 29, 1987, p. H6761). The answer, of course, is that they did it because their members supported their doing it (Democratic members always could vote to defeat a rule they didn't like, and only eight voted against this one), and that support was forthcoming because Democrats perceived that those rules were in their interest.[47] In the next section, we will conclude this account by discussing a few more examples of the strategic use of control over the agenda in 1987.

Agenda Management and Wright's Priorities

The Clean Water Act and the Highway Bill. The first two elements of the Democrats' 1987 agenda to receive action were the Clean Water Act and the Omnibus Highway Reauthorization (symbolically numbered H.R.1 and H.R.2 respectively). Both were holdover issues from the previous Congress. The water bill had been passed unanimously by the House and Senate in 1986, but Reagan had pocket vetoed it on the ground that it was too expensive. The highway bill had passed both houses, but had died in the conference committee because of disagreements between the House and the Republican-controlled Senate. Wright saw these as unfinished business—popular programs that had wide support, even among House Republicans. (They were also personally important to him. Wright had served on the Public Works Committee, which had jurisdiction over both bills, and would have become its chairman if he had not been elected majority leader.)

The Speaker and the bills' supporters believed that it would be politically advantageous—both on these bills and more generally—to put them quickly before the president (who opposed both). Thus the membership of Public Works was appointed early, and the committee acted with remarkable speed to report the bills. In order to avoid having to renegotiate all the agreements made on the legislation in the previous Congress, and to prevent delay, the party and committee leaders decided to seek a closed rule for both bills. The Rules Committee obliged. Many Republicans opposed the rules when the bills came to the floor in January, but the Democrats were virtually unanimous and the closed rules were adopted. The bills passed almost unanimously.

The Senate acted quickly as well, and as he had threatened, President Reagan vetoed both measures. The next step for the Democratic leadership was to secure the votes to override the vetoes. The Clean Water Act was easy. Republicans had forewarned the president that they would not stick with him, and both houses passed the override by wide margins. The highway bill was more difficult, because Republicans began to worry that another override so soon would undermine the president for the rest of his term. Thus the Democratic leaders needed every one of their members' votes they could get. Wright had Steering and Policy declare the veto override to be a party vote, an indication that it was one of the votes that would be examined when future committee assignments were made. He told a whip meeting that "this override has far-reaching implications. . . . This is Armageddon as far as I'm concerned" (Barry, 1989, p. 192). Tony Coelho, the party whip, sought to maximize the effect of the whip organization. "I want 100 percent of the Democratic vote," he said. "I want the southerners to know they can vote against the president" (Barry, 1989, pp. 192–93). He came close. On the successful override vote seventy-two Republicans were opposed, but only one Democrat voted with them.

The Budget Resolution. Wright wanted quick action on the budget resolution as well, even though it was related to the sensitive matter of a tax increase. In early February, the leadership set a deadline of March 26 for the House to complete action on the resolution. On the tax increase, the Speaker continued to press the issue. He defended his view on talk shows and in interviews, claiming that more taxes were necessary to pay for needed programs without increasing the deficit. He argued that "Democrats have to demonstrate that we can govern, and tell the hard truth, when it's necessary" (*CQWR,* Mar. 7, 1987, p. 426). This issue meant that Wright had to deal not only with the Budget Committee, but also with Ways and Means, which would have to report any tax increase.

It was not just a matter of increasing taxes, but how it was done. Wright wanted an increase that would fall primarily on the wealthy, like a freeze in the scheduled cut of the top tax rate or a tax on the sale of stocks and bonds. This brought him into conflict with Ways and Means chairman Rostenkowski, who had been quoted as supporting an increase in the gasoline tax. Wright was angry, both because this was a regressive tax and because of other things Rostenkowski had said in the interview. In reaction, he said, "Rostenkowski will damn well do what the Caucus wants him to. You know, he can be removed as chairman of that committee" (Barry, 1989, p. 176).[48]

Wright also pressed the Democrats on the Budget Committee to draft a plan consistent with party views (at least in his perception of them).[49] He held luncheon and dinner meetings (the latter at his home) with them. They resisted his call for more taxes, fearing public reaction. Wright responded by saying, "You all asked to be on this committee. It's a leadership committee. You are all part of the leadership. When you're in the leadership you do tough things" (Barry, 1989, p. 149).

When the Budget Committee met to begin marking up the budget resolution, the Republicans refused to participate, voting "present" on the amendments that were proposed. They "wanted panel decisions to be identified strongly as Democratic budget priorities" (Wehr, 1987, p. 517). The final Democratic plan was reported on a 21 to 14 party-line vote. Then the leadership crafted a special rule for consideration of the budget that would maximize the Democrats' political advantage. The basis for initial consideration was a plan that assumed budget cuts which would have resulted if the targets under the Gramm-Rudman-Hollings law were not reached. (The cuts would have been around 20 percent.) Then four alternative plans, including the Democratic budget and the president's original proposals, would be offered as substitute amendments. (Thus members knew that if they rejected all of the alternatives, they would have to vote in the end on enormous budget cuts. If, however, any substitute were adopted, that problem would be avoided.)

The rule, moreover, structured the alternatives in a king-of-the-mountain procedure; if more than one were passed, only the last approved would be adopted. The order of the alternatives (all of which were made unamenable) was, of course, not random. The president's budget (containing many politically unpopular cuts) was first, followed by plans proposed by conservative Republican William Dannemeyer of California and by the Democrats' Black Caucus. The Democratic leadership plan was last. The rule was adopted, with no Republicans in favor and only two Democrats against. The first three alternatives were soundly defeated, with none receiving more than fifty-six votes. Then the Democrats' plan was approved 230–192. No Republicans supported it; nineteen Democrats defected.

Budget Reconciliation and Welfare Reform. Both of these matters were on Wright's list of priorities, and the House's handling of them demonstrates that the Democrats' willingness to let the leadership employ the tools of agenda management was not without limit. The members would protect their own interests.

Both measures involved political difficulties. The reconciliation bill included budget compromises and a tax increase; the welfare-reform bill was costly, and unpopular among conservatives. The leadership first sought to merge the two issues together through agenda management. The rule proposed for floor consideration of reconciliation simply included the 148-page welfare-reform package as a self-executing amendment. If the rule were adopted, welfare reform would be automatically passed. This went too far for some Democrats. Many moderates and conservatives thought the welfare plan was too costly as passed by the Ways and Means Committee. Forty-eight of them joined with every Republican to defeat the proposed rule.

Thus the House had to deal first with reconciliation without welfare reform. A new rule was adopted, and the bill was passed through what Republicans regarded as another piece of unfair leadership manipulation. When the customary fifteen minutes for the vote on passage of reconciliation ran out, the margin stood at 205 to 206 against. The fifteen minutes is, however, only a minimum time guaranteed under the rules, so Wright held the vote open while party whips found Jim Chapman of Texas and persuaded him to change his vote. This yielded a 206 to 205 victory, and, as noted earlier, Chapman was later rewarded with a seat on Appropriations.[50]

That still left welfare reform, with various Democratic divisions on the issue. The bill, as reported by Ways and Means, had an estimated cost of $5.2 billion. Many Democrats wanted to see the price reduced. Indeed, Thomas Carper (D, Del.), a deficit-conscious member of the class of 1982, drafted his own less costly plan, which he wanted to offer as a substitute amendment on the floor. The Rules Committee turned Carper down, however, permitting only one amendment, a Republican substitute (*CQWR*, Nov. 21, 1987, p. 2876). Some opponents of the Ways and Means bill began organizing to defeat the rule, and the leadership pulled the bill from the floor schedule because they doubted that they had enough votes to pass the rule. It was delayed again in early December for the same reason. Shortly before the scheduled vote a letter, signed by seventy-nine House Democrats, was delivered to Speaker Wright.[51] It voiced opposition to the restrictive rule and indicated support for permitting a vote on additional alternatives. The signatories included not only moderates and conservatives, but also liberals like Mike Lowry, then chairman of the Democratic Study Group. The *degree* of restrictiveness of the rule was in large measure a response to the wishes of Ways and Means chairman Rostenkowski, and many members on other committees resented it. For example, Dennis Eckart (D, Ohio), a member of Energy and Commerce, indicated that his committee was able to handle controversial legislation without barring amendments. "But when Ways and Means reports a bill, . . . it's like it was carved in stone and delivered by hand from Mount Sinai" (Knudsen and Rovner, 1987, p. 3037).[52]

In response to these sentiments from the rank and file, the leadership reconvened the Rules Committee to change the proposed rule. They still refused to permit Carper's substitute, but did allow an amendment by Michael Andrews, a Ways and Means Democrat from Texas, which cut the bill's cost by $500 milion. This was enough for many members; twenty-two Democrats who had opposed the reconciliation rule (including sixteen southerners) switched to support the revised welfare-reform rule, and it passed 213 to 206. The Andrews amendment was adopted overwhelmingly, the Republican substitute was defeated, and the bill was passed 230 to 194. Eighty-eight percent of Democrats and only 7 percent of Republicans voted aye. The leadership got both elements of its agenda passed, but only in a form that the Democratic membership was willing to support.

The Defense Bill. Even though it wasn't one of Speaker Wright's agenda issues, one of the best illustrations of the combined impact of the main elements we have been discussing is the action on the fiscal 1988 defense authorization bill. Earlier chapters showed that defense matters had frequently been very divisive for House Democrats, but those divisions began to moderate in the late 1970s. As sentiments in the Caucus changed, so did Jim Wright's views. We saw how Wright had been pressured by the Caucus to change his position on MX. In later years, he voted more consistently with the liberals on defense matters. When he was elected Speaker, one of his first moves was to urge the Caucus to adopt a resolution supporting reversal of the administration's decision to violate the arms limits of the SALT II treaty (Walsh, 1986, p. A4). The leadership then took over the handling of arms-control amendments in the supplemental appropriations bill (Hook, 1987, p. 1488).

When the defense bill came to the floor in 1987, many members of both parties wanted to offer amendments.[53] Republicans wanted to move the bill in the direction of more support for President Reagan's positions, and many Democrats wanted to place further restrictions on the administration. This presented a complex set of choices to be managed by the leadership and the committees on Armed Services and Rules. The debate began under a rule that governed only the choice whether the original committee plan for $306 billion in spending should be trimmed back, by a substitute drafted by Les Aspin, to the $289 billion figure authorized in the Democratic budget resolution. The Aspin substitute won, with only twenty-one Democrats opposing it.

The Rules Committee then proposed an additional rule governing a small initial set of amendments to the bill. (A third rule was planned to cover the rest.) It specified the order in which amendments would be considered, and all were themselves unamendable. The ordering of amendments was important. Aspin "ensured that votes on important 'anti-Reagan' amendments would be separated by roll calls on less crucial issues, so that moderates and conservatives would be able to cast a 'pro-defense' vote following particularly controversial amendments on which the leadership wanted a vote against the administration position" (Towell, 1987a, p. 901). This kind of procedure offers protection for members who personally want to support the party position, but would have trouble "explaining a string of votes" (Kingdon, 1989, pp. 41–43; Fenno, 1978, pp. 144–45) to constituents back home. On the first set of amendments, the Democrats won all the major ones, and the maximum number of Democratic defectors was twenty-eight.

Then the Democrats had a problem. Because of the large number of amendments members wanted to offer, Rules had been unable to complete work on the planned third rule by the time the House completed action on the amendments that were already scheduled. Thus the next day the House would have to either suspend action on the defense bill or consider the new rule on the same day it was reported. That, however, required a two-thirds vote, which Republican opponents could easily block. The leadership and the Rules Committee came up with a simple, but remarkable, solution. Rules proposed a brief new rule, to be passed by the House by *majority* vote, which *waived* the two-thirds requirement for the final rule they would report the next day. Over vociferous Republican objections, but with only two Democratic nay votes, the rule passed.

The final rule covered a large set of amendments, again strategically ordered, and most unamendable. The rule also contained a number of king-of-the-mountain provisions for groups of amendments on the same subject.[54] One set, for example, dealt with SDI funding. Four amendments were permitted; one for funding increases and one to dismantle the program were easily defeated. The third amendment (by John Rowland [R, Conn.]) provided for only a small funding cut, and the last, offered by Charles Bennett (D, Fla.), cut $400 million. "In crafting the rule, Democratic leaders stipulated that Bennett's would be the last amendment voted on, so that members could first cast a 'pro-Reagan' vote for Rowland and then vote for Bennett. For whatever reasons, 21 members voted for both amendments" (Towell, 1987b, p. 974). This procedure not only provided political cover for moderate and conservative Democrats who wanted to support the Bennett amendment. It also meant that if Bennett were successful, his position would become part of the bill even if the Rowland amendment also passed, and by more votes. As it happened, Rowland's amendment narrowly failed and Bennett's passed. Eventually the bill passed 239 to 177, with only eighteen Democrats siding with the president in the negative.

Some Conclusions

This chapter has recounted the Democratic leadership's growing use of the enhanced powers granted by the reform movement, with particular emphasis on the Wright speakership. It was in the One Hundredth Congress that the combined effects of increased party homogeneity, increased powers for the leaders, and greater leadership willingness to use those powers reached their zenith. Conditional party government had a wide reach in 1987–88.

These developments, as we have also seen, were not without their difficulties. The party still had its dissident members, albeit fewer of them, and they occasionally gave victory to the Republicans. In other instances, like the rule on the reconciliation bill, the leadership underestimated the degree of division in the party. This was sometimes due, moreover, to Wright's failing to keep sufficiently familiar with sentiments among the membership. Democrats from various segments of the party have indicated that Wright was too much of a loner, that he didn't consult widely enough, and that he didn't listen adequately to colleagues (Barry, 1989, pp. 480, 580, 650). If the exercise of party government in the House is indeed possible only in those instances where there is significant consensus, then this was a consequential shortcoming.

On the other hand, it is also clear that there was widespread satisfaction with the Speaker's aggressive leadership style. We have seen that leadership strategies often reflected a partnership between party and committee leaders. Wright was invited to intervene in the intercommittee disputes on the catastrophic health insurance bill. The closed rules on the highway bill and the Clean Water Act were endorsed by committee Democrats. Evidence presented in chapter 5 and elsewhere (Rohde, 1990a) indicates that during the 1980s, committee bills came to reflect better the preferences of House Democrats, and the party leadership therefore had incentives to provide protection for these bills against floor action that might overturn the agreements committee Democrats had reached. As Smith (1989, p. 191) said, during this time "the necessity of firm majority control of the amending stage was widely accepted by House Democrats."

But it is important to recognize that these leadership actions were not designed to reinforce committee autonomy, as might have been the case in the prereform days of committee government. Rather, committee bills were protected because they reflected the widespread preferences of the Democratic membership. If a committee proposal contained important provisions that were contrary to the wishes of House Democrats, the leadership could be forceful in using its powers to undermine those decisions. This is most clearly demonstrated by the strategies pursued in connection with the defense authorization bills in recent years. Democratic leaders worked with Les Aspin and other Armed Services Committee Democrats to shape the special rules governing floor consideration to maximize the chances of reversing major decisions by the committee.

Not every effort by Wright was successful, nor was every tactical move approved, but the Speaker created an ambitious agenda that reflected party priorities, and saw it through the House virtually intact. Who would have anticipated such leadership ambition and success, looking forward in late 1986? As *Congressional Quarterly Weekly Report* said in its wrap-up discussion of the One Hundredth Congress, "Congress has indeed enacted more major legislation than many thought possible in an election year, under a lame-duck president and with control of government divided between the parties" (Hook, et al., 1988, p. 3117).

5 | Republican Reactions, Presidential Agendas, and Legislative Consequences

The preceding chapters have described the relationships among changes in the electoral base of House Democrats, the reforms of the 1970s, the degree of political consensus among those Democrats, and the style and actions of their party leadership. We will conclude our analysis with a discussion of three additional considerations: developments among House Republicans, the impact of recent presidents on partisanship in the House, and the effects of the resurgence of partisanship on the pattern of legislative outcomes.

House Republicans

To this point we have appropriately focused on developments within the Democratic party. Democrats were in the majority throughout the period, and most of the reforms that we have claimed were important applied only to them. However, electoral and institutional change also affected the Republicans, which in turn had an impact on the dynamics of partisanship in the House.

Republican Factionalism

Like the Democrats, Republicans in the House have experienced divisions over policy. The data in table 1.1 showed that Republican party-unity scores exhibited their own decline and resurgence over time. The Republicans' internal divisions were also the result of disagreements among factions within the party.

120

Traditional Conservatives. The largest and most durable faction within the Republican party has been the traditional conservatives, the long-time counterpart of the northern urban liberals among the Democrats. These members opposed most of the initiatives of the national Democratic party, and formed the bedrock of the conservative coalition with southern Democrats (Sinclair, 1982). During the Nixon administration the most conservative elements of this group formed the Republican Study Group, their party's equivalent of the DSG, with the intention of providing support for conservative initiatives by the president. In the words of one of their members, William Armstrong (R, Colo.; now a senator), "The Republican Study Group is the Republican regulars . . . We're the essence of the party" (*CQWR,* June 26, 1976, p. 1636). While many Republican moderates disputed this characterization, the group did boast seventy-five members in 1976, over half the House Republican membership.

Some referred to the group as the Reaganite wing, long before Reagan became president, because they shared his "hard" conservative views. Like the DSG among the Democrats, the Republican Study Group wanted to pressure the party leadership (conservatives attempted a number of times to remove moderate John Anderson of Illinois from his post as chairman of the Republican Conference),[1] and to espouse the "right" positions. As one member said, the group "reminds House Republicans of what the traditional Republican position is even when the leadership and the White House deviate. . . . I like to think we have an influence in keeping our party more conservative" (*CQWR,* June 26, 1976, p. 1636).

By the time Ronald Reagan became president, the conservative wing found it less necessary to organize for the purposes of exerting pressure, since the administration (particularly in the first term) was largely expressing their views. President Reagan spoke for a limited role for the federal government domestically, and for a strong defense effort to block the Soviet Union from extending its influence. These were two of the main perspectives shared by congressional conservatives. Yet there were points of conflict. Conservatives were, for example, very unhappy when the president agreed to substantial tax increases in 1982, although the eighty-nine Republican votes against the plan came primarily from the most right-wing members, including the aggressive "new" conservatives we will discuss next. A more serious conflict occurred in 1985, when Republicans were responsible for the 202 to 223 defeat of the special rule for floor consideration of the tax-reform bill, Reagan's major domestic initiative that year. (Only 14 Republicans supported the rule, while 164 opposed it.)[2] They believed that the president had compromised too much with the Democrats to secure support for passage of a bill. In the words of Dick Cheney (R, Wyo.), the administration "basically sold out to Rostenkowski. They cut out the Republicans in the House . . . and tried to jam it through and it didn't work" (*CQWR*, Dec. 14, 1985, p. 2614). During the following week President Reagan made a visit to Capitol Hill to talk about the issue to a closed-door meeting of House Republicans, and also made a large number of individual contacts. In response to this White House lobbying, fifty-four Republicans switched their votes and supported a rule for consideration of the bill, and tax reform eventually passed.

"New" Conservatives. During the late 1970s, new viewpoints became visible among House conservatives. One revolved around a group called the Conservative Opportunity Society (COS). The group grew out of the activities of the thirty-five-member Republican class of 1978, which contained a large proportion of activist conservatives. These new members did not conflict very much with more senior conservatives on substantive policies; rather, disagreements centered around the goals House Republicans should pursue and the means to achieve them. In the view of many of the freshmen, senior Republicans had been out of power for so long that they had become a "professional minority," settling for attempts to make modest adjustments in legislation processed by the Democratic majority. The newcomers wanted instead to make the Republicans the majority party and thereby control outcomes. Looking for ways to achieve this end, the freshmen held more than forty class meetings during their first eighteen months in office. "Many have made clear their unhappiness with the party's leaders, especially [Minority Leader John] Rhodes, who they say is not combative enough" (Cohen, 1980, p. 1144).

An important event for these members was the agreement of President Reagan and traditional conservatives like Senate Finance Committee Chairman Robert Dole (R, Kan.) to respond to increasing deficits with a large tax increase. To the junior conservatives this kind of compromise with the Democrats was both a betrayal of principle and politically foolish. Public opposition to taxes was, they believed, one of the vehicles that could bring the Republicans majority status; the party should not throw away that advantage by joining a tax increase. They failed in attempts to block the increase, but a majority of the eighty-nine negative Republican votes came from the classes of 1978 and 1980 (Pitney, 1988a, p. 10). Then in 1983, COS was formed by about a dozen of these junior members, with Newt Gingrich (R, Ga.), a former history professor, as chairman.

COS was to be a group of "conservative populists," which would ultimately help to elect a Republican majority (Pitney, 1988a, p. 11). The views of COS Republicans regarding legislative tactics will be discussed below. With respect to issues, they emphasized a strong defense posture, vigorously opposing a proposed nuclear freeze, supporting the Strategic Defense Initiative, and claiming that Democrats held naive ideas about the dangers of communism. On domestic issues they argued for policies to stimulate 'economic growth and against the constraints of government bureaucracy. They also supported "traditional family values," for example, standing for school prayer and against abortion.[3] Yet given their orientation toward producing an electoral majority for House Republicans, their positions were not uniformly conservative. For example, COS members supported limited economic sanctions against South Africa, to demonstrate, in Gingrich's words, that they stood for "an integrated conservatism, not a segregated conservatism." This reflected, John Pitney (1988a, p. 24) said, "COS hopes that its stand on South Africa will appeal to blacks and young voters." The influence of COS grew within the House GOP. By 1985 it had over forty members (Lemann, 1985, p. 22), and in 1989 Gingrich was elected Republican whip.

Another strain of new conservatism among House Republicans is identified with the Christian Right. This is not a completely separate group; it overlaps to a degree with COS (Gingrich, for example, is identified with it) and with traditional conservatives. What is distinctive about its members is the central role their religiosity plays in shaping their political style, and the issues they tend to push. They place the greatest emphasis on "family values" issues like abortion, homosexuality, and school prayer, rather than domestic economics or foreign policy. It appears that their members have declined since the early 1980s.

Moderates and Liberals. While the conservatives have been the dominant faction among House Republicans, there has also been a significant moderate group, plus a smattering of liberals. There has always been friction between the moderates and their conservative colleagues, as the attempts to remove John Anderson from his leadership post illustrate, but the Republicans' continuing minority status in Congress has led them to value every seat their party could get, so inclinations toward purges have been minimal (*CQWR*, Aug. 19, 1972, pp. 2051–54).

Various organized groups have appeared over the years to buttress the moderate Republicans. The oldest of these is the Wednesday Group, which has persisted from the early 1970s to the present. It has been mostly a discussion group, rather than one oriented toward legislative action. In 1981 another group appeared, its members calling themselves the "Gypsy Moths" (in contrast to the Boll Weevils), for the purpose of representing the moderates' legislative views to the Reagan administration (Broder, 1981; Arieff, 1981a; Stampen and Davis, 1989). They supported Reagan's initial budget and tax proposals, but began to break away from the president on budget issues late in 1981, because he had gone back on promises to them about future budget cuts (Arieff, 1981b, p. 1951). The Gypsy Moths became less active when the Democrats achieved their governing majority after the gains made in the 1982 elections, but from their numbers a new organization developed, called the "'92 Group" (Cohen, 1985; Ornstein, 1985). Formed in 1985 with about thirty members, the group chose its name to illustrate its goal of winning a Republican majority in the House in 1992. The members saw themselves as a counterweight to COS, and sought to develop moderate Republican legislative alternatives which they hoped would help to broaden the party's electoral base.

Like the southern conservatives in the Democratic party, the Republicans' minority faction has also had an identifiable geographic base: the Northeast.[4] Figure 5.1 presents data on party loyalty among northeastern Republicans, showing the proportions in two categories: those who supported the party less than half the time (opponents), and those who voted with it on at least 70 percent of the party votes (loyalists).[5] By the mid-1960s, the proportion of loyalists had fallen below 50 percent, and the proportion of party opponents began increasing. In the 1970s and 1980s, opponents accounted for about one-third of northeastern Republicans.[6] These data offer some interesting comparisons and contrasts with those for southern Democrats. Like the southerners, northeastern Republicans have lost numerical strength within their party. Throughout the 1950s, they comprised more than a third of the Republican House delegation, but during the 1980s they accounted for less than one-fourth.[7] Thus a fairly constant proportion of party opponents among northeasterners means declining influence for those moderates and liberals within the Republican Conference. On the other hand, figure 5.1 shows that opponents never outnumbered loyalists, while opponents peaked at over 60 percent of southern Democrats and loyalists fell below 20 percent. This shows that Republicans didn't face as great a problem with deviant members on partisan issues. The data also show that while the proportion of members with very low loyalty scores has declined to vanishing levels among southern Democrats, the proportion has remained substantial among Republicans from the Northeast. This leads one to wonder whether Republicans have experienced increases in homogeneity during the postreform period comparable to those we saw among Democrats in chapter 3.

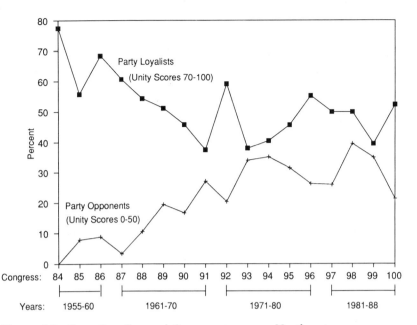

Figure 5.1 Party Loyalists and Opponents among Northeastern
Republicans, 84th–100th Congresses

Variations in Republican Homogeneity. Figure 5.2 presents data on Republican cohesion on party-unity and nonunity votes.[8] On party-unity
votes there is a pattern of decline and resurgence that is similar to that of
the Democrats, until the Reagan years. Cohesion is relatively high in the
earlier Congresses, drops off in the Nixon years, and then rebounds
somewhat. In the fourteen Congresses through the Ninety-seventh, the
difference in mean cohesion between the two parties exceeds five points
only six times.[9] In more recent years, however, there is a sharp difference by party. Republican cohesion returned to a level comparable
to, but somewhat lower than, that of the 1960s. The resurgence among
Democrats, on the other hand, far exceeded those earlier years. In the
Ninety-ninth Congress, Democratic cohesion on unity votes exceeded
that of Republicans by 17 points, and by 20 points in the One-
Hundredth.[10]

On non–party-unity votes the pattern is somewhat different. Although for Democrats the pattern of changing cohesion was similar on
the two kinds of votes, among Republicans cohesion increased somewhat through the mid-1960s, stayed fairly level between the Ninety-first
and Ninety-seventh Congresses, and then fell off again. This is roughly

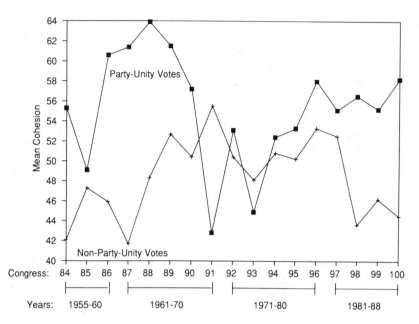

Figure 5.2   Mean Republican Cohesion, Party-Unity and Non–Party-Unity Votes (Consensual Votes Excluded): 84th–100th Congresses

opposite to the pattern on the unity votes. Yet despite this difference, Democratic cohesion on nonunity votes was generally higher than that of Republicans. In only four scattered Congresses was Republican cohesion greater,[11] and in five Congresses the level for the Democrats was higher by 13 points or more.[12] These differences will receive a more detailed treatment in future analysis than the space available here permits, but the data do show that Republicans never experienced the degree of internal division that beset the Democrats in the 1960s and 1970s. Republicans also didn't exhibit the more recent growth of homogeneity demonstrated by the Democrats (especially on those matters that divided party majorities).

One last perspective on unity on partisan votes is offered by figure 5.3, which shows mean party-unity scores for northeastern and other Republicans. The scores were similar in the early years, but a gap opened up during the Kennedy-Johnson Congresses. From the Nixon presidency on, both lines are fairly stable. The range from high to low for each is no more than 10 points. This is similar to the earlier data on northern Democrats (for whom the range for the same years was 12 points), but it is a marked contrast to the change for southern Democrats. Their average unity increased 30 points. These data conform with the earlier conclusions: regional division on partisan issues was never as great among Republicans as among Democrats, but in recent years the pattern has been reversed. Considering all the voting data, Republicans have not experienced the same increase in homogeneity that the Democrats have exhibited.

Strategic Responses to Minority Status

Charles Jones pointed out two decades ago, in his study of the minority party in Congress (1970, chap. 2), that minorities have a number of strategies open to them and that the range of those strategies is shaped by various political conditions inside and outside the Congress. Since Jones wrote, the changing conditions within Congress that we have been discussing affected minority strategies, and led to disagreement among Republicans about what course they ought to pursue.

Before the reform era, when committees had a greater independent impact on policy outcomes, Republicans had the option, in many cases, of aspiring to play a prominent role through committee participation. As they accrued committee seniority, their future held the possibility of becoming ranking minority members of subcommittees and commit-

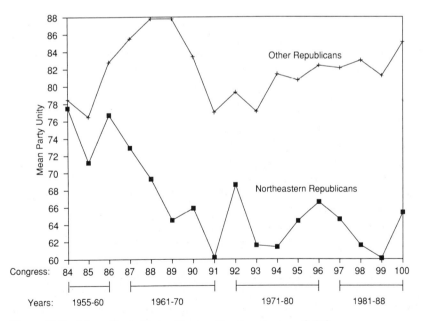

Figure 5.3   Mean Party-Unity Scores, Northeastern and Other Republicans: 84th–100th Congresses

tees. As one senior Republican, speaking about that period, told Norman Ornstein (1985, p. 32), "To a junior Republican there was something to look forward to, even if he wasn't going to be in the majority. It wasn't the same as being chairman, but it was the next best thing." Ornstein points out that on top committees like Appropriations and Ways and Means, "there was a major constructive policy role for senior Republicans to play. . . ."

Since the reforms and the increase in Democratic homogeneity, however, things have become quite different. Both within committees and on the floor, Republicans' ability to have an impact has declined. Increasing Democratic unity has reduced the Democrats' need to seek Republican support. Unless the majority is divided, in most instances it can do as it pleases. As Henry Waxman (D, Cal.) succinctly put it, "If we have a united Democratic position, Republicans are irrelevant" (*CQWR*, June 21, p. 1393). On committees, the party caucuses created by the Subcommittee Bill of Rights, the increased influence of party leaders, and the potential of pressure from the Democratic Caucus have all focused more legislative activity on creating agreements among Democrats.[13] This has reduced the influence of senior Republicans. As John McCain (R, Ariz., who left the House to run for a Senate seat) said (*CQWR*, June 21, 1986, p. 1393), "The only difference between a freshman Republican and a ranking Republican is that the ranking Republican gets to ask questions first. . . ."[14] Moreover, even in those cases where the conservative coalition still is able to control the shape of a bill (e.g., sometimes on Armed Services), the majority is frequently able to reverse those victories through amendments on the floor. Former minority leader John Rhodes (1976, p. 33) quoted Tip O'Neill as saying, "Republicans are just going to have to get it through their heads that they are not going to write legislation." The changes over the last decade have made that claim even more accurate.

As their impact has declined, House Republicans have grown more frustrated. There is widespread agreement among them that their lot will not change much unless they can attain majority status, but there has been disagreement about how to achieve that goal. More traditional Republicans believed that their party should seek to participate in the legislative process and to influence issues, building a record that Republican candidates could take to the voters. They generally saw House elections as separated, local contests. The more aggressive new conservatives, especially the COS group, viewed the matter more in national terms. They saw the traditional strategy as too "soft," reflecting too much acceptance of minority status. The COS conservatives and their sympathizers wanted to confront and harass the Democratic majority, in order to demonstrate to the country that their views were more similar to the electorate's than those of the Democrats. As Newt Gingrich said, "I have a much greater commitment to doing what's necessary to become a majority in the House rather than function as a strong minority. . . . As a result some things I do really antagonize the Democrats" (Cohen, 1980, p. 1142).

These confrontational sentiments were initially pressed by Gingrich's class of 1978, and were fueled by the large conservative group elected with Reagan in 1980. "The 1978 class was the first class to look the establishment Republican Party in the House in the eye and say, 'We don't want to be like you,'" said a Republican consultant. "The 1980 class did the same thing, but they were the followers" (Hook, 1988, p. 2264). In the words of Daniel Lungren (R, Cal.), another member of the class of 1978, "We didn't come here accepting that things take time and compromise. We wanted to challenge the institution and raise issues that ought to be raised" (Cohen, 1984, p. 414).

As we indicated above, Republicans' frustration gradually intensified as growing Democratic homogeneity increased the tendency toward party government in the House. Republicans loudly voiced their complaints about party balances on committees that were disproportionately weighted toward the Democrats, and about inadequate minority staffing (Granat, 1985, p. 535). There were, however, two events during Tip O'Neill's speakership that increased support within the Republican Conference for the advocates of confrontation. The first involved a direct conflict between O'Neill and Gingrich.

One of the tactics used by the COS activists was to use "special orders" (speeches after the House has completed legislative business for the day) to attack the Democrats on foreign- and domestic-policy issues, and for (in their view) unfair manipulation of House procedures. These speeches were not directed at other members—the House chamber was usually empty when they were delivered—but at the national audience of C-SPAN, the television network that broadcasts daily live coverage of House proceedings. The audience was small (estimated at about 200,000), but it was attentive, and larger than the activists could routinely reach any other way. For a while, Republican opinion on these speeches was mixed, and Democratic leaders trivialized them. Majority Leader Wright said, "If a fellow wants to waste the time of the television audience with bombast, the rules permit it. . . . But I suggest that the public knows it's phony as a $3 bill" (Granat, 1984c, p. 246).

Within a few months, however, the Democrats' patience had worn thin. On May 8, Walker of Pennsylvania and Gingrich used a special order to read into the *Congressional Record* a conservative Republican report which criticized Democrats' foreign-policy views over the previous fifteen years, and which cited many Democratic representatives by name. Gingrich claimed, in part, that Democrats believed that "America does nothing right and communism . . . rushes into vacuums caused by 'stupid' Americans and its 'rotten, corrupt' allies" (Reid, 1984, p. A6). Incensed, two nights later O'Neill ordered the cameras to pan the chamber during another special order (by Walker) to show the viewing audience that no one was in the House chamber listening to these impassioned speeches.

Now it was the Republicans' turn to be angry. Minority Whip Trent Lott (R, Miss.) said his colleagues were "absolutely united in our anger" over O'Neill's action (Reid, 1984, p. Al), and Minority Leader Michel wrote to the Speaker claiming that he had singled Walker out for "public ridicule" and complaining that he had made the decision "without prior consultation" (Granat, 1984c, p. 1167).[15] O'Neill explained his action in a speech on May 14, and Gingrich spoke again the next day, defending the foreign-policy report that had set the stage for the conflict. O'Neill then lost his temper and attacked Gingrich for questioning the patriotism of Democrats, saying it was "the lowest thing that I have ever seen in my 32 years in Congress" (Granat, 1984a, p. 1167). Lott claimed that this was an improper personal attack on Gingrich, and the presiding officer agreed that O'Neill had violated House rules. This was the first such rebuke for a Speaker in memory.

The COS members were gleeful that they had so provoked O'Neill, but other Republicans were less pleased. After the 1984 elections, Mickey Edwards (R, Okla.)—himself a very conservative Republican—challenged the COS strategy of confrontation in interviews and in a letter to his GOP colleagues. "This is not a philosophical issue," Edwards wrote. "Instead, it's a matter of whether conservatives get elected by Washington hoopla and forming ourselves into one great 'team' or by localizing campaigns effectively" (NJ, Dec. 15, 1985, p. 2402). In another letter in February, Edwards argued that Republicans had to "view the next two years not as a Holy Crusade against Tip O'Neill and the Democrats. . . ." Instead they should seek to localize and "individualize" House races, and "to demonstrate to young voters our ability to provide both acceptable policy and acceptable performance." In a follow-up interview, Edwards said, "I don't want to change the United States Congress into a high school fraternity, always looking for ways to throw pillows and have water fights, always looking for ways to attack the Democrats" (Granat, 1985, p. 537).

Disagreements over tactics persisted, but Republican sentiments were moved further toward support for confrontational tactics by a dispute over who was entitled to an Indiana House seat after the 1984 elections. Indiana officials had declared the Republican challenger, Richard McIntyre, to be the winner of the Ninth District by thirty-four votes over the Democratic incumbent, Frank McCloskey. Jim Wright introduced a resolution to declare the seat vacant pending a recount, and the House passed it on a party-line vote. The Republicans were angered by what they saw as a blatantly partisan political move, and they were further frustrated by the slow handling of the matter by the special task force of the House Administration Committee set up to consider the case. They tried to seat McIntyre, pending completion of the investigation, by calling for a vote on the matter on a day when many Democrats were absent, but they failed by one vote (Pitney, 1988b, pp. 10–11). After much conflict, the task force declared the Democrat to be the winner by four votes, and on April 22 the full House Administration committee agreed 12 to 0 after its Republican members had walked out in protest.

House Republicans were extremely angry. As a protest they kept the House in session all night on April 22. They attacked the committee recommendation in floor speeches, while wearing buttons that read "Thou Shalt Not Steal." The only GOP member of the three-man task force called the decision "a rape." On April 25 the Republicans tied up House business by repeatedly calling for roll-call votes on routine parliamentary matters (Plattner, 1985a). Finally, on May 1 the House voted 236 to 190 (with ten Democrats joining all the Republicans in the minority) to accept the committee's recommendation and seat McCloskey. After the vote, Republicans walked out. "Michel described the walkout as 'just the beginning' of GOP efforts to create public awareness of 'the autocratic, tyrannical rule of the Democratic majority.'" Newt Gingrich said the GOP would continue to use "guerilla warfare." Even moderate Republicans said that it would be difficult for Democrats to get their cooperation on issues like the budget (Plattner, 1985b, pp. 821, 825). While disruption of House proceedings was minimal in subsequent months, Republicans continued to attack what they regarded as Democratic mistreatment throughout the Ninety-ninth and One Hundredth Congresses.

As we noted earlier, one of the Republicans' devices for protest was to call for roll-call votes on the routine daily motion to approve the House *Journal* for the previous session. Since these votes have no direct legislative consequences, and are thus "pure protest" votes, an examination of them can provide an interesting picture of the pattern of "traditional" versus "confrontational" sentiments among House Republicans. Table 5.1 shows the relationship between frequency of opposition to approval of the *Journal* and a member's party loyalty, seniority, and region. The data indicate that members with higher party-support scores and fewer years of service more frequently opposed *Journal* approval. This accords with the characterization of the advocates of confrontation as young

Table 5.1 Protest Voting on Approval of the House *Journal* among Republicans, 99th Congress, by Tenure, Party Unity, and Region

	Percent of Times Opposing Approval of the *Journal*			
	0–49	50–89	90–100	Total (N)[a]
Party Support Score				
0–69	67	27	7	101 (30)
70–79	54	33	13	100 (63)
80–89	43	24	33	100 (42)
90–100	32	23	45	100 (47)
Tenure (Previous Terms)				
0 or 1	60	26	15	101 (55)
2 or 3	56	30	14	100 (66)
4 or more	28	26	46	100 (61)
Region				
South	26	30	45	101 (47)
Northeast	40	21	40	101 (43)
Midwest	24	26	51	101 (51)
West	10	34	56	100 (41)

[a]Percentages may not add up to 100% due to rounding.

conservatives. Regionally, opposition is less frequent among northeasterners and more frequent among members from the Midwest and West. The only possible surprise in these results is that southern opposition is not higher. This is mainly due to relatively infrequent opposition among senior southerners (i.e., those serving four or more terms).

Responses to Democratic Agenda Management

Republicans and Special Rules. As the discussion in earlier chapters indicated, an increasing amount of GOP discontent has revolved around procedural matters, particularly special rules. Data presented there showed that the mean party difference on special-rules votes has increased dramatically. Figure 5.4, which presents the mean proportion of each party voting aye on nonconsensual votes on special rules since the Ninety-first Congress, shows that this has occurred both because of increased Democratic cohesion on such votes and because of deteriorating Republican support. After the Ninety-first Congress, when over 60 percent of both parties, on average, supported contested rules,[16] the two parties have moved sharply in opposite directions. In the first session of the One Hundredth Congress, mean support for rules among Democrats was 94 percent, while among Republicans it was 23 percent.

Vocal Republican resentment of Democrats' partisan use of special rules reached its zenith in 1987–88, in response to the "artful crafting" under Speaker Wright. Within the Rules Committee, the Republicans were almost always simply outvoted. When the committee met to draft the resolution to govern debate on the 1987 Contra-aid moratorium, Trent Lott (R, Miss., a member of Rules and the GOP whip) said to the panel's Democrats, "I view this whole process as a sham. . . . You're slam-dunking us, and you've got the votes to do it" (*CQWR,* Mar. 14, 1987, pp. 460–61). Similarly, except for the few instances of failed rules noted previously, Democratic numbers and cohesion kept Republicans from having any impact on rules on the floor.

Lott charged that "the Democratic leadership in this Congress now has a set formula for these rules: the restrictiveness of a rule is in direct relation to the importance of the legislation it makes in order" (*Congressional Record,* July 22, 1987, p. H6457). Of course, as Bach and Smith (1988) note, the requests for restrictive rules sometimes come from bipartisan groups on the committee of jurisdiction. In the eyes of disgruntled Republicans, however, this doesn't make such rules any less partisan in impact. That is, while the interests of some committee Republicans in passing a piece of legislation may be sufficiently strong to get them to support a restrictive rule, the broad range of their party colleagues may still see that as contrary to their goals. For example, in May

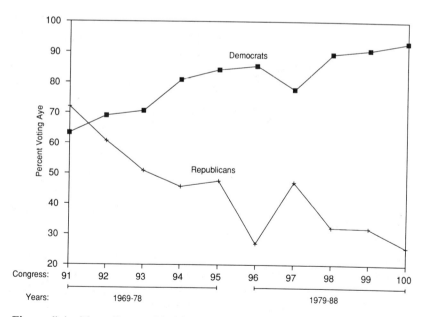

Figure 5.4   Mean Percent Voting Aye on Special Rules, by Party (Consensual Votes Excluded), 91st–100th Congresses

of 1987, Richard Cheney (R, Wyo.) was urging his colleagues to support a compromise restrictive rule for a bill from the Interior Committee, on which he served. Walker of Pennsylvania, one of the COS activists, opposed the rule. When Cheney pointed out to him that there was bipartisan agreement within the committee on the compromise, Walker responded,

> Let me . . . say to the gentleman that one of the problems with democracy is that it does tend to get a little messy. I mean, there might actually be Members who would come to the floor and offer amendments to the gentleman's bill. That would be a real tragedy. . . . The fact that there is a bipartisan consensus to shut down that kind of democracy does not strike this gentleman as being a very good idea. I mean, we have bipartisan bad ideas around here. I think they may be one of them.

Cheney replied that he shared Walker's concerns about restrictive rules. However, recognizing the interlocking nature of the Democratic leadership's powers to control the agenda, he pointed out that "at one time the bill was going to be brought up under the Suspension Calendar and that would have been even more restrictive than the procedure here today."[17] Walker was not persuaded, and nearly two-thirds of the Republicans sided with him against the rule.

A similar situation arose on the defense bill. Here again, Walker was complaining about the selection of amendments by the Rules Committee. He said, "I think the selection of amendments is a very conscious thing. It is meant to protect some philosophies on this floor, while denying other philosophies their full right." William Dickinson (R, Ala.), the ranking Republican on Armed Services, responded that the restrictive rules were really the fault of neither Armed Services nor Rules. Because of the enormous number of amendments proposed, Rules had to act as a traffic cop. Dickinson had worked closely with Aspin and the members of Rules to winnow down the amendments, saying the House "cannot soak up the entire summer dealing with one bill from one committee." Walker replied that "the route that the gentleman just described is exactly the direction that the majority is seeking to go. The more they can confirm the committee process around here, the more they dilute the ability of the minority to have any effect on legislation."[18] This view is certainly a far cry from the days of conservative-coalition domination of committees! Sixty-two percent of the Republicans voted with Walker and against Dickinson, without avail.

Protests and Rules Changes. House Republicans sought to dramatize their complaints about the Democrats' use of procedures for partisan ends through media interviews and public protests. On Constitution Day (September 17, 1987, the two hundredth anniversary of the ratification of the Constitution), they sought to create a media event by nailing a list of their complaints to the door of Speaker Wright's office in the Capitol. Their frustrations were exacerbated when no media coverage resulted; Wright didn't even learn of their action until a week later (Barry, 1989, pp. 388–89). During debates on special rules, Republicans continually offered statistics showing that restrictive and closed rules were being used much more frequently, and Trent Lott issued a statement in November 1987 attacking the Rules Committee's grants of blanket waivers of points of order for major bills (*CQWR*, Nov. 29, 1987, p. 2958).

In May of 1988, the Republican leadership launched another public-relations assault against their perceived procedural disadvantage. They prepared an elaborate set of speeches, with supporting statistical evidence, on the unfair patterns of special rules and on Democratic responsibility for the lack of congressional productivity (*Congressional Record*, May 24, 1988, pp. H3576–91). Copies of reprints from the *Record* were sent to the media and to academics who study Congress. At the end of the One Hundredth Congress, Richard Cheney—the newly selected minority whip—wrote an attack on Democratic practices for *Public Opinion* (Cheney, 1989), a magazine published by the American Enterprise Institute (a Washington think tank).

While the Republicans complained about the Democrats generally, the specific focus of their anger was almost always Speaker Wright. During the May 1988 protest, Lott said, "By resorting to these 'creative rule-alteration procedures—CRAP' the speaker is destroying the comity and uniformity that is so essential to the proper functioning of the House. . . ." (*Washington Post*, May 25, 1988, p. A3). Robert Walker claimed that Wright "is willing to run over us. . . . When he loses battles, instead of gracefully acknowledging defeats, he cheats." And even Cheney, not usually one of the combative conservatives, said, "I feel the Speaker is playing fast and loose with the powers of his office" (Pianin, 1987, p. A10).[19] Perhaps the most extreme language of all was Newt Gingrich's characterization of Wright as "the least ethical Speaker of the twentieth century" in a number of newspaper interviews.[20] Gingrich attacked Wright and a number of other Democrats on ethical grounds, and in May of 1988 he filed a formal complaint against the Speaker with the House Committee on Standards of Official Conduct, better known as the House Ethics Committee. At the same time, seventy-two Republican members sent a letter to the committee, calling for a formal investigation of Gingrich's charges (Kenworthy, 1988). The ensuing investigation eventually led to Wright's resignation from the House.

Republican reaction to their circumstances was not, however, limited to protests; they also responded with revisions of their procedures. This was not the first time that the House GOP had tried to deal with the problems of minority status through organizational changes. Between 1959 and 1967, they adopted a number of new procedures, including revitalization of the Republican Policy Committee and creation of the Committee on Planning and Research. There also were a number of revolts against party leaders (Jones, 1970, pp. 153–60).[21] Then during the reform era of the 1970s, the Republicans adopted some procedural changes, including seniority reforms that included Conference ratification of ranking members on committees (Ornstein and Rohde, 1978, p. 290). The changes of the mid-1980s are of particular interest, however, because they are clear responses to the Democrats' active partisan leadership.

The first steps taken in 1986, before the problems with Wright, were based on the report of a Conference task force on rules and procedures chaired by Richard Cheney (Wolfensberger, 1988, p. 38). Further changes, made during 1988, resulted from recommendations of committees chaired by Robert Lagomarsino of California and Jan Meyers of Kansas (*NJ*, Feb. 13, 1988, p. 412; Wolfensberger, 1988, p. 39).[22] The Conference adopted rules that permitted the party leader to designate certain issues as "leadership issues." On such issues each member of the "elected or designated Republican leadership" is obliged "to the best of his ability, to support positions adopted by the Conference, and the resources of the leadership shall be utilized to support that position."[23] Further, any Republican committee member who proposes to offer a motion to recommit on a bill is obliged to consult with the party leader to ensure that the motion reflects the majority view of the Conference as much as possible.[24] In addition, the ranking minority member of each committee has the "obligation to ensure that each measure on which the Republican Conference has taken a position is managed in accordance with such position" on the House floor (Conference Rule 14).

The rules also create Republican caucuses on every committee, which are required to meet before the organizing meeting of the full committee, and periodically thereafter by the call of the ranking member or a majority of committee Republicans. Finally the Conference decided that it would elect the ranking Republican on the Budget Committee, rather than leave that selection to the party leader. These changes parallel—and are considerably more explicit than—the Democratic "collective control" reforms that were designed to make persons who are granted power by the party more responsible to it. They grew out of dissatisfaction among Republicans over Conference Chairman Jack Kemp's support for the tax-reform bill in 1985 after the Conference had adopted a motion opposing it, and over the positions taken by some ranking minority members of committees while managing bills (Wolfensberger, 1988, p. 38).[25]

The Conference also adopted new rules designed to strengthen the influence of Republican party leaders. A new twenty-one member Committee on Committees was created. As in the previous system, committee members have as many votes as there are Republicans in their state delegations. The innovation is that minority leader and whip have twelve and six votes respectively. Newt Gingrich said, "It makes the leadership the balancing weight. . . . It's part of a series of steps House Republicans have been taking to increase [Minority Leader] Michel's capacity to lead" (*CQWR*, Dec. 10, 1988, p. 3475). Another step was to grant Michel the power to name the GOP members of the Rules Committee (*CQWR*, Sept. 17, 1988, p. 2625). In another parallel to Democratic practices, Michel also began creating task forces to deal with particular bills, like catastrophic health insurance and welfare reform in 1987. The Republicans had responded to their perceived domination by the Democrats by modeling their organizational changes on the DSG reforms of the 1970s. This demonstrates that at least the GOP believed that those reforms played a significant role in the Democrats' ability to shape House outcomes to their advantage.

Of course the Democrats react to Republican complaints by arguing that they have done nothing unfair in their management of the agenda. In 1987, Majority Leader Thomas Foley claimed, "The House of Representatives probably provides more opportunities for minority expression and participation in a meaningful sense than any other legislative body in the world" (Cohen, 1988b, p. 27). And Speaker Wright responded to the GOP's attacks by saying, "They complain about the procedures when they have no strong complaint about policy. . . . What I'm doing isn't cheating. It isn't bending the rules. The legality is clear" (Pianin, 1987, p. A10). Thus the Democrats don't claim that they aren't engaging in agenda management to advance their cause; they just claim that they are not violating minority rights. They see such practices to be appropriate for the majority as long as they can muster the votes to support them. For example, when Foley was attempting to gather support from the Democratic class of 1986 for the restrictive rule on the 1987 reconciliation/welfare-reform bill, he said to them, "It's a question of who's running this House" (Barry, 1988, p. 442).

The Democrats believe that they are the majority, and that they therefore have the responsibility to manage the work of the House. The reality is that in a partisan environment, the minority—by definition—lacks the numbers to affect many outcomes.[26] That reality was illustrated during the debate on one of the rules connected with the defense bill, in an exchange between Robert Walker and Butler Derrick (D, S.C.), a member of the Rules Committee and the floor manager for the particular rule. Walker was complaining about how a great number of amendments were to be considered in a very short time. Referring to an earlier exchange with Derrick, he said, "My problem is that we were told earlier today that the Rules Committee was in the process of intense deliberations here and we are getting their very best judgement on these things." Derrick responded, "I said earlier we were giving these matters a lot of deliberate consideration. We did. I did not guarantee that the gentleman would agree with the results" (*Congressional Record,* May 7, 1987, pp. H3297–98).

It is alleged that Republican Speaker Thomas Reed once said that the right of a minority is to draw its salaries, and its function is to make a quorum. The role of the minority in the postreform House is not so limited as that. It is clear, however, that the majority leadership doesn't see that role to include shaping the content of major legislation, at least not if they can help it.[27] Republican frustrations will probably continue so long as Democrats retain sufficient homogeneity to permit them to employ procedures to their advantage across a wide range of issues. As Foley said in an interview late in 1987 (Cohen, 1988a, p. 27), "We are getting awfully good at counting votes, we say modestly. This is a kind of situation where if we do not have the votes, we don't fight in the ring. Consequently, it creates a situation where the Republican contender doesn't get into the ring unless he is supposed to lose. If it looks like he is going to win, we don't get our fighter in the ring."

Presidents and Partisanship

This analysis has focused primarily on decisions and developments within the House, devoting only limited space to important interactions with the outside environment. Thus, for example, in order to keep the length of this presentation within desired bounds, our discussion of (and evidence on) the impact of electoral change was brief, even though we have argued that it is the primary cause of the resurgence of partisanship in the House. Similarly, a full consideration of congressional interactions with the president, and their relevance for partisanship, would require a much more extended treatment than is possible here.[28] However, the potential impact of the president on aspects of our argument is very large, so we must give some attention to the most salient elements, leaving fuller consideration to later analyses.

The research on partisanship and party decline discussed in chapter 1 saw an important connection between the president and congressional partisanship. For example, Brady, Cooper, and Hurley (1978, p. 388) argued that if the presidency and the House were controlled by the same party, party voting would be relatively high, while with split control it would be lower. They said that when there was undivided control, the president's requests would set an agenda for the majority party, and that the president would give the leadership a source of leverage to increase cohesion. Similarly, Patterson and Caldeira (1988) included a variable for divided control of government in their analysis of levels of party voting from 1949 to 1984. They argued (p. 119) that the "president's legislative programme provides the lion's share of the congressional agenda," that the president's support would strengthen majority-party partisanship, and that this in turn would "contribute to a stiffening of the cohesiveness of the minority party."

Thus these and other analysts generally share the view that common partisan control of the presidency and Congress enhances partisanship, while divided government reduces it. However, viewing the question in the context of the theoretical arguments we have been presenting would seem to imply that the relationship between partisan control and partisanship in congressional-executive interactions is not so straightforward. Rather, the implications for partisanship, in voting and in other areas, will depend on the various factors we have discussed: the president's relative ability to influence members' preferences, and the impact of the president on the agenda—in terms of both the issues that are raised and the specific alternatives that are supported or opposed.

Presidents and Agendas

There is universal agreement that presidents have a major role in setting the congressional agenda (Light, 1983; Kingdon, 1984; Sundquist, 1980, 1981; Fishel, 1985).[29] Indeed, for many, the president's is the dominant or exclusive role (Sundquist, 1981, pp. 147, 426–27), although others have argued that Congress has long played an important, independent part on particular issues (Orfield, 1975). Many analysts have asserted the corollary that the congressional parties lack the capacity to put forward a competing program. James Sundquist argued (1980, p. 199) that "the party position in the Congress is either the president's program or none at all."[30] As we have noted, the hypothesized relevance of party control to this is that when the same party controls the presidency and Congress, the majority leadership will rally the party behind presidential proposals. If there is divided control, however, the view of the literature is that the president will bargain with the Congress over issues and alternatives, muting and compromising partisan differences in the process.

These arguments were surely shaped by the researchers' observations of the patterns of postwar presidencies. During the Kennedy and Johnson administrations, when there was united party control, the presidential agendas were expansive and activist, depending relatively heavily on increased government spending (Light, 1983). These proposals largely reflected the preferences of a majority of congressional Democrats and their constituencies (although not generally those of the conservative committee leaders), and the majority's party leaders did rally their members (with varying success) over the course of those eight years. During the Eisenhower and Nixon-Ford administrations, on the other hand, control was divided. The presidents and the Democrats in Congress tended to disagree on directions and specifics, presenting the potential for stalemate. Frequently the executive negotiated agreements with party and/or committee leaders to resolve policy impasses. Thus, the analysts saw, united government increased partisanship, while divided government reduced it.

Yet these are not the only possibilities, as our theory implies and as the Carter and Reagan administrations demonstrated. Rather, the impact of party control of the two branches is—like party government in the House, in our characterization—conditional. *If,* under united government, the president's proposals reflect the views of the dominant faction in the majority party, and *if* the majority party is relatively homogeneous on the major issues and the minority party doesn't have incentives to go along, then the result will be a fairly partisan pattern of support. This is to some degree a reasonable characterization of the Kennedy-Johnson years (at least until the 1966 elections). In the case of divided government, *if* parties are internally divided, and *if* the president does not push radical departures from the status quo, and *if* the administration's inclination is to compromise a significant share of the differences with congressional Democrats (all fair characterizations of the Nixon administration), then partisanship should be muted.

What if, however, the conditions cited above are not met? What if, under united government, the president represents a different party faction than the congressional majority? What if he doesn't work well with Congress, and chooses as priorities those issues and solutions that split, rather than rally, his party? Wouldn't we expect partisanship to be lower than if these conditions didn't obtain? And under divided government, what if the preferences of the two congressional parties are relatively homogeneous and opposed? What if the president favors major changes in governmental policy, moving further and further from the preferred position of the congressional majority? Wouldn't we expect partisan conflict to be magnified? In our view the Carter and

Reagan presidencies show that these contrasting expectations are justified.

Carter's Agenda. Jimmy Carter came to Washington with a large agenda for the Congress to deal with. During his first year in office he recommended about eighty legislative proposals (Arieff, 1980, p. 3096). These proposals were rooted in the 1976 presidential campaign (Fishel, 1985; Jones, 1988b, pp. 82, 85), in which Carter ran as an outsider, against the Washington establishment.[31] The press had great difficulty pinning down whether he was a liberal or a conservative, and he did not try to make their task easy. He did, however, admit to being a "fiscal conservative," while also saying that he was liberal on issues like civil rights and the environment (Jones, 1988b, p. 127). Furthermore, during his presidency he tried to maintain a broad appeal by emphasizing those issues that would not clearly brand him ideologically. "Instead, he tried to stress issues that ostensibly crossed ideological lines, such as energy, transportation deregulation, welfare reform, cutting wasteful water projects, promoting human rights[,] and nuclear proliferation, to name a few" (Arieff, 1980, p. 3097).

These issues, moreover—and the proposals related to them—were reflections of Carter's own beliefs and his conception of the presidency. Jones (1988, pp. 2–3) contends that Carter conceived of his role as a representative as that of a trustee, in the manner advocated by Edmund Burke. That is, his responsibility was to protect the public interest and not be responsive to political pressures. It was to do what was *right*, not what was popular. Such a president "can be expected to identify particularly thorny issues and insist that they be handled whatever the political cost" (Jones, 1988b, p. 79).

Reflecting his outsider's approach, Carter had a negative view of Congress and the federal government before, during, and after his presidency. These views were conveyed in his 1976 campaign speeches, and (so one of the members of the Carter administration said) "the man that believed those speeches believed . . . that there's something fundamentally corrupt about the governmental process in Washington. . . . *He was a common cause monarch*" (Jones, 1988b, p. 81; Jones's italics). Carter saw the president as the spokesman for the national interest, while he perceived Congress as responsive to special interests, as the following quotation from his memoirs indicates: "Members of Congress, buffeted from all sides, are much more vulnerable to these groups than is the President. One branch of government must stand fast on a particular issue to prevent the triumph of self-interest at the expense of the public" (Carter, 1982, p. 88).

Carter's varied issues preferences and his negative attitude toward Congress caused problems for his agenda in the House. The leadership generally supported him (although there were never good personal relations). Speaker O'Neill, for example, said, "I'm a partisan Democrat. . . . The President of the United States is the leader of my party" (Malbin, 1977, p. 942). However, the various elements of Carter's agenda cut across or exacerbated Democratic divisions (Sinclair, 1981a; 1982, chap. 8). Environmental, energy, and reorganization proposals produced support and opposition among Democrats and Republicans, among liberals and conservatives. While he advocated reducing government bureaucracy and opposed special interests, he also proposed the creation of two major new government departments: the Consumer Protection Agency and the Department of Education. These were widely viewed as political payoffs to major liberal elements of his electoral coalition. On the other hand, liberals were angered by Carter's unwillingness to support greater spending on matters they considered important.

Similar conflicts arose in foreign and defense policy. Liberals liked Carter's support for human rights, his proposal to return the canal to Panama, his decision to cancel the B-1 bomber, and his efforts to reach a strategic arms agreement with the Soviets. But they opposed his support for increases in conventional weapons in Europe, and sought to cut his defense proposals. Finally, some Carter proposals, like that to reduce water projects, simply ignored the political interests of Democrats in Congress regardless of ideology.

Because of these differences in viewpoint and emphasis, Carter faced widespread criticism in Congress during his whole administration, especially from northern liberals. For example, in May of 1977 Senator Edward Kennedy (D, Mass.) attacked the administration for failing to produce a health-insurance proposal, and Senator George McGovern (D, S.D.) said that liberals "will not be a cheering section for tinkling symbols [sic] that signify nothing" (CQWR, May 21, 1977, p. 989). Eventually, of course, these conflicts coalesced in Kennedy's challenge to Carter's renomination in 1980. That split the party, and made it even more difficult to advance the president's agenda. As Speaker O'Neill said late in 1979, "Everything fell apart. . . . We came back after our August vacation and it was clear Kennedy was going to run. . . . The members . . . were thinking, 'How am I going to protect myself?'" (CQWR, Dec. 22, 1979, p. 2880).

Reagan's Agenda. Like Carter, Reagan was a former governor who ran as an outsider against the Washington establishment. He also came to office with a substantial agenda rooted in the presidential campaign

(Fishel, 1985; Light, 1983; Jones, 1988a).[32] Finally, like Carter's, Reagan's agenda was shaped by his own policy views. But most decidedly *unlike* Carter's, his agenda did not cut across or mute ideological conflicts. Reagan was an unabashed conservative, and his ideology was, as Paul Light said (1983, pp. ix–x), "the central factor in the choice of issues for his agenda. . . . To a greater extent than any recent President's, Reagan's definition of good policy—that is, his image of what the world should be—shaped his legislative agenda. Though Reagan also made some decisions on the basis of electoral pressure . . . the bulk of the administration's program centered on the President's own conservative ideology."

In another contrast to Carter, Reagan's efforts to advance his agenda were given a major boost by the character of his election victory. Carter, who had once held a substantial lead in the polls over Gerald Ford in 1976, ended up winning by only a very narrow margin of victory. The Democrats, moreover, gained only one House seat and nothing in the Senate.[33] Reagan, on the other hand, beat Carter by a surprisingly large margin, particularly in the electoral vote (489 to 49), and the Republicans gained thirty-three House seats and a dozen Senate seats. The latter gains gave them Senate control for the first time since 1953–55. The Democratic leadership in the House saw these results (correctly or not) as an endorsement by the electorate of a shift on domestic policy in the conservative direction, and they believed they didn't dare risk trying to block consideration of Reagan's proposals. Speaker O'Neill wrote in his memoirs,

> I could have refused to play ball with the Reagan administration
> by holding up the president's legislation in the Rules Committee.
> But in my view, this wasn't a politically wise thing to do. Despite
> my strong opposition to the president's program, I decided to give
> it a chance to be voted on by the nation's elected representatives.
> For one thing, that's how our democracy is supposed to work. For
> another, I was afraid that the voters would repudiate the
> Democrats if we didn't give the president a chance to pass his
> program. (O'Neill and Novak, 1987, p. 344)

So the Congress considered the major elements of Reagan's agenda in 1981, and the president was very successful on items like domestic-spending reductions, tax cuts, and defense increases (Jones, 1988a, p. 38). In subsequent years, however, Reagan faced reduced popular support for himself, or more Democrats in Congress, or both. Despite this changed context, he sought to press ahead with his conservative agenda. Reagan was, moreover, disinclined to compromise from the beginning of his administration (Sinclair, 1983, pp. 120–21), and he didn't moderate this tendency a great deal as time passed. For example, as late as the middle of 1987 a *Washington Post* story (July 6, 1987, p. A1) was headlined "Reagan Mood Is Uncompromising, Efforts on Bork, Economic Agenda Reflect a Rightward Turn." His attitudes, however, reduced his chances of success. Conservative Democrats charged in 1986 that Reagan

> has produced a stalemate with his demands for higher defense spending and no new taxes.
> "I haven't noticed any real willingness to compromise," Stenholm [of Texas, Chairman of the Conservative Democratic Forum] complains . . . (Calmes, 1986a, p. 912)

Thus Reagan's insistence on his favored alternatives reduced the propensity of moderate and conservative Democrats to support him and accentuated partisan polarization.

Reagan's early successes, moreover, undermined the possibility of further gains. The ability to secure passage of a proposal depends not only on the nature of the proposal, but also on the location of the status quo, i.e., the current government policy. If the status quo were toward the liberal position on an issue (as it was on domestic spending, for example, when Reagan took office), then a proposed move in the conservative direction would have a better chance of success than if the status quo were already at a conservative-favored point. Thus Reagan's victories on his major issues in 1981 made further conservative gains on those issues more difficult to achieve. Similarly, the constraining effects of budget deficits made it less likely that liberal alternatives would be proposed on issues, which might have divided Democrats and given Reagan a counterpoint around which to rally supporters.[34]

Shaping Preferences and Marshaling Support

A president's success will depend not only on his ability to get Congress to consider his agenda, but also on his ability to shape members' operative preferences toward his preferred positions.[35] When party control is unified, a president's ability to reinforce cohesion within his own party will lead to success. When party control is divided, a president who cannot persuade members of the congressional majority to cross party lines will have trouble passing his program.

President Carter had considerable difficulty in getting Democrats to go along with his initiatives, especially in the first year or two. This was partly due to the nature of his agenda, which activated rather than reduced intraparty divisions. His difficulties were also due, however, to the way in which the administration dealt with Congress. "Carter quickly began to garner brickbats for his apparent reluctance to consult steadily with members of Congress as he formulated his legislative proposals—and to lobby them assiduously once his initiatives were in their hands" (Hagar, 1977, p. 2637). The disinclination toward consultation stemmed from Carter's suspicion of the motives of congressmen and their responsiveness to special interests, and from the view that he was the trustee of the nation's interests. Thus it was natural to concentrate program development in the White House (Jones, 1988b, p. 79; see also Sinclair, 1983, pp. 115–18). These factors were also related to the problems with lobbying Democrats. As Jones said (1988b, p. 84), "Carter thought Congress should support the president because he spent time on an issue, demonstrated public support, and personally avoided the strictly political (by his definition)." Finally, other factors causing difficulty in Carter's attempts to secure support for his program included the failure to set priorities among the elements of his large agenda (Jones, 1988b, p. 126) and the inherent problems of dealing with the unsettled power relationships in Congress immediately after the reform period (Jones, 1988b, chap. 3; Edwards, 1980, pp. 193–96).

Because of the character of Reagan's electoral victory in 1980, he had considerable success in putting together majority support in the House during his first year. This might be referred to as "the politics of hope and fear." House Republicans hoped that Reagan's electoral margin, and the congressional gains that accompanied his victory, marked the beginning of the long-awaited realignment that would finally give them a majority in the House. Thus they were inclined toward great cohesion behind Reagan's major initiatives. On the other hand, Democrats (and particularly southerners) feared the prospect of a Republican realignment. Many of them believed that a majority of voters had endorsed a policy shift toward conservatism, and were concerned about the political consequences to them if they opposed Reagan.[36] This concern induced enough of them to join with the cohesive Republicans that Reagan succeeded in getting many of his major proposals passed.

After 1981, however, reductions in Reagan's approval level made it difficult to hold Republicans together, and even more difficult to induce Democrats to support him. Moreover, with fewer Republican votes available after the 1982 elections, the number of Democrat defectors necessary to give the president victory was much harder to achieve (Rohde, 1989b, pp. 141–43). In addition, many Democrats came to believe that the threat of imminent realignment was a "false alarm." The elections of 1982 (with its significant Democratic gain in the House) and 1984 (when Reagan's enormous popular landslide produced few congressional gains) indicated that few of them were in danger (Rohde, 1989b, pp. 158–60). The hopes and fears of 1981 receded, and with them much of the resources necessary to produce Reagan victories. Finally, Reagan appeared to be more contemptuous of congressional Democrats as time passed,[37] and less inclined to be actively involved in pressing legislative initiatives. These tendencies also undermined chances for success.

Carter and Reagan: Some Effects on Partisanship

In our discussion above, we argued that divided government will not necessarily reduce partisanship, nor will unified government necessarily enhance it. More specifically, we contended that a number of factors during the Carter administration (particularly differences with congressional Democrats over what issues and alternatives should comprise the agenda) reduced congressional partisanship. On the other hand, we argued that during the Reagan administration, the president's conservative agenda and unwillingness to compromise in the face of a more homogeneous Democratic party in the House amplified partisanship after the first year or two.

Figure 5.5 presents the data on the mean party difference by Congress on nonconsensual votes. Before the Carter years, the pattern appears roughly consistent with the expectations of earlier researchers.

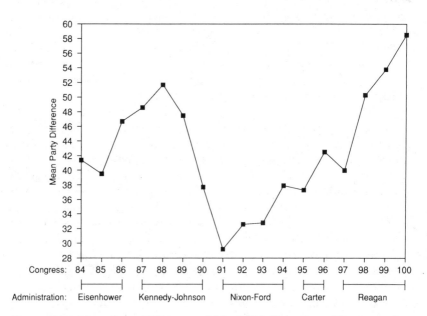

Figure 5.5 Mean Party Difference, 84th–100th Congresses (Consensual Votes Excluded)

Partisanship in voting increased in the last Eisenhower Congress after the Democratic landslide in the 1958 congressional elections, but then moved even higher during the Kennedy-Johnson years. It declined again after the 1966 midterm elections, when the Democrats suffered heavy losses and Johnson's approval ratings had fallen to very low levels, and then declined even further with the advent of the Nixon administration. Continuing the pattern for the Congresses after second midterms, the level of partisanship increased somewhat after the 1974 congressional landslide gave the Democrats two-thirds of the House seats. The later data, however, appear to be consistent with our expectations regarding the Carter and Reagan years. There is no enhancement of partisanship visible as a result of the coming of united government under Carter, although there was a slight increase in his second Congress. During Reagan's first Congress, partisanship did decline slightly, but it increased sharply after the 1982 elections and continued to grow in subsequent years.

One might argue, however, that these aggregate figures don't tell the entire story. We know, for example, that the mix of vote types varied greatly over this period. Also, the aggregate totals cover all votes, not just those on which the president had a position. Furthermore, these data concern only floor voting, and thus convey no information on partisanship in other arenas, such as the shaping of legislation in committees. These are all important considerations, and we will try to shed some light on them by narrowing our focus.

Rather than considering all votes, we will limit this segment of the analysis to votes on initial regular passage of bills and joint resolutions.[38] Thus we are considering those significant legislative proposals needing presidential approval that came to a floor vote on final passage. In terms of the agenda, this is the policy alternative the House has decided to endorse after consideration by its committees, and after collective action on the House floor.[39] Regarding these bills, we first ask, In what proportion of the cases where the president took a position did he favor passing the bill? Figure 5.6 displays those data for the Eighty-fourth through the One Hundredth Congresses.[40]

In the last three Eisenhower Congresses, the president endorsed between 59 and 86 percent of the bills. During the united-government years of the Kennedy-Johnson administrations, the president and Congress almost always agreed; the proportion of bills favored by the president was 95 percent or higher in every Congress. The level remained almost as high in the first two Nixon Congresses, then fell to a level below the Eisenhower figures during the next four years under Nixon-Ford. Under Carter, the president again was heavily in agreement with Congress's choices, although the level was below that under

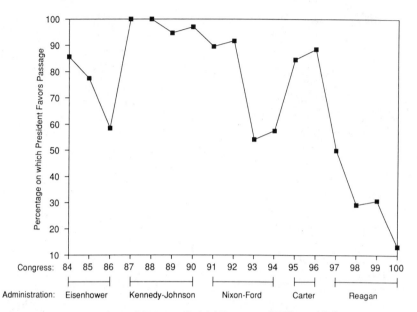

Figure 5.6 Proportion of Votes on Initial Passage of Bills and Joint Resolutions on Which the President Favored Passage, 84th–100th Congresses (Votes on which the president took no position are excluded)

Kennedy-Johnson. Finally, during the Reagan years, the proportion of bills endorsed by the president started out lower than at any previous point in the series (50 percent) and declined substantially from there. In the One Hundredth Congress, the president approved of only nine of the sixty-eight bills (13 percent).

Clearly it would not be reasonable to conclude from these data alone that Reagan was a less successful president than his predecessors (nor that Carter was less successful than Kennedy). We have noted that Reagan's agenda was relatively ideological and ambitious, and that he was victorious on those early proposals that were his highest priorities. Moreover, these data tell us nothing about instances in which proposals that the president opposed never even got to the floor. What they do show is that (given the example of the Reagan administration) divided government does not necessarily lead to compromise and negotiated accommodations between the president and the House. The data don't clearly tell us who won, but they do clearly show that interbranch and interparty disagreement was higher under Reagan than in previous divided administrations.

Figure 5.7 shows the mean party difference on votes on initial passage of bills and joint resolutions, controlling for presidential positions. The series for cases where there is no presidential position provides a baseline for comparison. It shows a pattern of decline from Eisenhower through the middle of the Nixon-Ford years, then a steady increase to a level about 10 points higher than that at the beginning of the series.[41] The other two series show a consistent pattern (the missing points are due to a lack of cases):[42] under divided government, the highest levels of party conflict are when the president opposes passage; under united government, the greatest conflict occurs when he supports passage. Consider these patterns in light of the previous research linking partisan control of government to the level of congressional partisanship. Under united government, congressional-presidential agreement on a bill presented for a vote on passage would usually enhance party cohesion within the majority party, while disagreement would divide the party. (The incentives for the minority party are less clear, but the majority pattern alone would exert a powerful impact on partisan voting.) Under divided government, on the other hand, instances of presidential opposition to bills exert no conflicting incentives for majority partisans between the inclination to oppose the president and the in-

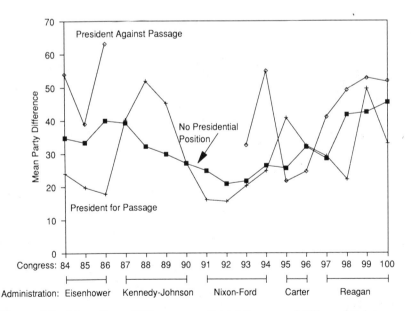

Figure 5.7 Mean Party Difference on Initial Passage of Bills and Joint Resolutions, by Presidential Position (Consensual Votes Excluded)

clination to support the product of the committees (modified, perhaps, on the floor). This would enhance majority cohesion. Instances of presidential endorsement involve a product which received support from at least a segment of the majority party in committee and/or in the amending process, so they will almost always produce division within the majority.

The point of all this is that the overall pattern of partisanship is not an automatic consequence of united versus divided government, but is instead conditionally based on the mix of the different strategic situations. If, under divided government, most of the votes involve bills which the president finds sufficiently satisfactory to endorse (which are probably the product of conservative-coalition support in committee and on the floor), partisanship in voting on them will indeed be muted. This was the case in the first four years under Nixon. If, however, the character of most bills is such that presidential opposition is provoked (as was the case under Reagan), then partisan voting will be stimulated.

The pattern can be more clearly illustrated by laying out the data for Congresses during the three Republican administrations in parallel fashion. This is done in table 5.2. (Unfortunately, there are not sufficient data to compare the Kennedy-Johnson and Carter years.) These data show that while there is some difference across administrations (e.g., the third Reagan Congress displays much higher partisanship than the parallel Congresses for his predecessors), most of the temporal

Table 5.2 Mean Party Difference on Initial Passage of Bills and Joint Resolutions under Republican Presidents, Controlling for Presidential Position (Consensual Votes Excluded)

| Congress | President Opposes Passage | | |
	Eisenhower	Nixon-Ford	Reagan
First	—	[N=2]	41.1 (14)
Second	54.0 (4)[a]	[N=1]	49.2 (26)
Third	39.0 (7)	32.6 (20)	52.8 (23)
Fourth	63.1 (14)	54.9 (15)	52.0 (43)

Congress	President Supports Passage		
First	—	16.1 (22)	29.2 (11)
Second	24.0 (11)	15.6 (14)	22.2 (13)
Third	19.8 (18)	20.3 (21)	49.6 (8)
Fourth	17.8 (18)	24.8 (19)	33.1 (5)

[a]Numbers in parentheses are number of cases.

comparisons yield relatively similar levels of party conflict. The pronounced differences involve comparisons within administrations between instances in which the president endorses passage and those in which he opposes it. This indicates that circumstances of compromise and of conflict between president and Congress under divided government do produce similar response patterns across time, but the mix of conflict and compromise will vary depending on characteristics of the president and Congress. Under Reagan there was both a more ideologically conservative president, and a more homogeneous majority party opposing him, than there had been in the past. Instead of the tendency toward compromise and reduced partisan conflict under divided government expected by previous researchers, this led to a much higher proportion of bills unsatisfactory to the president, and thus to higher levels of partisanship in voting. Thus there appears to be strong support for our theory's implications regarding the conditional nature of consequences of divided or unified government.

Some Legislative Consequences

In this section we will conclude our analysis by discussing some consequences of House reform and increased partisanship for legislative outcomes. We will first consider the changing level of party victory over the period covered by this study, and then turn to a discussion of effects on the shaping of legislation in the House.

Patterns of Party Victory

Most previous studies of congressional partisanship analyzed either the level of party voting or levels of party unity, or both. There is, however, another consideration related to partisanship which is rarely considered, but may be the most consequential: the relative frequency with which each party wins or loses on votes when it is in conflict. It is the effect on winning or losing that ultimately makes the levels of party cohesion interesting, as the examples we have been presenting illustrate. Therefore it will be useful for us to consider the impact of changing partisanship on the legislative fortunes of the two parties.

Focusing on victory also reminds us that maximizing party loyalty is not always necessary, particularly for the majority. Except for those instances where a two-thirds margin is required, victory requires only that the majority party get more votes for its preferred position than the minority secures for its side. In concrete terms, the Democrats don't even have to reach the same level of cohesion as the Republicans when the two are in conflict. They have only to hold the number of their defectors to a level "near" that of the Republicans. How "near" depends on the number of seats each party holds. For example, if the Democrats were to hold 261 seats (their average for the Eight-fourth through One Hundredth Congresses), they could tolerate forty-three more defectors than the Republicans and still win. This is a party-unity level of 84 percent for Democrats if Republicans are perfectly cohesive. Thus most of the time the Democratic party and its leadership does not need to induce every Democrat to side with the party, and trying to do so wouldn't be worth the cost in terms of bargaining or of interpersonal conflict. The majority party leaders will, therefore, probably tolerate a certain amount of disloyalty with relative equanimity.[43] The pressures to conform will become apparent only when defectors have caused party defeats, as in the case of the Boll Weevils in 1981.

Table 5.3 presents data on party voting, including the proportion of votes on which the parties were opposed that were won by the Democrats.[44] It also shows the share of seats the majority held in each Congress. During the Eisenhower administration the Democrats won a little over 60 percent of the contested votes until their numbers were swollen by the 1958 landslide. That pushed their success rate over 70 percent. The arrival of a Democratic president more than compensated for the loss of some seats, and the level of Democratic victories moved even higher. Then in the Eighty-ninth Congress, the two-thirds majority provided by the Johnson landslide boosted the Democrats' success rate over 88 percent. Even though southern Democratic loyalty had fallen to an average of 55 percent, the large number of northern Democrats almost guaranteed that the party position would carry.[45]

The trend of rising Democratic success ended in the Ninetieth Congress. Although the Democrats still controlled the presidency, their heavy losses in the 1966 elections (leaving them with even fewer seats than they held before the 1964 landslide), in conjunction with low southern loyalty in response to Johnson's agenda, left their share of unity votes won at the level of the Eisenhower years. Then under Nixon the Democrats' success rate declined even further. It bottomed out in the Ninety-second Congress when the majority party, with over 58 percent of the seats, won less than half of the party-unity votes. (Not coincidentally, average party unity for southern Democrats in the Ninety-second Congress also fell below 50 percent.) Majority-party success rebounded a bit in the Ninety-third Congress, and then shot up to 76 percent in the Ninety-fourth as a result of the large Democratic gains in the 1974 elections. This clearly illustrates the impact of a larger number of seats going to the majority: the Democrats won 15 percentage points more of the votes, although there was no noticeable gain in average unity for northerners or southerners.

Table 5.3 House Party-Voting Data, 84th–100th Congresses

Congress (President)	Democrats percent of House Seats[a]	Mean Party-Unity Scores (Percent)				Unity Votes won by Democrats (percent)
		Repub-licans	Demo-crats	North. Demo-crats	South. Demo-crats	
(Eisenhower)						
84	53.3	78	80	86	73	63.5
85	53.8	74	78	85	70	62.1
86	64.9	81	80	86	70	72.2
(Kennedy-Johnson)						
87	60.0	81	81	92	68	77.4
88	59.4	82	83	94	68	75.8
89	67.8	81	79	91	55	88.6
90	57.0	79	75	90	51	61.5
(Nixon-Ford)						
91	55.9	72	71	83	50	57.9
92	58.6	76	70	82	46	48.3
93	55.8	73	74	85	54	59.6
94	66.9	76	75	85	53	76.0
(Carter)						
95	67.1	77	73	81	55	71.3
96	63.7	79	76	83	61	73.2
(Reagan)						
97	55.9	78	78	86	60	59.2
98	61.8	78	82	89	67	76.5
99	58.2	76[b]	83[b]	89[b]	71[b]	77.8[b]
100	59.3	81[b]	86[b]	91[b]	76[b]	81.2[b]

[a]Source: Ornstein, Mann, and Malbin (1990, pp. 47–48).
[b]Excluding procedural protest votes (see n. 44).

Then the Democrats regained the presidency. Reflecting the negative response among liberals to some aspects of Carter's program, northern Democratic unity declined and the party won a smaller share of the unity votes than it had under Ford. With the advent of the Reagan administration, Democratic success declined sharply. The comparison of the Ninety-seventh Congress with the Ninety-third is striking. In both cases there was a Republican president and the number of seats held by each party was almost the same, and while Democratic unity was up a bit, so too was Republican unity. As a result, the percentages of votes won by the Democrats in the two Congresses were virtually identical.

In subsequent Congresses under Reagan, increasing Democratic cohesion made itself felt, and the majority's success rate shot up. Here it is useful to compare the One Hundredth Congress with the Ninety-fourth. Each is the fourth Congress of a Republican administration. Although the Democrats held thirty-three fewer seats in the One Hundredth, their average party unity was 11 points higher. As a consequence, they won over 81 percent of the unity votes, compared to 76 percent in the Ninety-fourth. Indeed, the only Congress in which the Democrats won a greater share of the votes than in the One Hundredth was the Eighty-ninth, when they held the presidency and over two-thirds of the House seats. From the point of view of party victory on roll-call votes, the impact of increased partisanship is clear.

Floor Amendments

One of the earliest major reforms discussed in chapter 2 was the adoption of recorded teller voting and electronic voting in the Legislative Reorganization Act of 1970. Liberal Democrats had contended that the inability to put members on the public record on amendments, coupled with the great powers of committee chairmen to influence members' votes on nonrecorded amendments, undermined their ability to change committee policies that were more conservative than the majority preference in the chamber. In the liberals' view, moreover, unrepresentative committee policies were frequently the norm because senior committee Democrats (especially chairmen) had disproportionate influence over the content of bills, and were disproportionately southern and conservative.

The reforms adopted in the 1970s, however, undermined these institutional biases. The power of committee chairmen was substantially reduced. Moreover, Democratic committee caucuses were institutionalized, and the final say on committee activities and on the distribution of power within the committee (e.g., subcommittee chairmanships and assignments) was vested in that group. In addition, the recorded-teller-vote rule made members' votes on amendments visible to constituents, and electronic voting made it feasible to have record votes on a large number of amendments each Congress. If these reforms accomplished what was intended, then the measures reported from committees should have become, over time, more representative of the views of House Democrats, making it less necessary for them to press for amendments on the floor on conflictual issues. If, however, aspects of a bill did not satisfy Democrats, then the new amendment rules should have made it easier to secure desired changes.

Steven Smith's (1989) detailed study of floor politics in Congress provides information that bears directly on these points. His data show (p. 34) that Democratic sponsorship of amendments in the House decreased from about 70 percent of all amendments in the Ninety-first and Ninety-second Congresses to less than 60 percent in the Ninety-third through Ninety-ninth. If one focuses only on amendments decided by recorded votes, which presumably involve greater conflict, the Democrat-sponsored proportion declined from 63 percent in the Ninety-second Congress to about 50 percent thereafter. The results regarding amendment adoption are even more striking. Smith found (p. 150) that before the reforms, controlling for party and seniority of amendment sponsors, junior Democrats were least successful at getting amendments adopted, while senior Democrats were most successful. Republican success fell in between. After reform every group's success rate increased, but junior Democrats quickly moved ahead of Republicans, and in the Ninety-ninth Congress they surpassed even senior Democrats.

When Smith controlled for party and whether the sponsor was a member of the committee of jurisdiction (p. 151), parallel patterns were apparent. Before reform, committee Democrats were much more successful than any other group, with the others being about equal. Postreform, the gap between committee and noncommittee Democrats closed, and by the Ninety-ninth Congress their success rates were only a few percentage points apart. Smith summarized these results (p. 151): "Reforms of floor procedure stimulated Republican amending activity disproportionately, perhaps to the surprise of Democrats, but the reforms also were associated with increased success among rank-and-file Democrats, just as many Democratic reformers had in mind."

We can supplement Smith's findings in a number of ways with our own evidence. He considered data on all amendments, many of which involved little or no disagreement. We can narrow the focus by dealing only with amendments decided by recorded votes, and by excluding the subset of those that were consensual. Thus we consider only those amendments about which there was some noticeable conflict. Second, we also restrict our attention by considering only first-degree amendments. As Weingast (1989a, b, c) and Smith (1989, pp. 183–87) pointed out, second-degree amendments (i.e., amendments to amendments) can be used by committee members to counter attempted changes in bills, and thus they do not necessarily indicate any dissatisfaction with the committee's product. First-degree amendments are attempts to change committee-adopted decisions. Finally, Smith considered amendments in terms of the partisan affiliation of the sponsor. This does not, however, always reflect the character of the coalition backing the proposed change. It is frequently in the interests of amendment backers to have a Republican sponsor an amendment favored by liberal Democrats,[46] or to have a Democrat (frequently southern) propose an amendment backed by conservative Republicans.[47] This gives a bipartisan cast to the effort and may increase the chances of success. Here we will instead classify amendments by which party provides a greater proportion of positive votes. If the percentage of Democrats voting aye exceeds the proportion for Republicans, the amendment will be termed Democrat-favored.

Figure 5.8 shows the proportion of amendments favored by Democrats from the Ninety-second Congress on.[48] In the first Congress, Democrats favored about half of the amendments. This fell to about 40 percent in the remaining Nixon-Ford years, and to 30 percent under a Democratic president. Reflecting Reagan's influence over the agenda in his first two years, the Democrat-favored proportion increased again to 47 percent, but then tapered off. In the One Hundredth Congress, the Democrat-favored proportion of amendments had fallen back to the level of the Carter years.[49]

In figure 5.9, we see the proportion of amendments adopted according to which party favored them. In the Ninety-second Congress, Republican success was much higher, but in the next two Congresses, that rate declined while Democratic success increased. Republican success was then greater in the Carter and first Reagan Congresses, but in the Ninety-eighth through One Hundredth, Democrat-favored amend-

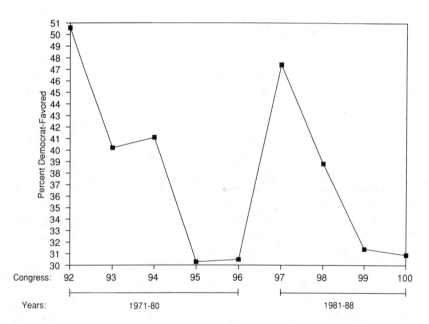

Figure 5.8 Proportion of Amendments Favored by Democrats, 92d–100th Congresses (Consensual Votes Excluded)

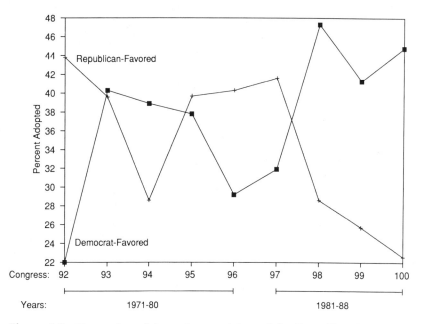

Figure 5.9 Proportion of Amendments Adopted, by Party Favoring Amendment: 92d–100th Congresses (Consensual Votes Excluded)

ments were much more likely to be adopted than Republican-favored ones.

Finally, figure 5.10 shows the mean party difference on amendments. Partisanship was stable on Democratic amendments under Nixon-Ford, declined somewhat under Carter, and then increased under Reagan to levels markedly higher than those of the Nixon years. On Republican-favored amendments, the mean party difference was quite stable over time until after Reagan's first Congress, when it grew substantially. On both categories of amendments, average partisanship was over 12 points higher in the One Hundredth Congress compared to the Ninety-seventh.

Both Smith's data and our own support our theoretical expectations. After the reform era, Democrats favored a smaller proportion of amendments (except for the early Reagan years), presumably because the content of committee-passed measures became more satisfactory to them. On Democrat-favored amendments, the proportion adopted increased over time, while the proportion of Republican amendments was steady, and then declined. After the 1982 elections, when northern Democrats and loyalist southerners had enough combined votes to control outcomes routinely in committee and on the floor, Democrat-

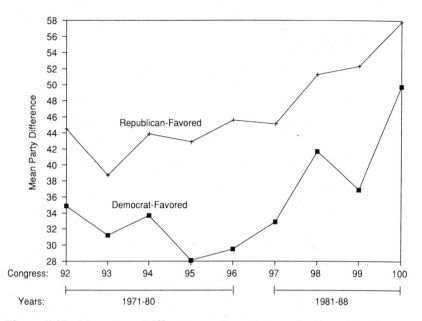

Figure 5.10   Mean Party Difference on Amendments, by Party Favoring Amendments: 92d–100th Congresses (Consensual Votes Excluded)

favored amendments were much more likely to pass than were Republican amendments. Moreover, partisanship rose on both types of amendments, but it began and remained higher on Republican-favored proposals. The politics of floor amendments in the House has predominantly become a matter of Republicans trying to change the committees' products, and Democrats voting more cohesively over time to protect committee bills,[50] a remarkable change from the prereform era.

Bill Passage

We can conclude our analysis by examining data on bill passage that parallel those we offered in the discussion of amendments.[51] Figure 5.11 displays the proportion of bills and joint resolutions that were favored by Democrats on initial regular passage.[52] The share of Democrat-favored bills increased under Kennedy-Johnson, then declined at the beginning of the Nixon administration. In the Ninetieth Congress, the majority party was able to shape only three of every five bills to its satisfaction. Democratic success increased over the Nixon-Ford Congresses, but it actually declined in the first Carter Congress. The conflict between the White House and House Democrats over the agenda apparently impeded the majority party's ability to control the content of legislation. During the first Reagan Congress, the Democrat-favored share of bills declined again, reflecting the Republican–Boll Weevil coalition. After that, however, Democrats dominated outcomes. In the Ninety-ninth Congress, nine of every ten bills were Democrat-favored, the highest level since the Eighty-ninth Congress,[53] and in the first session of the One Hundredth, *every* bill that came to a vote was Democrat-favored. The combination of Democratic homogeneity, the tools granted by reform, and the vigor of the majority leadership under Wright gave the Democrats a more consistent control over outcomes than had control of the presidency and two-thirds of the House seats in 1965–66.

Finally, figure 5.12 shows the data on mean party difference on these bills and resolutions. If almost all bills receive majority support, then Republican-favored bills will—virtually by definition—involve a divided Democratic party. Therefore we would expect that in those cases partisan differences will be muted, and the data confirm that expectation. The mean party difference is remarkably stable over time on Republican-favored bills, with the exception of the Ninety-ninth and

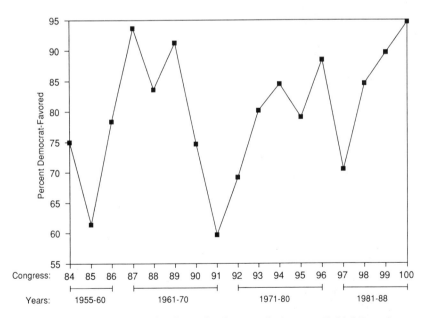

Figure 5.11 Proportion of Bills and Joint Resolutions on Initial Regular Passage That Were Democrat-Favored (Consensual Votes Excluded)

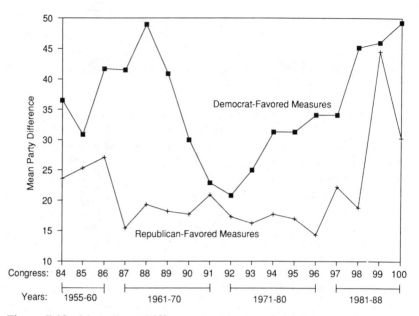

Figure 5.12   Mean Party Difference on Votes on Initial Regular Passage of Bills and Joint Resolutions Controlling for Which Party Favored the Measure (Consensual Votes Excluded)

One Hundredth Congresses, where there were few cases.[54] On Democrat-favored bills, on the other hand, we see the familiar pattern of reduced partisanship in the Ninetieth through the Ninety-second Congresses compared to earlier years. Then from the Ninety-third Congress on there is a steady increase until the Ninety-eight through the One Hundredth Congresses, when the relatively high levels of party conflict exhibited in the Kennedy-Johnson years were equaled or exceeded. In both the shaping of legislation during the amending process and the collective judgments on the product of that shaping, a cohesive Democratic majority has come to control most outcomes.

Summary

This chapter has considered varied facets of the causes and consequences of the resurgence of partisanship in the House. First, we discussed House Republicans, considering their factional patterns, their strategic responses to minority status, and their reactions to the activities of the Democratic leadership in the 1980s. The analysis indicated that divisions among Republicans were never as serious as those among

Democrats, but neither has the GOP experienced as great an increase in homogeneity. As Democrats increased in cohesion and became more frequently able to arrive at an internal consensus on policy matters which did not require Republican assent, the GOP members became increasingly frustrated. They reacted to being cut out of the policy-making process on major issues, and to what they regarded as the Democrats' unfair procedural manipulations, with visible anger and vocal protests. They also responded by adopting rules and procedures to strengthen their party's organizational structure and their leadership. These changes were patterned after the previous procedural revisions among Democrats, a striking indication of the Republicans' belief in the efficacy of the Democrats' actions.

We next discussed the impact of the Carter and Reagan presidencies on partisanship in the House, arguing that previous analyses of the relationship between divided government and partisanship did not sufficiently capture the varied theoretical possibilities regarding the issue. Specifically, we saw that Carter's agenda divided the Democratic party and tended to mute partisanship in the House, while Reagan's ideological agenda and personal style reinforced and exacerbated partisan divisions.

Finally, with regard to the pattern of legislative outcomes, we saw that over the last two decades the proportion of amendments that received greater support from Republicans than Democrats increased, the success rate of Republican-favored amendments declined, and the degree of partisan division on those amendments increased. This shows that committee bills were becoming more satisfactory to Democrats than to Republicans. The patterns of partisan support on bill-passage votes, after the amending process was complete, demonstrated that there too the results more often reflected Democratic preferences.

6 | Conclusions and Future Prospects

We have presented a set of arguments, with supporting evidence, intended to explain the increased partisanship apparent in the House of Representatives during the 1980s and to describe some of its consequences. This chapter will draw together the various elements of the theoretical explanation to make clear how they are interrelated, and will briefly recall the patterns in the relevant evidence that has been presented. After that, we will close the analysis with a discussion of possible future changes in the major elements of the theory, which might then alter the patterns we have discerned. In particular, the discussion will focus on the impact of two changes that have already occurred: the transition in the presidency from Ronald Reagan to George Bush, and the transition in the speakership from James Wright to Thomas Foley.

Theory and Evidence: A Summary

It is probably useful to attempt to capture the essentials of our argument in a few sentences, and then go on to discuss in more detail how the parts fit together. The main driving force behind the resurgence of partisanship in the House is the exogenous influence of electoral change. The elections of the late 1950s and the 1960s brought to the House many new liberal Democrats. These members found institutional arrangements (especially the disproportionate powers of committee chairmen) to be biased against their interests and in favor of those of the "conservative coalition." They sought to redress the institutional imbalance through the reforms of the 1970s, which weakened chairmen and strengthened the majority party. After the reform era,

162

electoral forces again had an impact through national and district-level changes that resulted in electoral coalitions of representatives that were more similar within parties and more different between them. These changes resulted in party caucuses in the House that were more homogeneous with regard to policy preferences, and which therefore found it easier to find common ground on previously divisive issues. This increased homogeneity also provided the basis for more aggressive use of reform-granted powers by the Democratic party leadership. Finally, partisanship was enhanced in the 1980s by the impact of individual personalities: Democratic leaders, who were progressively more willing to use their powers to advance partisan interests, and President Reagan, whose inclination to press his relatively extreme policy views made it easier for Democrats to arrive at satisfactory compromise positions within their party. As a result of all these factors, outcomes in the House—in committee and on the floor—more frequently reflected the preferences of House Democrats. We will now review more fully these aspects of the theory and their interrelationships.

Electoral Forces, Member Goals, and the Rise of Reform

In 1958 and the early 1960s, many Democrats with liberal policy preferences were first elected to the House. As we noted in the discussion of members' goals, the assertion that these junior Democrats were concerned about policy outcomes does not imply that this was the exclusive, or even the paramount, goal for all of them. Many of these representatives were primarily concerned with getting reelected, some had higher office in mind, and others wanted power in the House. However, it is also true that for many Democrats there was little or no conflict between policy goals and others. Recalling our distinction between personal preference (the policy outcome actually preferred by a member) and operative preference (the outcome the member supports when all relevant political influences are taken into account), for many northern Democrats the two types of preferences were the same. Both they and their supportive (i.e., reelection and primary) constituencies favored expanded government services, efforts to influence the economy, new civil rights laws, etc. Thus for them the pursuit of policy interests was an electoral advantage. Moreover, even when there was goal conflict, members often found it possible to balance reelection and policy interests by taking some electoral risks and compromising some policy positions.

When these new Democrats got to the House, they found that although their party was in the majority and theoretically could control outcomes, in reality the conservative coalition of southern Democrats and Republicans stood as an effective roadblock to the achievement of their policy goals. This was possible for four related reasons: (1) committees dominated the policy-making process, (2) committee chairmen and other senior members had disproportionate power within committees, (3) conservative southern Democrats held power positions on committees out of proportion to their numbers in the party (especially on the most important committees), and (4) these conservatives were able to ally with the Republicans against the majority of their own party because the seniority system automatically granted and protected their positions of influence on committees. As Richard Bolling said (1968, p. 223), these circumstances resulted in a situation in which "the majority of House Democrats has not had effective control of the House."

Liberal House Democrats began searching for ways to improve their situation. The Democratic Study Group was formed to provide like-minded members with useful legislative information and to rally them behind liberal initiatives. It became clear, however, that this wasn't going to be sufficient, and (when their situation worsened with Richard Nixon's election in 1968) the DSG leadership tried to devise changes in the institutional arrangements in the House that would give them greater influence over policy outcomes.

Diverse Goals and the Patterns of Reform

As we saw in the discussion of the reforms in chapter 2, the effort to alter the rules operated on three distinct tracks. These reforms were intended to alter the conditions that permitted the conservative coalition to prevail against the majority of Democrats. The DSG leaders who devised the series of reform packages saw them as means to advance liberal policy goals. More important, this was the main reason that they publicly articulated in trying to rally support for reform among House Democrats. They argued that senior committee conservatives didn't support party positions, that the unrestricted use of the seniority system made this possible, and that the proposed reforms would change things. However, the DSG leaders also recognized that members were not solely motivated by policy concerns. Other interests had to be protected in the reform process, and those interests sometimes provided additional incentives for supporting reform.

The first, and most essential (from the liberals' point of view), reform track was the set of measures that undermined the powers of committee chairmen. The Subcommittee Bill of Rights protected the operating independence of subcommittees, providing guaranteed staff and explicitly establishing jurisdictions. In addition it removed the appointment of subcommittee chairmen and members from the control of committee chairmen. Some limits were also placed on the dominant and independent influence of committees on policy outcomes within their jurisdictions. One aspect of this was the adoption of the recorded teller vote, which altered the relationship between the committees and the floor. Members chose to put their decisions regarding proposed changes in committee bills on the public record. They thereby pitted the pressures of their interest in reelection and policy against the influences that committee leaders could bring to bear, another recognition of the mixed goals pursued by congressmen.

Committee independence and influence was also counterbalanced by the measures that strengthened Democratic party leaders, the second reform track. The transfer of Democratic committee-assignment powers to the Steering and Policy Committee, coupled with direct Speaker control over Rules Committee appointments, expanded leadership influence over members' access to the most desirable spots in the committee system. Other changes (multiple referral, influence over special rules, expanded ability to use suspensions) increased the leaders' ability to shape the floor agenda to enhance the prospects of committee products they endorsed, or to undermine those they did not.

Finally, the third track of reform was designed to ensure that the new distribution of power that resulted from the first two tracks did not result in new independent and autocratic practices. It put in place mechanisms of collective control for each of the significant repositories of power granted through the Democratic party. Top party leaders could, as had always been true, theoretically be replaced at the beginning of any Congress, but this power was never used (or needed). However, the leadership's accountability to the members was enhanced through regular and special meetings of the Democratic Caucus, and through weekly meetings of an expanded whip system, which provided avenues for members to communicate their concerns and complaints. Committee chairmen (and subcommittee chairs on Appropriations) were made responsible to the Caucus through regular secret-ballot votes at the beginning of each Congress, whereby House Democrats could approve or reject their occupancy of those positions. Employing these procedures, the Caucus rejected chairmen five times between 1974 and 1988. Similarly, other subcommittee chairmen were made responsible to party caucuses on their respective committees, and this power was also exercised a number of times. These new rules were all designed to accomplish the goal that Rep. Don Fraser set up at the beginning of the reform effort: "to make the people who held positions of power . . . responsible to rank and file Democrats" (Sheppard, 1985, p. 40).

Thus the reform movement was a multifaceted effort intended to revise the balance of power within the House and to increase rank-and-file influence over party and committee leaders. However (again recognizing the diversity of member goals), there was never any intention that party influence would be equal across all committees. Committees like Merchant Marine and Veterans' Affairs were not the targets of the reforms; they would rarely deal with bills that would sharply divide Democrats from Republicans, liberals from conservatives. The same was generally true of those more important committees that were closely linked to members' reelection goals because they provided tangible benefits to be delivered to constituents (e.g., Agriculture, Public Works, Interior). Rather, the reforms were primarily concerned with the top committees that made national policy on matters that frequently provoked partisan division, committees like Appropriations, Budget, Ways and Means, Energy and Commerce, and Armed Services.

The obligation to support party positions, moreover, was not intended to apply equally to all members. There was no intention to create a system of party responsibility like those that operate in parliamentary democracies, imposing on every member the requirement to support every party position. Instead, obligation was to be imposed on members "who held positions of power"—party leaders, committee chairmen, members of prestige committees. In effect, seeking and accepting positions of influence within the committee or party leadership meant accepting an implied contract: such leaders were obliged to support—or at least not to block—policy initiatives on which there was a party consensus. If these expectations were violated, members risked the loss of their influential positions. Party support was also expected from representatives who aspired to these positions. Taken together, these elements define the system that we have termed conditional party government. Committee and party leaders were to be responsible to the members, not vice versa. Members were to be free to pursue their own goals within a generally decentralized system. The exceptions were to be limited to those areas that were of concern to the party collectively, and, among those, to issues on which there was a reasonably wide consensus among party members. Moreover, the degree of responsibility was roughly proportional to the amount of power the members had been granted by the party. Party and top committee leaders had the greatest obligations.

Electoral Forces Again: The Increase in Party Homogeneity

In earlier chapters we argued that regional differences among Democratic voters played a prominent role in producing the deep divisions that were apparent within the House Democratic party in the 1960s and 1970s. As new issues (like civil rights, the Vietnam War, and expansion of government services) rose to prominence—issues that found different preferences among northern and southern Democratic voters—sharply different patterns of positions were taken by northern and southern Democratic congressmen. Then, gradually, the composition of each party's electorate began to change. Most profoundly, the Voting Rights Act added large numbers of black voters to the electorate, most of whom identified with the Democratic party and had relatively liberal policy preferences. At the same time, many conservative white voters jointed the Republican party in the South. Some of these were northern migrants; others were disaffected Democrats who were choosing a new and more hospitable home for their conservative preferences. As a consequence of these changes, and some concurrent shifting among northerners, the policy positions of the coalitions of voters supporting congressional candidates became more similar within the parties across regions, and more different between the parties.

As we saw in chapter 3, in the wake of these shifting patterns of preferences among voters, the positions supported by members of Congress also changed, especially among southerners. Some southern conservatives were replaced by (usually even more conservative) Republicans; others were succeeded by moderate to liberal Democrats. In still other instances, the same representative continued serving, but supported Democratic party positions more frequently in response to the liberalization of their supportive constituencies. In the North there were changes too, with the number of Democrats (most of whom were party loyalists) increasing, and the number of moderate Republicans declining.

This trend toward increased party homogencity was reinforced by the operation of those reform provisions that were intended to enhance collective control of those in power positions. Senior Democrats, and more junior members who wanted leadership or prestige committee positions, were encouraged to support party positions and discouraged from allying with the Republicans. The combined effect of these electoral and institutional forces was similar to the new pattern among voters: the responses of members within the parties to many issues became more similar, and collectively the responses of the two parties became more divergent. Even on issues that we examined which were previously very divisive for Democrats—civil rights, defense, and budget policy—more common ground was found in the 1980s, frequently resulting in partisan victories over the Republicans.

Increased Use of Leadership Power

The growth of preference homogeneity among Democrats (at least in terms of operative preferences, but probably also with regard to personal preferences) increased the scope of conditional party government. Within that set of issues that were of partisan interest, there were more and more instances in which there was sufficient consensus to support employment of the expanded powers that were granted to the leadership by the reforms. There were more issues on which the Steering and Policy Committee could declare important floor votes to be party policy, to be taken into account when committee assignments were made. There were more bills on which Democratic members were willing to support the use of restrictive rules to limit amendments, and votes to approve these rules increasingly provoked sharp partisan opposition from Republicans. Important bills often required action by multiple committees, and the Speaker increasingly played the role of arbiter in instances of intercommittee conflict. While the scope of the party leadership's activities had been expanding under Speaker O'Neill, the aggressive use of these powers was sharply increased when James Wright succeeded to the position. He articulated an agenda that he believed reflected party views, and then pressed that agenda to passage despite facing opposition from the president and House Republicans in almost every instance.

As Democratic homogeneity grew and the leadership increasingly employed its powers, the party's whip system was expanded to serve the interests of both leaders and rank-and-file Democrats. Members wanted an effective means to communicate their preferences and complaints to the leaders. The leaders, in turn, needed this communication to assess the degree of party consensus, and also wanted the resources it provided to persuade reluctant or undecided colleagues on important votes. The perceived effectiveness of the strengthened Democratic leadership in advancing party interests was well reflected in Republican moves to grant similar increased powers to their leaders.

Presidential Influences on Partisanship

In discussing the influence of the president on partisanship, we noted that many analysts had argued that divided government would tend to reduce partisanship, while united government would enhance it. However, we contended that this generalization was not theoretically valid in all cases. Rather, the degree of partisanship would depend not only on whether partisan control was divided or united, but also on the nature of a president's preferences vis-à-vis those of members of Congress, and on the inclination of each side to compromise.

These hypotheses were supported by evidence from the Carter and Reagan administrations. Carter pressed a wide-ranging agenda that divided rather than rallied his party, reducing instead of increasing partisanship. Reagan initially proposed policy shifts in a conservative direction that found substantial support among southern Democrats as well as Republicans. However, he attempted to build on his early successes with further conservative initiatives. These revealed the different preferences of Republicans on the one hand and southern conservatives and moderates on the other, and made it easier for Democrats to arrive at a consensus on alternatives to presidential proposals. The result was an increasing proportion of bills on which the combination of committee and floor action produced results that found the two parties on opposite sides and President Reagan opposing passage.

Partisanship and Legislative Outcomes

Our analysis concluded with the presentation of evidence that showed how the pattern of legislative outcomes in the House had changed as a result of the resurgence of partisanship. The proportion of amendments that were Democrat-favored declined, and the Republicans' ability to get amendments they favored passed also decreased. This indicates that committee bills were better reflecting the preferences of House Democrats. Taking the combination of committee and floor action into account, the proportion of bills that were more favored by Democrats also increased. Finally, Democratic victories on floor votes on which party majorities opposed one another grew to levels that were generally higher than previous Congresses in which the presidency was in Democratic hands.

The combination of greater homogeneity in both parties based on changing electoral conditions, and the employment of institutional powers to buttress that homogeneity and advance party-favored initiatives, created the context for the operation of conditional party government. It didn't function on all issues, because members didn't intend it to. And it didn't function in some instances because there wasn't sufficient consensus to offer a chance of party victory. But during the 1980s, the Democratic majority was more and more frequently able to arrive at party positions on a wide range of nationally important issues in the face of determined opposition from House Republicans and a popular Republican president. This is not the American equivalent of parliamentary party responsibility, but it is a remarkable change from the way the House used to operate, and to a situation that involves a much stronger role for parties than most analysts thought was possible.

Changing Perspectives on Politics in the House

Kenneth Shepsle (1989, p. 238) said that when scholars talk about Congress, they have in mind "a textbook Congress characterized by a few main tendencies and described in broad terms." Probably none of the aspects of this textbook-Congress characterization would find unanimous support among analysts, but they would secure widespread agreement. We would argue that in light of the cumulative research described here—both the original findings and the reported results of others—certain aspects of the shared picture of politics in the House need revision, at least as a matter of emphasis.

The Role and Impact of Parties and Leaders

The most significant change relates to the perceived importance of parties and their leaders. As we noted in chapter 1, Collie (1986) found few examples of research in journals in 1985–86 that dealt with congressional parties, and those that did mostly indicated that they were unimportant. These views, and others we discussed, are more recent ratifications of the shared view, dominant over the last quarter-century, that parties and leaders in the House are weak and relatively inconsequential. That perspective was succinctly articulated by David Mayhew in his *Congress: The Electoral Connection* (1974, p. 27): "The fact is that no theoretical treatment of the United States Congress that posits parties as analytic units will go very far. So we are left with individual congressmen, with 535 men and women rather than two parties, as units to be examined. . . ." Mayhew was writing in the midst of the reform era, when both legislative parties were experiencing deep divisions. Levels of party loyalty were low, the incentives for party support were weak, and party leaders were usually disinclined to try to influence outcomes. Thus the textbook picture was fairly accurate for that time.

However, inherent in Mayhew's characterization is the view that members are connected either to parties *or* to electoral incentives. He indicated that if legislators' interests are not linked to their parties through organizational arrangements as they are in parliamentary systems, then they will respond to their constituencies and not be supportive of their party.[1] What this characterization does not recognize is that members may be linked to their parties *through* their constituencies. We can imagine a hypothetical election system in which all politicians are motivated only by the desire to win elections, all voters decide whom to support based solely on a common set of issues, and all voters who support the more liberal position belong to the Democratic party while all conservatives are Republicans. In this system the party primaries in each district would naturally choose Democratic candidates who espouse more liberal positions than do the chosen Republican candidates. Then the general-election outcome would depend on the partisan balance among voters in each district. Once in office these members would tend to support the conflicting positions of their respective parties, solely on the basis of their own electoral incentives.

Of course the real-world context of congressmen that we have been discussing is not nearly so neat and simple as this hypothetical world, but the evidence indicates that in the wake of changes in the electorate over the last twenty-five years or so it is closer to that situation than it used to be. Both the earlier literature on party voting and more recent analyses have indicated that northern and southern Democrats, for example, disagreed on many issues largely because the positions of their constituents were different on those issues. In contrast, even when party voting was at its nadir, there was a relatively high level of agreement on issues (and of party loyalty) among northeastern Democrats and among midwestern Republicans. This was because the views of their respective constituencies were fairly similar.

As the cumulative effects of electoral changes began to be felt during the 1970s and 1980s, the supportive constituencies of party candidates became more similar in their policy views across regions. This does not mean that northern Democrats' constituencies and southern Democrats' constituencies became identical. It just means that they tended to become noticeably more similar than they had been, and in particular that northern and southern Democratic constituencies tended to become more like one another than the latter were like Republican constituencies. As a consequence, the positions taken by northern and southern Democratic representatives became more similar—in their election contests, in their committees, and on the House floor. Thus there is no *necessary* conflict between evidence of high party loyalty and the view that members are motivated solely by electoral interests, although we have argued that other motivations are at work as well. Parties in the House have become more cohesive, and in turn more active and influential, and this has happened partly as a *consequence* of congressmen's individual electoral interests. It is perhaps useful to refer to the level of partisanship that is the result of exogenous, electorate-based forces as the "natural level of partisanship." Then we can talk of the actual level of partisanship as higher or lower than this natural level due to other factors, like organizational and personal influences.

Our textbook picture must change not only to encompass stronger parties in the House, but also to include stronger and more influential party leaders. Much of the literature on party leadership we discussed emphasized the restrictions context exerted on leaders, and that literature generally expected that leaders would remain weak because their context wouldn't permit anything else. Cooper and Brady (1981, p. 423), for example, expressed doubt that Speaker O'Neill (and by in-ference his successors) could even be as strong a party leader as Rayburn, whom they had described as very much at the mercy of strong committee chairmen and a divided party. Yet in the preceding pages we have seen that perhaps O'Neill, and certainly Wright, headed a stronger leadership. This is not a demonstration that Cooper and Brady and their contemporaries were incorrect in their theoretical arguments, but rather that the context of the leaders has changed in ways that were not foreseen.

The interaction of increased Democratic homogeneity with enhanced leadership powers has created conditions under which there is substantial membership support for (and even demand for) strong leadership action on behalf of a range of party-supported initiatives. And recently, parallel conditions have increasingly developed within the Republican party. It is important to emphasize that these developments provide general support for, not refutation of, the contextual theory of leadership. This newly strengthened leadership is not analogous to the powerful party heads of parliamentary systems or to the House speakerships of Cannon and Reed—leaders who commanded their memberships. Instead, these are leaders who are strong because (and when) they are agents of their memberships, who want them to be strong. When the legislative situation involves an issue that party members care about and on which their preferences are homogeneous, the stage is set for maximal use of the leadership's powers. If, however, the party is deeply divided, then leaders will be reluctant to use the tools at their disposal, and they can appear as weak as the leadership looked immediately after the reform era.

Despite this general support for the contextual theory, we must recall the argument for a qualification to that view: that there is an asymmetry between the circumstances which constrain leaders and those which are permissive. When conditions won't support strong leadership activity, then leaders who want to exercise power and those who do not will probably yield roughly the same results. When the membership is permissive or demanding of strong leadership, however, leaders who are aggressive and enthusiastic will likely exhibit substantially more activist behavior than will leaders who are reluctant about the exercise of their powers. Yet even reluctant leaders must, in these situations, be responsive to demands for action by the membership. We will return to this point below when we contrast Speakers Wright and Foley.

Southern Democrats and Their Party

Much of what needs to be emphasized regarding southern Democrats was touched on in the preceding section. A great deal of the literature on Congress has used a North-South regional breakdown among Democrats as a surrogate for contrasting political preferences of members. Indeed, some analysts have facetiously argued that one of the few verified "laws" in political science is the statement "except in the South."[2] Southern Democrats were always seen to be different from their northern counterparts, largely because the constituencies they represented were seen to be different. While it is clear that those differences between constituencies and members have not disappeared entirely, evidence we have discussed demonstrates that the differences are substantially reduced from earlier levels. We must, therefore, recognize that even though sectional differences among Democrats may still be pronounced on some issues, on many others those differences have become surprisingly small, and thus the usefulness of region as a general surrogate for preference is questionable.

The Consequences of Reform

We emphasized in chapter 1 that most analysts have argued that the reforms of the 1970s in the House resulted in a decentralized, and even atomized, power structure, which so effectively reflected the many diverse and conflicting preferences in the country that the institution was often incapable of taking collective action. For example, in one of the general treatments of reform, Rieselbach (1986, pp. 110–11) concluded that "Congress has become more decentralized, more responsive to a multitude of forces inside and outside its halls, and, as a result, more hard pressed to formulate and enact coherent, responsible public policies. Structural reform has enlarged the number of power centers involved in making policy, and party power cannot mobilize them in support of programs that either challenge or sustain the president." In a similar vein, Sheppard (1985, p. 244) argued that instead of improving congressional performance as the reformers wished, the reforms "give rise to a whole new layer of resistance." Therefore, he claimed, "While there may be many positive aspects of a system in which members have great opportunity for individual initiative, such a system also *predestines the House* to remain inchoate, difficult to lead—and undirected" (emphasis added).

In contrast to these views, the analysis we have presented shows that during the 1980s party power was indeed often able to mobilize the House's power centers in support of programs that challenged the president, and that the House was less difficult to lead than it had been, and was far from undirected. Moreover, it seems clear that while the majority party and its leadership were not always successful in their efforts, to the degree they were it was not in spite of the reforms, *but rather partly because of them.*

Each of the three tracks of reform played a part in creating conditions which enhanced the natural partisanship of the more homogeneous membership. (1) The role of committee chairmen as power centers independent of the Democratic party and its leaders was substantially reduced. (2) The new powers granted to the leaders permitted them to shape the floor environment to the party's advantage, and to provide incentives (e.g., committee assignments, whip appointments, etc.) for individuals to support the party position. (3) Those reforms directed at collective control of power offered special incentives for those members who were most able to influence outcomes—party leaders, committee chairs, subcommittee chairs—to go along with positions behind which the party was united.

It is important to note that this argument in no way contradicts the view that the House is generally characterized by decentralized decision processes within which individuals seek to serve the interests of their districts and enhance their electoral security. Nor does it contradict the view that these tendencies toward decentralization were enhanced by the reforms which strengthened subcommittees and increased individuals' resources. As we stated earlier, much of the House's legislative activity involves routine issues of distributive policy or reauthorization of established programs. The details of these issues are very important to individual members' interests, but provoke little controversy. However, the comparatively small set of issues that involve real conflict increasingly finds congressmen's preferences divided along partisan lines. Within that issue set, the effects of the reforms are profoundly felt because they have increased the chances of getting the House to adopt a position favored by a strong majority of the majority party.

The reforms passed by the House in the 1970s were not a substitute for shared policy preferences among Democrats. They could not create consensus where none existed. The homogeneity that developed in the late 1970s and the 1980s was a necessary precondition to their having their intended effect. But once the increased homogeneity existed, the reforms permitted the Democrats to achieve a level of partisan success that was higher than electorate-based incentives alone would have done.

Agenda Setting and the Impact of Divided Government

As the discussion in chapter 5 indicated, the predominant view of analysts has been that the president plays the dominant role in agenda setting regarding the issues that will be considered and even the programs that will be proposed. Within this context most researchers have also argued that the consequence of divided government has been either muted partisanship and compromise, or stalemate and inaction. James Sundquist (1980, p. 199) put the matter succinctly, shortly before the beginning of the Reagan administration, when he discussed the consequences of weak parties and party leaders: "But the party position in Congress is still either the president's program or none at all. Neither in the House nor the Senate, even in the periods of divided government, has the majority leadership presumed to put forward any alternative program of its own. . . ."

While this perspective would have received almost universal assent at the time it was written, clearly things have changed. As Barbara Sinclair's (1989a) analysis showed, the House Democratic leadership had begun articulating an agenda during the early Reagan years, and our analysis showed that this trend reached a peak at the beginning of the Wright speakership. Wright devised a list of priorities that reflected Democratic views (or so he believed), and saw them all through House passage despite the opposition of the president and of House Republicans in almost all instances.

In the case of these priorities, partisanship was not muted by divided government, although compromises were eventually reached in some instances. Nor was stalemate the result, and certainly not inaction. Clearly the president did not set this agenda; he opposed it. Yet not only did every one of the ten items on Wright's list of priorities (see table 4.2) pass the House; every one of them eventually became law in one form or another.[3] The Clean Water Act and the Highway Reauthorization passed the House initially with wide support, and both were enacted over Reagan's veto. Compromise versions of the Savings and Loan Rescue, Welfare Reform, and the Farm Credit Bill were enacted by bipartisan majorities. In each of these three instances the House Democrats and the White House got some of what they wanted and gave up other things.

On Catastrophic Health Insurance, a compromise was reached between Democrats and Republicans without an endorsement from the president. However, he did eventually sign it into law. Reagan vetoed the conference report on the Omnibus Trade Bill. The Democrats responded by stripping out the provisions he found most objectionable—those requiring advance notification of plant closings—and then passed the two parts again as separate measures. The president signed the trade bill, and then (due to concerns about voter sentiments in the upcoming presidential election) much more reluctantly permitted the plant-closing bill to become law without his signature.

The bill providing relief for the homeless was the only item on Wright's agenda that the president did not formally oppose. He did, however, oppose the conference report on the measure, which was almost unanimously supported by Democrats, but which a majority of Republicans voted against.[4] The conference report on the budget resolution narrowly passed (215 to 201), with the support of only three Republican representatives. Interestingly, the compromises worked out within the Democratic party on the issue were reflected in the fact that the thirty-four Democratic votes against the resolution were divided between the most liberal and the most conservative elements of the party.[5] Finally, the conference report on the reconciliation bill reflected agreements made at a budget summit between congressional Democrats and the administration. While this compromise outcome made no one completely happy, it did include $9 billion in new taxes aimed primarily at corporations, along the lines of Speaker Wright's most controversial proposal at the beginning of the Congress. As a consequence, three-fourths of House Republicans opposed the measure.[6]

In light of the pattern of events during the Reagan years, and particularly during the One Hundredth Congress, the widely held view of Congress's role in agenda setting and the impact of divided government needs some modification. The majority party in the House *can* propose a program different from that offered by the president. The Democrats did so in the One Hundredth Congress. Moreover, under divided government the House majority party *can* challenge (and defeat) the administration. On Wright's priority measures, the Democrats either secured a compromise result in which each side got part of what it wanted, or they prevailed outright. Moreover, this priority list doesn't include other relevant items, such as the wide range of Democratic alternatives proposed on defense policy and Wright's leadership in opposition to Reagan's policy in Nicaragua.

These results do not, however, mean that it is *easy* for the House (or the Senate) to devise its own agenda or to challenge the president. Only if certain conditions are present will this occur. Homogeneous preferences on policy within the majority party are required. Sharply contrasting views held by the president and disinclination to seek compromise will enhance the likelihood that the House majority will seek independent solutions on policy. Moreover, the likelihood of congressional victory on conflictual issues will depend on the degree of popular support for the Congress's views versus the president's. This all means that there will always be issues—and perhaps many of them—on which congressional alternatives can't be arrived at because there is too much disagreement within and between members' constituencies. Yet it is important to recognize the possibility that a partisan majority can create and secure passage of its own agenda despite presidential opposition, to recognize that this *has* happened, and to recognize the conditions under which it may happen again.

Some Thoughts Regarding the Senate

This analysis has focused on the House, but it would seem useful and necessary to say something about how the different elements of the theoretical argument might apply to the Senate. Such a comparison is interesting because the pattern of readily available evidence indicates that the resurgence of partisanship in the Senate, while present, has not been nearly so pronounced as in the House. One would hope that we could find plausible hypotheses regarding differences between the houses on theoretically relevant variables to help to explain these contrasting patterns.

The contrast between the two bodies is most apparent in data on floor voting. In the two decades from 1969 to 1988, the frequency of party-unity voting (i.e., party majorities opposing one another) in the House went from a low point of 27 percent (1970) to a high of 64 percent (1987), a range of 37 points.[7] In the Senate, the variation was between 35 percent (1970) and 52 percent (1986), only 17 points. Data on average party-unity scores also indicate higher levels of loyalty in the House during the 1980s among Democrats in general and southern Democrats in particular.

One possible source for explanations of these differences is electoral forces, which have been the principal explanatory factor for the changes in the House. It would seem that the effects of district versus statewide elections would be very potent. The constituencies of senators will, on average, be considerably more heterogeneous than those of House members. No state can be as dominated by urban interests as a district in Manhattan, and no state can be as focused on automobile manufacturing as the Seventh District of Michigan, centered on Flint. The diversity of Senate constituencies increases the variety of winning electoral coalitions that candidates can put together. This may lead to greater preference conflict within the parties in the Senate, and less difference between them.

Also, the liberalizing impact of black enfranchisement in the South was unequally distributed across districts within states. Thus while in some districts the effect would be strong and in others negligible, the statewide effect would be the diluted average of these two. For example, 58 percent of the population in the Second District of Mississippi is black (leading to the election of black Democrat Mike Espy in 1986), while only 19 percent of the Fifth District (served by conservative Republican Trent Lott for sixteen years, until 1988) is black. The black population of the state is in between at 35 percent, and both senators are Republican. Thus the natural level of partisanship produced by electoral forces may be lower in the Senate than in the House.

Another possible explanation lies in differences in institutional arrangements and leadership powers. First, the distribution of power across individuals is much more equal in the Senate. The potential for extended debates (commonly known as filibusters) has no parallel in the House, and it vests considerable power in minorities. This has become even more true as time pressure has increased due to the Senate's growing workload (Oppenheimer, 1985). Individual senators also have greater access to desirable committee positions. In 1989, 86 percent of the senators were members of one of the four most desirable committees, while the same was true of only 30 percent of the representatives.[8] Senators also serve on more committees and subcommittees than do representatives, which gives them more vantage points from which to influence legislation. In the senate, moreover, committees have long been less important, and the floor more important, than in the House (Fenno, 1973). Senators have been less inclined to specialize in their committees' jurisdictions, even though those obligations covered a broader range of legislation. For example, Smith (1989, p. 143) shows that from the 1950s through the 1980s, a higher proportion of floor amendments was offered in the Senate compared to the House by members not on the committee with jurisdiction over the legislation. Thus a wider range of members tends to participate in legislating on any given issue in the Senate.

Growing out of the more equal distribution of power across individuals is the fact that power is also more evenly divided between the two parties. Because of the potential for filibusters and the related need to employ frequently unanimous consent agreements to deal with bills on the floor (Smith, 1989, chap. 4), the minority party has a much greater potential to block action in the Senate. Thus the Senate majority party has usually had to make accommodations with the minority, whereas the House majority party (if it can hold its votes) can usually work its will.

Third, the Senate majority-party leadership simply doesn't have the kinds of tools at its disposal that the House leaders do. Senate leaders can offer few incentives to encourage loyalty; as noted, assignments to top committees come almost automatically to senators. Similarly, Senate leaders don't have powers over the agenda analogous to those possessed by the House majority leadership. There is no Rules Committee to shape floor action with the assent of only a bare majority of the body. Instead, the need to use unanimous consent agreements puts the ultimate control over the agenda in the hands of the broad spectrum of the Senate membership.

Finally, the Senate parties haven't employed mechanisms like those in the House directed toward the collective control of power. It is not that such mechanisms don't exist. Party leaders in both parties in the Senate can be voted out at the beginning of any Congress, and both parties adopted rules in the early 1970s that would permit the party caucuses to remove top committee leaders (Ornstein and Rohde, 1978, pp. 290–91). These procedures have not, however, been used to encourage party loyalty. No Senate committee chairman has been successfully challenged because of too-frequent support for the other party's positions, or for any other reason. Due to these and other factors, parties (and especially the majority party) in the Senate have less influence over outcomes than in the House, and they can do less for (and to) members.

A third area for explanations of the difference in partisanship between the institutions, at least regarding floor voting, is a difference in the respective agendas. To be sure, since both houses must act on bills for them to become law, the issues dealt with will tend to be generally the same. That does not mean, however, that the mix of votes on these issues will be the same. That could be one source of variation. Also, the proportion of types of votes may be different. For example, the Senate may vote on more amendments than the House. That also could make a difference.

These are some of the reasons that may account for the greater resurgence of partisanship in the House over the past two decades. There are surely others we could discuss. It is important to note, however, that we are talking about differences in rates and levels of change. The direction of change has been similar in both institutions; partisanship has increased. The exploration of these similarities and differences should provide fertile ground for future research.

Future Prospects

In this final section, we will try to look ahead and assess the prospects for continuation or change in the patterns we have been exploring. One advantage of a theory is that it tells us what factors we must consider when discussing likely change or continuity.

Electoral Forces and Party Homogeneity

If the configuration of electoral forces is the primary factor in explaining the resurgence of partisanship, then we need to begin by asking, What is the likelihood that events will occur that will undermine the new levels of consensus within the parties? In particular, what are the chances that new or more serious splits will develop within the Democratic majority? Alternatively, is it likely that a Republican majority could take control, or that Democratic numbers will be so reduced that effective rule would be restored to a conservative coalition?

The relevance of these questions was underscored in September of 1989 when the Democrats lost a major confrontation with President Bush and the Republicans over the question of whether to cut the capital gains tax. Six Democrats on the Ways and Means Committee (including five southerners) joined with Republicans to report the cut, and on the floor the party split, providing a comfortable margin against a leadership move to delete the provision from the bill. This was the first major test for the Foley leadership, which was soundly beaten. As a result, the media began writing about the divided and dispirited Democrats. The story in *Congressional Quarterly Weekly Report* (Sept. 30, 1989, p. 2529) was headlined "Rout of Democratic Leaders Reflects Fractured Party."

Despite the vivid coverage, the capital gains loss appears to have been a classic case of an event that was less than met the eye. To be sure, it was a significant loss for the leadership, and it was not the only matter that divided the party. It did not, however, seem to reflect any general dissolution of Democratic cohesion, before or after the event. Overall in 1989, party majorities opposed one another on 55 percent of the floor votes. This was 8 points *higher* than in 1988 (although it was 9 points lower than at the high point of 1987). In terms of average party unity, Democrats exhibited only a small decline: down 2 points from 1988 (to 86 percent) for all Democrats, and down 4 points (to 77 percent) for southerners. Indeed, Republicans exhibited a greater decline in loyalty (down 5 points to 75 percent), and average southern Democratic unity remained higher than the average for all Republicans. Most important for majority-party control, the Democrats won 83.6 percent of the votes on which the parties were opposed. That level is almost the same as their winning percentage (84.9 percent) in the One Hundredth Congress.[9] Despite a new administration in which the president has enjoyed high levels of popularity, and despite the two ethics controversies which led to the resignations of Speaker Wright and Majority Whip Coelho, the Republicans have been no better able to rally their own troops or to divide the Democrats.

Nor does the future, at least in the near term, seem to hold much likelihood of Democrats losing actual or effective control of the House. At the end of the 101st Congress, they held a 259 to 176 majority, an 83-vote margin. This will require the Republicans to secure a net gain of forty-two seats to win a majority. With high reelection rates for incumbents, and the GOP's modest success in winning open seats during the 1980s (Abramson, Aldrich, and Rohde, 1990, p. 256), this is a daunting task, to say the least. The Republicans believe that the shifting of district lines and the likelihood of many open seats due to retirements in 1992 will give them a chance to take control, but even the usually optimistic Newt Gingrich estimates the odds at only one in seven.

It is easier to imagine the GOP making some gains to narrow the Democrats' margin of control, thereby creating the potential for the remaining conservative Democrats to provide the GOP routinely with the margin of votes to win in committees and on the floor. That will, however, depend in part on where their gains are made, and in part on their ability to be more cohesive than the Democrats. Regarding the first issue, if the Republicans gain seats primarily from districts where their presidential candidates have been doing well, it is likely that they will mostly be replacing those Democrats who already vote with them most often (see Rohde, 1988, table 10). That will not yield much progress. On the other hand, replacing those Democrats who vote frequently with their party (which would make the most difference to restoring the conservative coalition) will mostly mean winning in southern districts where the Democratic party has been stronger, or against more entrenched northern incumbents, both of which will be difficult.[10]

Therefore it seems that party interactions and legislative outcomes in the House will, in the near future, hinge more on the relative cohesion of two party contingents that are relatively similar to those that serve today. This will depend to a large degree on the nature of the issues that are dealt with, and how the members of the respective parties (and their constituents) respond to them. It will also depend on the strategies of the party leaderships, which we will discuss in the next section.

Regarding Democrats and issues, it doesn't appear likely that their degree of consensus will significantly increase or decrease. Some issues (like capital gains) will remain so divisive as to prevent victory, others will involve divisions (as on child care) that are difficult but possible to work out, and many will yield routine intraparty compromises. Neither across-the-board homogeneity nor frequent unbridgeable fissures are in prospect.

Despite the changes in Eastern Europe and the possible end of the cold war, defense will not quickly disappear as a problem issue for House Democrats. While both northern and southern Democrats will favor defense reductions (as will, for that matter, most Republicans), the southerners will tend to support smaller cuts. As one southerner said, "It's all relative. People will be more pragmatic, but end up in the same position relatively."[11] For example, the changing international situation led members on the left wing of the Democratic party to seek deep immediate defense reductions. However, when they met with Speaker Foley, he told them that their views had the support of only "one-third of Congress," and couldn't carry the day (*Washington Post,* Mar. 7, 1990, p. A20).

Party leaders and the chairmen of the Armed Services and Budget committees (Les Aspin and Leon Panetta, respectively) worked to achieve a Democratic consensus on defense funding. Agreement was reached in a meeting of the Democratic Caucus to support comparatively small immediate cuts in outlays, but much larger reductions in budget authority, which would result in substantial spending savings in future years (*CQWR,* Mar. 17, 1990, p. 842). As the budget process moved toward floor action, defense "hawks" called the figure in the Democratic plan "unrealistically low," but they were reassured by the party leadership that the eventual figure would be higher after negotiations with the Senate and the administration (*NJ,* May 5, 1990, p. 1101).

Disagreements about defense, coupled with differences on tax increases and the desirable aggregate level of spending, mean that Democrats will continue to have problems regarding budget policy. But here too, determined efforts to reach intraparty compromises are likely to continue to yield results that can rally member support. In 1990, for example (as in other recent years), Republicans on the Budget Committee forced Democrats to arrive at their own plan, which was reported on a straight party-line vote. When the resolution came to the floor, no Republican supported it and thirty-four Democrats voted against it, but it still passed 218 to 208. The Democratic opposition "included some conservatives dissatisfied with the defense spending figure and liberals opposed to domestic spending cuts" (Fessler, 1990, p. 1331), just what one would expect from a compromise result.

The budget situation illustrates that high levels of consensus may not necessarily be advantageous for a minority party. Republicans are strongly united against a tax increase, and favor spending cuts to control the deficits. This makes it difficult to secure joint action with southerners, who believe that deficit reduction must be accomplished by a mix of action on spending and revenues. One conservative southern Democrat said that it was impossible to craft a realistic budget plan "that didn't mention the 'T word.'" As a consequence of that fact of major efforts to get Democrats together, "the last 3 or 4 years I have supported the Democratic Budget over any alternative, because it's physically impossible to do better. We've been able to do better within the Democratic party than with a bipartisan budget."[12]

It appears that trends may cause the Republicans at least as much difficulty in maintaining consensus as they cause the Democrats. Disagreements about how quickly and deeply to cut defense face them too. Abortion is causing special difficulties for the Republicans as individual members decide whether to adjust their positions in light of the issue's new salience to the electorate. Also, conservative Republicans have had some problems with position shifts by President Bush. For example, GOP representatives had been fighting to change provisions of a bill designed to reverse some restrictive Supreme Court decisions on the scope of civil rights laws. They had been supporting a Bush administration proposal that was much narrower in scope. When the Democratic bill was reported by the House Education and Labor Committee on May 8, 1990, only one Republican supported it (*CQWR,* May 12, 1990, p. 1482). However, only a week later Bush met with a group of civil rights leaders and indicated that he had only "minimal" differences with the proposed bill (*Washington Post,* May 15, 1990, p. A1).

Even more jarring to Republicans was the White House's indication, in May of 1990, that it might accept tax increases as part of a "budget summit" agreement with congressional Democrats. GOP candidates and campaign consultants worried that the issues that had provided them a string of presidential victories, and congressional gains in 1980, were slipping away. As one Republican pollster said, "The problem is, the Republican Party has been the party of strong defense and low taxes. The strong defense issue has gone away and now this other issue is going away" (*Washington Post,* May 11, 1990, p. A24).

In summary, it does not seem likely that the Republican party will soon attain a House majority. It is more likely that effective control in the House could be restored to the conservative coalition, but that too is not very probable. One way this could happen is for the GOP to make great numerical gains, albeit falling short of the magic number 218. That, however, is only a bit more plausible than an outright majority. Another way would be for major divisions to resurface among House Democrats (or some combination of Democratic divisions and Republican gains). On this point we have argued that while further significant increases in Democratic homogeneity do not seem to be in the cards, renewal of intraparty splits does not either. Moreover, the effectiveness of the conservative coalition is partly predicated on Republican cohesiveness, and that may be problematic. Finally, new strength for the conservative coalition might arise if the buttressing effects of the majority-party leadership and their use of their reform-granted powers is undermined through the transition from Wright to Foley. It is that issue we address next.

Institutional Arrangements and Party Leadership: From
Speaker Wright to Speaker Foley

Any discussion of changes under Speaker Foley must emphasize that all
conclusions should be regarded as tentative. After approximately one
year under Foley, Democratic members who were asked to compare his
approach to that of his predecessor invariably prefaced their remarks
with comments like "It's too early to be sure," or "I'm not certain about
Tom yet." With that caveat in mind, however, it is clear from members'
perceptions and from other evidence that there is a marked difference
in style and attitude between Speakers Wright and Foley. This evidence
tends to support our earlier generalizations of the importance of the
personal dimension in leadership style when the context is tolerant regarding the exercise of power, but the leader's own view is more
restrictive.

From the time of his election to the speakership, Foley emphasized
that he sought to restore a sense of fairness to the House and to reduce
the bitterness between Republicans and Democrats. In his address to
the House he said,

> I understand the responsibility of the Speaker of the House, as
> other Speakers have understood it and practiced it, to be a
> responsibility to the whole House and to each and every individual
> Member, undivided by that center aisle.
>
> . . . I appeal specifically to our friends on the Republican side
> that we should come together and put away bitterness and division
> and hostility. (*Congressional Record,* June 6, 1989, p. H2284)

Long before becoming Speaker, Foley had often articulated his
aversion to strongly partisan conflict. When he was a candidate for majority leader he said, "I don't believe that the corrosiveness that has
come with the bitter partisanship in recent years is healthy" (*NJ,* Sept.
28, 1985, p. 2188). After assuming that post, he elaborated, indicating
that there were strategic reasons for his view: "I'm not going to be a
19th-century opposition-basher. . . . It doesn't attract people who
weren't already knee-jerk supporters. The task is to convince people
who are subject to being influenced or persuaded" (*CQWR,* Mar. 8,
1986, p. 549).

In addition to his own personal attitudes, Foley's approach has been
shaped by his political circumstances. He represents a mixed urban-
rural district, within which Republicans do very well in statewide races.
(Reagan carried it with 60 percent of the vote in 1984.) Foley's safe victory margins deteriorated during the 1970s. In 1978 he received only 48
percent in a three-way race, and in 1980 he got 52 percent in a two-

person contest. Beyond this electoral uncertainty which led him to moderate political positions, Foley's viewpoint was influenced by his service on the Agriculture Committee, which he chaired from 1975 to 1981. This distributive-politics environment not only muted partisan conflict; it also made Foley sensitive to the attitudes and circumstances of the many southern Democrats with whom he served.

As Speaker, Foley has emphasized not only fairness to the Republicans, but also widespread consultation among Democrats. He said, "The reality is that in a modern, participatory Congress . . . the responsibility of leadership and the necessity of leadership is to constantly involve members in the process of decision and consensus" (*NJ*, Apr. 29, 1989, p. 1035). In this process, Foley places great emphasis on listening to the cross-section of Democrats in the whip meetings, and on entertaining the views of moderates and conservatives in the party. For example, one southern conservative who is a member of the Conservative Democratic Forum noted, "We're meeting tomorrow with the Speaker for an hour, and we've had periodic meetings with all the leaders—a much closer working relationship between our group and our leadership now than, say, in the early 1980s."[13] In order to reach out deliberately to the conservatives, Foley appointed Charles Stenholm, the chairman of the CDF, to a deputy whip post. As a moderate southerner said, "They made Charlie a deputy whip, and he's had a tremendous influence on a number of pieces of legislation recently. And I think the leadership is listening to him and to conservative southerners maybe a little more than they used to."[14]

During 1989, in addition to the turnover in the top Democratic leadership after the resignations of Wright and Coelho, the death of Claude Pepper brought a new chairman to the Rules Committee: Joseph Moakley of Massachusetts. Under Moakley the relationship between the Speaker and the committee changed, as did the committee's approach to drafting rules. In interviews, both northern and southern Democrats on Rules indicate that Foley allows the committee substantially more leeway than Wright did. For example, one member of Rules indicated that Foley "keeps his finger pretty much on what's going on, but on most of the legislation he doesn't get too much involved."[15]

Moakley used the flexibility granted to him to seek further reductions in interparty hostility, promising to be fair and to consult with committee Republicans. "The majority rules, but ruling doesn't mean trampling or rubbing somebody's nose in the dirt," he said (*Roll Call*, Mar. 12, 1990, p. 17). In a similar vein, Moakley noted, "I've learned a long time ago that the best way to get things done is not to surprise your opponents, although you don't have to give them everything they want" (*Washington Post*, Sept. 12, 1989, p. A19).

These changes in the Democratic party leadership produced a positive response from House Republicans. When on one occasion Foley declared that the Republican position had won on a voice vote—an event that would never have occurred under Wright—the GOP members gave him a standing ovation (*CQWR*, Mar. 3, 1990, p. 642). At the close of the House's 1989 session, Minority Leader Michel offered a resolution thanking the Speaker for the "able, impartial, and dignified manner in which he presided" over the House. Speaking in support of the resolution, Michel said, "I feel it is very important that we publicly recognize in a bipartisan fashion the great job the Speaker has done in restoring a sense of civility and comity to the House of Representatives" (*Congressional Record*, Nov. 21, 1989, p. H9596). Similarly, Moakley's approach also received a positive response. Gerald Solomon (R, N.Y.), a member of Rules, said (regarding the rule on the 1989 Defense authorization), "It was obvious that Joe Moakley went out of his way to try to be helpful to us in having Republicans' voice heard on the floor of the Congress" (*Roll Call*, Mar. 12, 1990, p. 17).

The new good feelings among Republicans and conservative Democrats were not, however, widely shared among Democratic liberals. They had long been concerned about Foley's moderate approach. Shortly before his election as Speaker, Barney Frank (D, Mass.) said, "His only fault is about half an inch too much caution" (*NJ*, Apr. 29, 1989, p. 1034). When Majority Whip Tony Coelho (shortly before his resignation) seconded Foley's nomination as Speaker before the Democratic Caucus, he said to his colleagues, "Tom has a deserved reputation for being a statesman, a velvet glove. . . . You must be the iron fist" (*Washington Post*, June 7, 1989, p. A4). While the majority of the majority party generally tolerated Foley's conciliatory approach through the end of 1989, complaints were heard more frequently during 1990. That dissent, and the leadership's behavior in light of it, again illustrates the central importance of contextual factors in shaping leaders' style.

By early 1990, many liberal Democrats had grown frustrated with the party's inability to contest Bush's defense policies and budget priorities. As Byron Dorgan (D, N.D.) said, "There is growing discontent among Democrats who want to hear the bugle, saddle up and ride off" (*Washington Post*, Mar. 15, 1990, p. A11). Liberals criticized Foley for failing to break a deadlock on child care for almost a year, for not pushing bigger defense cuts, and for not supporting Sen. Daniel Moynihan's (D, N.Y.) proposal to cut Social Security payroll taxes.

A striking example of the leadership-member interaction occurred in connection with the 1990 budget resolution. When the resolution came to the floor, it came under a restrictive rule, but not one designed for Democratic advantage. Such a procedure wasn't necessary. Once agreement was reached among Democrats on a level for defense spending, and it was clear that southern conservatives could live with the figure, it was sure that the Democratic proposal would carry the day. Therefore the Rules Committee permitted four substitute amendments (three different Republican proposals and the Black Caucus's budget) under a king-of-the-mountain rule, with the administration budget last. By that point the president's defense proposal and his deficit assumptions were hopelessly outdated by events, and his plan included what Democrats believed would be unpopular domestic cuts. They, therefore, thought they could get some mileage out of forcing Republicans to desert the administration ship on the vote. GOP members, however, fooled them and simply failed to offer the administration proposal.

Democrats were incensed. Budget Chairman Leon Panetta charged that the "failure even to offer the president's budget makes clear that the president offers no choices that are acceptable to either a majority of Democrats or a majority of Republicans" (*CQWR*, May 5, 1990, p. 1333). Rank-and-file Democrats, however, were even more angry at their leadership for letting the Republicans off the hook. Many thought that a new rule should have been passed, making it in order for a Democrat to put the Bush budget to a vote. As one liberal Democrat who was at the subsequent meeting of the Democratic whip organization said, "There were an awful lot of people who were damn mad at Tom Foley for not having a Democrat offer it, and cause them [the Republicans] a little heartburn. And because the whip organization is large enough, the Speaker got an earful, and he got it from around the country."[16]

While Foley continued to assert that he preferred legislative achievements to partisan conflict, it was clear that he was inclined to accept more such conflict in 1990 than before. For example, while he informed Democratic liberals that there were not sufficient votes to cut defense spending as much as they wanted, he also wrote a fund-raising letter that was sent out by the Democratic Congressional Campaign Committee, in which he criticized President Bush for not being willing to support greater defense cuts (*Washington Post*, Mar. 15, 1990, p. A5). Foley was also more willing to employ agenda-shaping rules to provide advantages to Democratic proposals, as the following examples indicate:

1. On the voter-registration bill (January 1990), which provided for automatic registration nationwide when persons receive or renew a driver's license, the rule permitted only one set of amendments considered as a group. (They were defeated.) Only six Republicans voted for the rule, while not even one Democrat voted against it

2. When the child-care bill finally came to the floor (March 29, 1990), the Democratic compromise was protected by a rule that permitted no Republican amendments at all, and no instructions on the motion to recommit. No Republicans supported the rule; Democrats voted 246 to 5

3. On the parent-leave bill (May 1990), the rule limited amendments, permitted amendments were unamendable, and a king-of-the-mountain procedure was employed. The vote on the rule was Republicans 18 to 146, Democrats 233 to 5

4. The rule for the bill expanding protections for the rights of the disabled (May 1990) permitted only eight of the forty-five amendments that had been submitted to the Rules Committee. Republican Tom DeLay of Texas had proposed eleven amendments, and not one was made in order. On the vote to bar Republican attempts to change the rule, Republicans voted 7 to 160 against, but Democrats were in favor 244 to 2

Republican reactions to these events also demonstrated that things had changed in 1990. Before the child-care bill came to the floor, Republicans complained that they were not being told about the Democrats' plans for the rule, with Newt Gingrich complaining of "Jim Wright–style machine politics" (*Roll Call*, Mar. 3, 1990, p. 14). When the rule was actually proposed, Lynn Martin (R, Ill.) of Rules charged that "the Democrats in this rule are slamdunking the minority and, more ironically, the Democrats are slamdunking democracy," while Representative Michel said that "we do not even have comity anymore. . . . The Majority has turned this House into a den of inequity" (*Congressional Record*, Mar. 29, 1990, pp. H1252, H1254). On the parental-leave rule, the GOP's anger was focused directly on Foley. Representative Solomon of Rules indicated that he believed that none of the Democrats on the committee had participated in shaping the restrictive rule. "Mr. Speaker," he said, "this was your call, this was a leadership call, inspired no doubt by the desire of members of the Democratic caucus to play hard ball with this issue and gag members on both sides of the aisle" (*Congressional Record*, May 9, 1990, p. H2160).

A month later, conflict over the proposed constitutional amendment to permit legislation making flag desecration a crime caused Solomon to use even stronger language in attacking Foley. Supporters of the amendment wanted to delay a vote so that they could organize pressure among constituents in favor of passage. However, Foley, believing he had the votes to defeat the amendment, refused. Solomon said, "Mr. Speaker, that is wrong. . . . I swear I cannot understand why you cannot be receptive to the veterans of this nation when you are kowtowing to ilk like the Communist Youth Brigade . . ." (*Washington Post,* June 21, 1990, p. A1). The amendment failed to pass.

Thus we see the interplay of leaders' own inclinations and pressures from the membership. In response to a widespread preference among Democrats for more activist leadership, Speaker Foley has adopted a more partisan mode of operation than he would like. Yet despite this change, he is apparently not as strongly partisan as many in the Democratic rank and file would prefer, and certainly not as partisan as someone with different personal tendencies (like Wright) would have been.

It appears likely that the Democratic leaders under Foley will be disinclined to take a partisan approach to legislative activity unless it is important to passage of a high-priority item for the party. In those circumstances, however, they will apparently accept the preferences of the Democratic Caucus and employ the tools at their disposal. This was aptly illustrated by the conflict over the rule for the child-care bill. The Republicans dramatized their anger over the leadership's behavior by crossing out printed quotations from previous statements by Foley and Moakley promising fairness to the minority. One of these was a quotation from Moakley that said, "We should all be distressed by the rising number of rule requests that seek restrictions for no justifiable reasons" (*Congressional Record,* Mar. 29, 1990, p. H1248). In an interview after the debate, the Rules Committee chairman said, "This is a justifiable political reason. . . . It's a party platform decided by the leadership." He indicated that the Democrats had no hope of picking up any Republican votes by being responsive to their wishes. As a consequence, "we couldn't afford to lose anybody [among the Democrats]. We had to tie this up in a tight package" (*Roll Call,* Apr. 2, 1990, p. 28).

Presidential Agendas and the Bush Administration

The other major political transition of 1989 was the replacement of Ronald Reagan by George Bush in the White House. The discussion in chapter 5 recognized that the president plays a major role in shaping the congressional agenda, and argued that the nature of the president's preferences and his willingness to compromise can have a major impact on the amount of partisan conflict in a situation of divided government. What effects can we anticipate in this regard from the Bush administration? After only a little more than a year of Bush in office, conclusions here must also be tentative, but some preliminary comparisons with the previous eight years are possible.

The most obvious point is that divided government has persisted; the Senate and House both remain in Democratic hands. Indeed, the 40.2

percent of the House seats won by the Republicans was the lowest proportion won by the party of a victorious presidential candidate in the nation's history. This dearth of political resources is one reason for the limited policy agenda of the Bush administration. Any inclinations of the new president to seek departures from the status quo against Democratic preferences were constrained by the small number of his fellow Republicans in Congress. On the other hand, temptations to propose ideas that Democrats might support were limited by Bush's eight years of service in the Reagan administration, and the fact that he had run for president on that administration's record. Moreover, new programs, regardless of their political stripe, were difficult to propose in the context of continuing large budget deficits.

Partly as a result of the limited political agenda, the first years of the Bush administration have been marked by less partisan conflict between the House of Representatives and the White House than we saw under Reagan. Other reasons include a contrast of personal styles, a different attitude toward government, and a greater willingness to compromise. Bush is a former member of the House, and he has many friends there on both sides of the aisle. Since taking office he has worked to cultivate previous and new relationships. Democrats and Republicans alike have been given personal tours of the family quarters during White House functions. Bush joined friends for lunch in the House dining room, and for paddleball in the House gym. More substantively, he has had numerous bipartisan groups of representatives to the White House to discuss legislative matters (*NJ*, Oct. 14, 1989, pp. 2509–10).

Beyond these stylistic contrasts, President Reagan often expressed the view that government and the people in it were the source of many of the nation's problems rather than the source of solutions. It is clear that Bush doesn't share this view. Shortly after his inauguration, the president told a group of senior civil servants that they were "some of the most unsung heroes in America," and said that he had "not known a finer group of people than those that I have worked with in government" (*Washington Post*, Jan. 27, 1989, p. A7). As a consequence, he is less likely to denigrate the federal government in general, and Congress in particular. He is also less likely to attack Democratic proposals merely because they entail governmental solutions. Finally, and partly as a result of these others factors, Bush is more likely to initiate or accept compromises with the Democrats, as agreements on the budget and Central America in 1989 illustrate.

While these characteristics of the Bush administration have reduced partisan conflict, and have rendered that which remains less hostile than in the Reagan years, this hasn't been translated into widespread legislative triumph for the new president. On the contrary, in terms of having his position supported on congressional roll-call votes, "George Bush fared worse in Congress than any other first-year president elected in the postwar era" (Hook, 1989, p. 3540). He won on only 63 percent of roll calls in both houses combined, compared to 82 percent under Reagan and 74 percent under Nixon in their first years. Moreover, Bush's success in the House was lower than in the Senate; he won only half of the eighty-six votes on which he took a position.[17]

It is clear that partisan disagreements played a large role in determining this rate of success. Of the twenty-eight presidential-position votes that did not find majorities of the two parties opposed to one another, Bush won 71 percent. Moreover, on the eight votes that involved Democratic majorities supporting the president in opposition to a majority of Republicans, Bush's position was successful every time.[18] However, on the remaining fifty-six votes, which found Republican majorities behind the president against the Democrats, his position carried only 30 percent of the time.

Unlike President Reagan in his first year, when he was successful on 74 percent of the House votes involving a presidential position, Bush did not have the benefit of the appearance of a popular mandate for his policy agenda. Reagan had led the Republicans to a Senate majority and a gain of thirty-three House seats in 1980. In 1988, on the other hand, Republicans lost seats in both houses. Moreover, in only 56 of 435 House districts did Bush receive a larger share of the vote than did the winning representative (*NJ*, Apr. 29, 1989, p. 1048). George Bush had no coattails, and Democrats had no reason to fear opposing him.

President Bush was not, however, left without political resources. Continued economic prosperity, the extraordinary events in Eastern Europe, and low levels of domestic political conflict all combined to give the president very high approval ratings. Thus while Democrats experienced little pressure to support him, Republicans were not pressured to oppose him. This permitted Bush a strong base of support from which to negotiate compromises, often with the threat of a veto in the background. And this was a threat that he exercised in practice: Bush vetoed ten bills in 1989, and every one was sustained by the Congress.

So we see that Bush's relationship with the Democratic House has been less conflictual and less hostile than Reagan's. The new president was less successful in getting the Congress to do what he wanted than was his predecessor at the beginning, but the Democrats have not been able to shape ultimate outcomes to the degree they were able to in the later Reagan years. It would appear likely that this pattern will tend generally to persist, although the degree of party conflict will probably slowly increase. While the styles of both Bush and the Democratic congressional leadership will continue to mute hostility, it seems likely that the Democratic rank and file will continue to press their leaders to challenge Bush. And the threat of presidential vetoes will probably not block this trend. As Speaker Foley said, "We don't just fall over dead every time a president says that he's inclined to veto something. If that were the case, he would never have to exercise a veto, would he?" (*USA Today*, Mar. 30, 1990, p. 4A). Moreover, if Bush's level of popular support eventually wanes (as would seem likely), he may have to either exercise the veto less frequently or experience being overridden by the Congress in some cases.

Conclusion

So in viewing future prospects for party conflict in the House in terms of various facets of our theory, it seems likely that because of electoral forces, relatively high levels of partisanship will persist. While the personal styles of leaders in Congress and the White House will probably mitigate this somewhat, contextual forces within the House will induce leaders of both parties to pursue conflicting legislative strategies in many areas. Thus the near future does not seem likely to produce any sharp contrasts to the general patterns we have outlined in the preceding chapters. Electoral, organizational, and personal forces have reshaped the politics of the U.S. House of Representatives. While in an earlier era it may have been possible for scholars accurately to assert that political parties were of little theoretical importance in explaining political behavior and legislative results in the House, that is certainly not true now. Parties are consequential in shaping members' preferences, the character of the issues on the agenda, the nature of legislative alternatives, and ultimate political outcomes, and they will remain important as long as the underlying forces that created this partisan resurgence persist.

Notes

For convenience, citations to *Congressional Quarterly Weekly Report* will be indicated as *CQWR,* and those to *National Journal* will be indicated as *NJ.*

Chapter 1

1. For two discussions of the relevance of Wilson's work to the modern Congress see Dodd (1987) and Rohde and Shepsle (1987).

2. Among the many works that discuss these Speakers, see Galloway and Wise (1976), Ripley (1967), and Jones (1968). For other sources see Jones and Ripley (1966).

3. A good brief account of the debate, with citations to relevant sources, can be found in Price (1984, pp. 104–8).

4. For example, James McGregor Burns argued in *Deadlock of Democracy* (1963) that the United States really had four major parties, two presidential and two congressional, and that the latter worked together to block the policy initiatives of the former. See also Broder (1971).

5. A discussion of the formation of the DSG and its activities may be found in Stevens, Miller, and Mann (1974).

6. Data on the frequency of party voting, and individual members' scores on the party-unity index (discussed below), have been published annually for both houses of Congress since the 1950s by Congressional Quarterly, Inc. an organization that provides journalistic coverage of Congress.

7. For some additional historical analysis of these types of data, see Clubb and Traugott (1977) and Cooper, Brady, and Hurley (1977).

8. See also Deckard and Stanley (1974).

9. The perspectives described here are drawn largely from discussions of the period through 1982. After that time, as we shall see, other patterns became visible.

10. One exception to this was Dodd and Oppenheimer (1981, p. 53), who said that the changes "substantially increased the prerogatives of the Speaker."

11. Others argued only that the tasks of the leadership had become more difficult. See Deering and Smith (1981, p. 267), Sinclair (1981, pp. 182–84), and Smith and Deering (1984, p. 258).

12. The literature on congressional elections is vast, especially over the last fifteen years. For a good introductory survey see Jacobson (1987) or Ragsdale (1985).

13. *Congressional Quarterly,* the original source of these data, defines the South as the eleven states of the Confederacy plus Kentucky and Oklahoma. We will employ the same definition in our analysis.

14. See the data in Cooper, Brady, and Hurley (1977, p. 138).

Chapter 2

1. Sheppard (1985, p. 38). The quotations are from an interview with Richard Conlon, DSG staff director from 1968 until his untimely death in 1988. The discussion of initial proposals in the next paragraphs is drawn largely from Sheppard.

2. One of the Executive Committee members—Morris Udall (D, Ariz.)—did challenge McCormack at the opening of the Congress. He lost, 178 to 58.

3. DSG members voted in support of Democratic programs 91 percent of the time, in contrast to 31 percent for non-DSG Democrats and 24 percent for Republicans. Cited in Sheppard (1985, p. 43). The full study can be found in the *Congressional Record,* Mar. 19, 1969, pp. H6749–52.

4. See "The Seniority System in the U.S. House of Representatives," *Congressional Record,* Feb. 25, 1970, pp. H5169–72.

5. For a discussion of the Hansen Committee and its operation, see Ornstein (1975).

6. John Aldrich (1989b) presents a theoretical argument that views some institutional reform efforts as attempts to alter institutional structures that, with the support of some relevant actors, frustrate the will of the majority. See also Aldrich (1989a).

7. The reader will note that these various motivations are reflections of the member goals discussed by Richard Fenno (1973, chap. 1). We will return to this point later in the chapter.

8. For example, the original proponents of the "Subcommittee Bill of Rights," discussed below, believed that the interests of the approximately 120 subcommittee chairmen would outweigh those of about 20 committee chairmen. See the last paragraph of the memo outlining the original proposal, in Sheppard (1985, p. 100).

9. The discussion in this section draws on Ornstein and Rohde (1978), Sheppard (1985), and Rieselbach (1986), as well as more specific studies cited below.

10. Brief discussions of the act may be found in Ornstein and Rohde (1978, pp. 282–83) and Sheppard (1985, pp. 45–63).

11. This would prevent a chairman from blocking committee action simply by leaving town, as Howard Smith of Virginia—longtime chairman of the Rules Committee—was famous for doing.

12. See Rohde and Ornstein (1974, pp. 1–3).

13. Teller votes were taken by having members who favored each side of a question file past designated counters (or "tellers"), who would get an accurate count of those pro and con. Under a recorded teller vote, each member would turn in a card with his or her name on it, so that positions could later be recorded. This method was chosen because it was quicker than a roll call (which could take forty-five minutes), but the distinction was rendered moot when the House moved to an electronic voting system for all record votes in 1973.

14. For a discussion of the adoption and impact of this procedure see Ornstein and Rohde (1974), Sheppard (1985, pp. 56–57), 62), and Smith (1989, pp. 25–36).

15. Using the new procedure, a challenge was launched against John McMillan (D, S.C.), the autocratic conservative who headed the District of Columbia Committee. He survived the challenge, 129 to 96, but the large vote against him demonstrated to all chairmen that the possibility of removal was real. See Ornstein and Rohde (1978, p. 284) and Sheppard (1985, pp. 77–78).

16. For more details, and a discussion of compliance, see Rohde (1974).

17. See *CQWR*, Jan. 18, 1975, p. 166.

18. The rejection of Patman illustrates that ideology was not the *sole* consideration in the chairmanship contests. Patman had always been a relatively liberal southern Democrat. He was opposed by members, however, "because of the high-handed way he ran his committee and his poor record as a legislative leader" (*CQWR,* Jan. 19, 1975, p. 114). At the time of the 1975 challenge, a Common Cause report criticized Patman for "directing the Committee in an incoherent and haphazard manner" (Sheppard, 1985, p. 201).

19. In subsequent years, two other House chairmen would be voted down by the Caucus. We will discuss these cases in chapter 3.

20. By the 101st Congress (1989–91), the committee was expanded to include the chairmen of Appropriations, Budget, Rules, and Ways and Means, as well as the Caucus vice chairman and the chairman of the Democratic Congressional Campaign Committee. The four deputy whips were replaced by the chief deputy whip, and the number of appointees by the Speaker was increased to eight.

21. Rules of the Democrat Caucus, Ninety-fifth Congress, section M VIIc.

22. For a comparison of the voting records of the two groups, see Rieselbach (1986, p. 77, n. 55). Analyses of the impact of the change can be found in Shepsle (1978, pp. 262–81) and Smith and Ray (1983).

23. For an analysis of the vote to enlarge the committee, see Cummings and Peabody (1963). Peabody (1963) discusses the changes in the committee resulting from expansion.

24. See Davidson and Oleszek (1977) for a detailed study of this effort.

25. With the exception of Appropriations, which we discuss below.

26. In 1977, the Caucus rejected Robert Sikes of Florida as chairman of the Military Construction subcommittee. Sikes had been censured by the House the previous year for conflicts of interest (*CQWR,* Jan. 29, 1977, p. 159).

27. All Budget members, including the chairman, are limited to serving on the committee three congressional terms out of any five successive terms.

28. This reform was employed in 1975 to compel a floor vote on a proposal to restrict the oil depletion allowance in the federal tax code. See Rieselbach (1986, p. 73, n. 29).

29. The Caucus twice rejected making the whip elective in the 1970s, but accepted it in 1987. We will discuss the reasons for this below.

30. All of the reforms we have been considering involve the internal distribution of power in the House. There were other aspects to the reform effort which are important, although they don't relate to our main theme. Probably the most similar other reforms were those intended to strengthen the Congress vis-à-vis the executive branch. It was primarily because of policy disagreements between the Democratic Congress and Republican presidents that these changes were seen to be needed. They included the War Powers Act, changes strengthening the Government Accounting Office, and the adoption of the new congressional budget process. Other categories of reform were "sunshine" rules (designed to eliminate secrecy), campaign finance regulation, and new rules on congressional ethics. For details see Rieselbach (1986) and Sheppard (1985).

31. Sheppard (1985, p. 228) asserts that the reformers relied on guile to achieve their goals before the 1974 elections, based on the fact that most reform measures had secured leadership support and were passed by voice vote. The lack of a numerical vote would not seem to be evidence of the absence of disagreement on reform any more than voice votes in the Committee of the Whole (before recorded teller voting) were evidence of no disagreement on policy. It would rather seem to be evidence, in both instances, that opponents saw no point in bothering with a numerical vote when the outcome was certain.

32. This finding is more striking due to Kingdon's deliberate choice of controversial issues.

33. For a more extensive discussion of the relationship between a member's own preferences and other influences in roll-call voting, see Rohde (1990b).

34. See, for example, Maisel (1982, chap. 2), and Fowler and McClure (1989), particularly the discussion of Fred Eckert (R, N.Y.).

35. Quoted in Jones (1981, p. 32, n. 19) from an article in *Science,* Mar. 30, 1979, p. 1321. On Waxman, see also Loomis (1988).

36. See the articles in Rapoport, Abramowitz, and McGlennon (1986) and the earlier studies cited therein.

37. See Ornstein (1975), Ornstein and Rohde (1977), Price (1978), and Smith and Deering (1984).

38. Explicit evidence regarding the different aspects of this characterization will be presented in the next two chapters.

39. For a discussion of theoretical issues related to this type of policy, see Weingast (1979) and Shepsle and Weingast (1981).

40. From 1953 through 1987, 141 record votes were taken on final passage of measures involving veterans' issues (both substantive and appropriations measures). The average percentage of the membership voting in favor was 97.5, and 102 of the measures were passed by suspension of the rules. The data set on which these statistics are based will be described in chapter 3.

41. These categories are meant to be exemplary, rather than exhaustive. Other useful categories could probably be offered, and specific measures may arguably fit more than one.

42. Rules, of course, is important across all issues because of its "traffic cop" powers. For a discussion of the link between member goals and these prestige committees, see Smith and Deering (1984, pp. 89–98). Their focus is primarily on how the committees affect the goals of actual and potential committee members. Here we are trying to emphasize how they affect the policy goals of *all* representatives. See also Cox and McCubbins (1990).

43. Of course this makes the recent increase in partisanship in voting even more striking.

44. The idea of the majority party's disproportionate interest in certain committees is an important element of Kiewiet and McCubbins's (1990) analysis of the Appropriations process, and more generally of the ongoing work of Cox and McCubbins (1989, 1990) on the committee system in the House. My thinking on this matter has benefited greatly from discussions with Cox and McCubbins, and I am grateful to them for sharing their ideas with me.

45. These varied circumstances of committees illustrate the need to make some important distinctions about committee influence and subcommittee government that are often not sufficiently emphasized in the general accounts in the literature. The first is the crucial point made by Smith and Deering (1982, chaps. 5 and 6, esp. pp. 197–98) that subcommittees can be independent (free from restrictions on activity) without being autonomous (in control of policy outcomes within their jurisdictions). The second is the variation in importance to members of the policies dealt with by committees, as we have been discussing. The lion's share of the jurisdictions of most subcommittees deal with issues that fall in the first three categories noted above. These subcommittees may have autonomy, because most members don't care about the outcomes or because shared preferences will automatically produce acceptable results. Those subcommittees that deal with the nationally important, divisive issues that were the concerns of the reformers may have independence, but it is unlikely that they have autonomy (again, see Smith and Deering, 1982, chap. 5 and 6). The numerical predominance of the first set of subcommittees may account for the literature's tendency to suggest that the reforms generally produced subcommittee autonomy.

46. It is probably worth emphasizing that this theoretical discussion, and the presentation of evidence that follows in subsequent chapters, deals with central tendencies and dominant influences. Given the diversity of goals and circumstances among representatives, there are some people our arguments will not

fit, and we could surely find quotations from individual members that would contradict every generalization offered.

47. Dodd and Oppenheimer's (1981, p. 35) analysis of conservative coalition support scores shows that by 1977 the proportion of moderates had increased considerably (compared to 1959) among *both* northern and southern Democrats.

48. The conception of party leaders or committees as agents of their parties, which draws on the literature on principal-agent models in economics, is finding broad application in theories of congressional behavior. See Fiorina and Shepsle (1989) and the sources cited therein for a discussion. Cox and McCubbins (1990, chap. 3) offer another perspective on the leader-follower relationship.

49. As Cox and McCubbins's (1990) and Kiewiet and McCubbins's (1990) analyses show, this argument also holds for election-oriented members who perceive that party failure would have a negative effect on their reelection chances.

50. See Peabody (1976, pp. 31–33). Peabody reports data on nine consecutive Speakers through Albert; Speakers O'Neill, Wright, and Foley make twelve.

Chapter 3

1. The discussion in this section draws heavily on Rohde (1990b), which considers some of the points in more detail.

2. Of course, member goals also affect other types of choices. See Hall (1987) for an analysis, with strong empirical support, of the link between goals and participation in committee decision making. More generally, see Hall (1986, chap. 7, pp. 5–8).

3. See Fenno (1978, chap. 6) for a discussion of expansionist and protectionist phases to members' careers.

4. See, for example, the analyses of Fiorina (1974, chap. 5), Asher and Weisberg (1978), and Brady and Sinclair (1984).

5. Of course, this measure was employed because alternatives were unavailable for the historical periods that were being analyzed.

6. Some of the arguments in this section were presented in Rohde (1990b).

7. Collie and Brady (1985, pp. 279–82), for example, show that levels of party voting and party cohesion vary across issues in three different time periods. More generally, see also Sinclair (1982).

8. Empirical evidence presented elsewhere (Rohde, 1989a, 1989b, 1990a) indicates that changes in the mix of issues and vote types do have an effect on voting patterns, but that the changes in the level of partisanship are not due only to this. Some relevant data are also discussed below. That is, preference changes and other factors also had an impact.

9. Recall that party-unity scores are the percentage of all votes with opposed party majorities on which a member supports his or her party. Scores through the Ninety-fifth Congress were obtained from ICPSR file 7645 ("Voting Scores

for Members of the United States Congress, 1945–82"), and were recomputed for each member to remove the effect of nonparticipation. From the Ninety-sixth Congress on, the scores were computed directly from the ICPSR roll-call tapes for each Congress. In the Ninety-ninth and One Hundredth Congresses there were many purely procedural votes which were used by Republicans to protest what they regarded as unfair treatment by the Democrats. These votes were excluded in computing scores to make the data more comparable over time. (Including these votes would have made northern and southern Democrats appear to be even more similar than do the data we actually use). In both Congresses, all votes on approval of the House *Journal* are excluded, and additionally in the Ninety-ninth Congress votes protesting House decisions on the seating dispute in an Indiana House election were excluded.

If a given seat had more than one occupant in a Congress, the member who participated in the most votes was counted. Scores for Speakers are ignored because Speakers rarely vote.

10. For a more detailed analysis, see Rohde (1991).

11. The generalizations in this paragraph are based on analysis in Rohde (1988, pp. 3–9). Supporting data will be found there on all points except candidate recruitment, for which analysis is not yet complete. Much detailed evidence on these matters will be found in Rohde (1991), chapters 3 through 5. Another perspective on the link between partisan changes in the electorate and in the Congress can be found in Schlesinger (1985).

12. For example, as we discuss later in the chapter, they urged and got an expansion of the leadership circle itself.

13. Blanchard became governor of Michigan and Wirth was elected senator from Colorado.

14. Gephardt was first Caucus chairman, then majority leader; Coelho was chairman of the Democratic Campaign Committee, and then majority whip, Panetta was elected chairman of the Budget Committee.

15. The increase amounted to $1.8 billion. See *CQWR*, Aug. 9, 1986, p. 1800.

16. See the discussion of defense and antiapartheid sanctions below, and in Rohde (1989b, pp. 144–48).

17. The fifty-seven freshmen comprised 21 percent of the Democrats in the House in 1983, and the survivors of the class still accounted for 19 percent of Democrats in 1989.

18. A 1981 CDF membership list can be found in Arieff (1981a, p. 1026).

19. They often came close to this on important administration initiatives. On three key budget and tax votes in 1981, the Republicans averaged *one* defection. See Rohde (1989b, p. 142).

20. It is worth noting that this account focuses on the major factions, and isn't exhaustive. Further elements included a populist caucus (Hagstrom, 1983), members tied to the remnants of urban machines, and individual variations.

21. The cohesion score is the absolute value of the difference between the percentage of the group voting aye and the percentage voting nay. In comparing these scores to party-unity scores, one needs to remember that they are analogous, but equivalent cohesion scores will be lower.

22. Consensual votes are those with majorities of 90 percent or more. Collie (1988) uses the term *universalistic* to describe this type of roll call because of the hypothesized link between those votes and the theory of universalism in distributive politics (Weingast, 1989; Shepsle and Weingast, 1981). The more neutral term *consensual* is used here to leave open the possibility that the proportion of near-unanimous votes may also increase or decrease due to other causes, such as changes in voting rules.

Due to the potential variation over time in the proportion of such votes, and to the fact that they will inflate cohesion scores, we will usually exclude them from our calculations. Note that they will be excluded automatically from party-unity calculations, which require opposed majorities. Thus failure to delete them from the analysis presented in figure 3.1 would be particularly misleading, since they would all appear with the nonunity votes, increasing those scores considerably.

This data series, and most others that follow, commences with the Eighty-fourth Congress because that began the unbroken series of years of Democratic control. Thus we are able to have a long time series without the need to control for changing party control.

23. A more extensive discussion of the impact of variations in the agenda on partisanship can be found in Rohde (1990a).

24. This latter group included purely procedural votes that were not linked to any particular legislation (e.g., approval of House *Journal*), and internal House matters like the authorization of funding for committees or the election of the Speaker. This does *not* include procedural matters like the passage of special rules or recommittal votes, which are included with the legislation to which they apply.

25. Of course some categories have so few votes in certain years that the scores vary sharply in consecutive Congresses. The generalizations apply to those categories with a relatively large number of votes.

26. Counting all record votes, the total went from 1,540 in the Ninety-fifth Congress to 1,273 in the Ninety-sixth to 812 in the Ninety-seventh. From that point on, similar totals have been achieved.

27. The impact of different issues will be dealt with further in the next section, and the role of various vote types in fostering increased cohesion will be addressed again in chapter 4.

28. There is no special substantive reason for beginning with the Ninety-fourth Congress. It was selected to provide class cohorts of sufficient size that averages would have some meaning. Pushing back further would have yielded cohorts of three or fewer members.

29. Other evidence on the increased homogeneity among Democrats, and that its cause was changes among southerners, is found in the large-scale analysis of voting dimensionality by Poole and Rosenthal (1991). They conclude, "The changes by southern Democrats have resulted in the 1980's being not only a period in which spatial mobility is low but also one which is nearly spatially unidimensional."

30. Most of these involved foreign or defense issues or votes involving the national debt.

31. For an earlier treatment of these issues, from which some of this discussion is derived, see Rohde (1989b, pp. 143–48). These matters will be discussed in considerably more detail in Rohde (1991).

32. Carmines and Stimson (1989) give a superb account of the role of racial issues in the transformation of American party politics. Specifically, they show how changes in elite behavior altered the popular perceptions of the parties, and then how voters adjusted their loyalties to reflect the changed perceptions.

33. The votes can be found in *Congressional Roll Call 1981* (1982, pp. 74H–77H).

34. The three votes can be found respectively in *Congressional Roll Call 1985* (1986, p. 44H); *Congressional Roll Call 1986* (1987, p. 110H); and *Congressional Roll Call 1988* (1989, p. 90H).

35. For all years except 1986, the votes included are those budget votes that were selected by Congressional Quarterly Inc. for inclusion in their annual list of key congressional votes. See appropriate volumes of *Congressional Roll Call*. In 1986, no budget votes were on the list, so the two final votes on the fiscal 1987 resolution were selected for table 3.4.

36. This description is based on *CQWR*, May 17, 1986, pp. 1079–81, and the quotation appears on p. 1081.

37. Some details of these measures will be discussed in chapter 4.

38. The total number of nay votes from Republicans and southern Democrats never exceeded four.

39. See *CQWR*, Aug. 16, 1986, pp. 1869–72.

40. See chapter 4 for a discussion of leadership use of special rules on these bills to advantage party positions.

41. In 1987 the vote was Democrats 227 to 18, Republicans 12 to 159; in 1988, Democrats 213 to 36, Republicans 39 to 136.

42. See Caucus Rule 7 in Galloway and Wise (1976, p. 172).

43. Actually the Caucus had dealt with policy matters a few times before this. Not surprisingly, the initial instances dealt with the Vietnam War. In 1971 it adopted a resolution calling for the withdrawal of U.S. troops before the end of the Ninety-second Congress, and in 1972 it instructed the Foreign Affairs Committee to report a resolution setting a date for termination of the war. See Ornstein and Rohde (1978, p. 289); *CQWR*, May 3, 1975, p. 915.

44. This quotation and the others in this paragraph are from *CQWR*, May 3, 1975, pp. 911–12).

45. Author's interview with a member of the Committee on Party Effectiveness, July 1989.

46. Ibid.

47. See *CQWR*, Mar. 9, 1985, pp. 456–59, and Feb. 8, 1986, p. 271.

48. The description in this paragraph draws on Cohodas and Granat (1985).

49. Author's interview, May 1990.

50. It's not clear, however, how much of an ideological interpretation can be placed on this case since at the same time the Caucus replaced nominee Joseph Fisher of Virginia with James Jones of Oklahoma. Here the winner was more conservative. Both contests are described in *CQWR*, Jan. 27, 1979, p. 152.

51. This discussion draws on the description previously presented in Rohde (1989b, pp. 149–52).

52. The description of the plan is taken from Broder (1981b), and all quotations are contained therein.

53. The party's dealings with CDF were not, however, limited to imposing sanctions. In 1985, the leadership responded to discussions with CDF leaders by supporting improved committee assignments for its members and stronger representation in the leadership (e.g., in the Speaker's Cabinet). See Rohde (1989b, pp. 151–52). A more extensive discussion will be found in Rohde (1991, chap. 6).

Chapter 4

1. Another activity of the committee—endorsing legislation—will be discussed below.

2. All data on whips from the 1970s on are taken from the *CQWR* biennial publications on congressional committees and subcommittees.

3. As the number of deputy whips expanded further, they were no longer assured spots on Steering and Policy. Only the whip and his chief deputy are guaranteed membership.

4. For example, compared to the seventeen whip polls in two years reported by Ripley, Dodd (1979, p. 39) said that fifty-three were conducted in the Ninety-third Congress.

5. The analysis by Waldman related to the whip system in the Ninety-fourth Congress (1975–76).

6. An account of the operation of the whip system in the Ninety-fifth Congress can be found in Cooper (1978). Sinclair (1983, pp. 56–67) discusses its activities through the beginning of the Reagan administration. The description offered here is taken from these two sources.

7. Author's interview, August 1989.

8. Author's interview with an at-large whip, July 1989.

9. The series begins with the Ninety-fifth Congress because earlier years had only one or two southern appointed whips. A similar pattern exists for northern Democrats, but the differences are very small. The top party leaders (e.g., Speaker, leader, whip, Caucus chairman, etc.) are excluded from these data.

10. Recall that this was the Congress in which the leadership sought to accommodate the Boll Weevils, giving them good committee assignments, for example. Whip system appointments may have been another part of this effort.

11. The other elements of the strategy are a service orientation, which will be briefly addressed next, and using the rules to structure the choice situation, which will be the main focus of the rest of the chapter.

12. Author's interview, August 1989.

13. Author's interview, July 1989.

14. Ibid.

15. Author's interview, August 1989.

16. Author's interview with an at-large whip, July 1989.

17. Author's interview with a member of the leadership, August 1989.

18. Research on multiple referrals includes: Oleszek, Davidson, and Kephart (1986); Davidson and Oleszek (1987); Davidson, Oleszek, and Kephart (1988); and Collie and Cooper (1989).

19. A third type—split referral, in which parts of a bill are assigned to various committees—is rarely used.

20. Rieselbach (1986, p. 107) reported similar conclusions from work by Eric Uslaner.

21. Multiple referral is also closely tied to the Speaker's expanded power over the Rules Committee, discussed below.

22. As the Ns in table 3.2 indicate, until the Ninety-first Congress record votes on suspensions were quite rare, and usually occurred when the leadership miscalculated and some controversy erupted on a "noncontroversial" bill. In the Eighty-ninth Congress, for example, there were only four roll calls on suspensions, and in all four instances the bill failed to pass. For a detailed discussion of the use of suspensions, see Bach (1986a, 1986b).

23. It is interesting to note that on the roll call that ensured adoption of the expansion of suspensions, every northern Democrat voted aye and every Republican voted nay, but the Republicans were joined by twenty-one conservative southern Democrats. It passed, 208 to 206. In 1977, on the vote that blocked the Republicans from offering amendments to the Democratic rules package, 100 percent of the Democrats opposed 100 percent of the Republicans.

24. In the Ninety-third Congress, from 57 to 60 percent; in the Ninety-fifth, from 62 to 65 percent. However, with the exception of the One Hundredth Congress, the share of consensual votes is fairly stable: never above 66 percent, never below 52 percent.

25. Many of the failures were later brought up under regular consideration, but they would then potentially be subject to amendment on the floor before passage.

26. For historical background on the Rules Committee see Robinson (1963), Kravitz and Oleszek (1979), Matsunaga and Chen (1976), and Rules Committee (1983).

27. In fact, in the official history of the Rules Committee, the description of the period beginning in 1973 is labeled "The Rules Committee as an Arm of the Leadership" (Rules Committee, 1983, pp. 212–30).

28. On this last point, see also Smith (1989).

29. These roll calls include both votes on passage of rules and votes on moving the previous question (thus preventing changes in the rule). See Bach and Smith (1988, pp. 96–98) for a discussion.

30. More details on these two examples can be found in Plattner (1985, pp. 1673–74). The Pepper quotation is on p. 1674.

31. Barbara Sinclair's analysis (1989a, pp. 15–22) of major legislation in four Congresses from the Ninety-first to the One Hundredth shows that leadership

involvement in agenda setting was greater in the One Hundredth than in any of the earlier Congresses.

32. Wright's agenda, as discussed in this section, includes ten bills. A list is presented below. This list does not cover all legislative initiatives pushed by the leadership, but rather isolates the main bills which Wright himself indicated he wanted to press. The information to construct the list came from Hook (1986, 1987), Walsh (1986), and Cohen (1987, 1988a).

33. Mike Lowry (D, Wash.) said, "Half the fights I had with Tip were over that very issue. . . . There's a tremendous core in the Democratic Caucus—maybe two-thirds—who wanted to move forward and be aggressive, but we could never do it because Tip just plain said 'no'" (Hook, 1986, p. 3070).

34. Author's interview, July 1989.

35. Author's interview. The interview took place in the summer of 1989, after Foley had replaced Wright as Speaker.

36. Author's interview, May 1990.

37. This account is drawn from Barry (1989, pp. 542–43).

38. The "journey" of the bill is described in issues of *CQWR* during 1988 as follows: May 21, p. 1400; June 4, p. 1516; June 11, p. 1629; June 18, p. 1667; July 9, p. 1913; July 30, p. 2087; Aug. 6, pp. 2149–51; and Aug. 13, p. 2294.

39. The data on bills and rules in this section include all bills and the concurrent budget resolution for which the House passed special rules governing initial floor consideration during 1987. They exclude rules providing waivers for conference reports and rules waiving points of order for consideration of appropriations bills. There were a total of fifty-five pieces of legislation that met these criteria.

40. In fact, they account for ten of the fourteen bills listed in the "Status of Major Legislation" charts published periodically in *Congressional Quarterly Weekly Report* during 1987.

41. This reflects the fact that a growing proportion of the House's legislative agenda has become routine and nonconflictual. See Bach (1988).

42. Author's interview, May 1990.

43. Author's interview, August 1989.

44. The statistics on passage votes include the vote to adopt the Democratic substitute on the budget resolution. However, the Democratic leadership wasn't universally successful in shaping the floor situation as it wanted. Three rules failed to pass in 1987. One involved an attempt to package welfare reform as part of the reconciliation bill. There was too much Democratic resistance to this, and they were separated. Both bills eventually passed separately (see below). Another case arose when Rules failed to make in order an amendment proposed by Public Works Committee chairman James Howard to the airport-improvement bill. A new rule was passed, permitting the amendment.

45. Author's interview, August 1989.

46. An analysis of Republican responses will be found in chapter 5.

47. For a theoretical discussion of the motivations for members to support restrictive rules on distributive legislation, see Krehbiel (1989). See also Weingast (1989b, 1989c).

48. A few days later, Wright also reacted to Rostenkowski's apparent departure, in another interview, from party policy on the trade issue, implying that members didn't really want to support the Gephardt amendment (to impose trade sanctions on Japan). Wright wrote a letter to Rostenkowski about the matter, in which he pointed out, "As Chairman of the House Committee on Ways and Means, Danny, you are the designated agent of the Democratic Caucus. . . ." Wright also referred to Rostenkowski and himself as "their [i.e., members'] chosen agent . . ." (See Barry, 1989, pp. 176–78; the quotations appear on p. 178). This indicates that the theoretical argument that leaders are, and perceive themselves to be, agents of the membership is more than just political-science jargon.

49. Clearly this was the agenda item about which there was the greatest member disagreement, at least initially. There was a lot of conflict, much of it about what was politically feasible rather than what was desirable in principle, before a consensus was reached. For useful accounts of this process see Barry (1989) and Palazzolo (1989).

50. Republican anger over Wright's action was extreme, and it was not abated by Democrats' pointing out that votes were often held open longer than fifteen minutes. For example, the parliamentarian indicated that up to that point in 1987, eleven votes had been held open longer than the reconciliation vote (Barry, 1989, p. 477).

51. See Knudson and Rovner (1987, pp. 3036–37), and Barry (1989, pp. 538–39).

52. For similar sentiments from a member of Armed Services, see Barry (1989, p. 539).

53. Over 200 amendments were proposed, and Rules eventually made over 125 of them in order (Bach and Smith, 1988, p. 125).

54. Aspin had made an agreement with the ranking Republican committee member, William Dickenson, that the Democratic position would go last three times and the Republican position go last three times. Because of a jurisdictional mix-up, the Rules Committee overrode the agreement with respect to one of the sets of amendments. See *Congressional Record,* May 7, 1987, pp. H3298–99.

Chapter 5

1. "Conference" is the Republicans' formal name for their party caucus. Anderson was also a member of the Rules Committee, and conservatives objected to the fact that on some important committee votes he sided with the Democrats.

2. Given the numbers, the opposition clearly included more than just Republican conservatives, traditional or otherwise. They were, however, the main source of the opposition.

3. For examples of COS positions, and their characterizations of the corresponding positions of the "liberal welfare state" taken from a Gingrich flier, see Pitney (1988a, p. 21).

4. For example, on a list of twenty-one Gypsy Moths published in the *Washington Post* (July 27, 1981, p. A4), fifteen were from the Northeast, six were from the Midwest, and none were from the South or West. In addition, Republican moderates and liberals have tended to come from central city or suburban districts. See *CQWR,* Aug. 19, 1972, p. 2054.

5. Note that this corresponds to figure 3.1, which presented similar data for southern Democrats.

6. Barbara Sinclair's (1982) study of voting alignments in the House showed that across the major issue categories she examined, northeastern Republicans were usually noticeably more liberal than their party colleagues from the 1950s on.

7. Part of this decline is due to the shift in House seats from the northeast to the Sun Belt through reapportionment, and part is due to greater Democratic success in the region. On the shift in the regional balance in House seats generally, see Abramson, Aldrich, and Rohde (1990, chap. 9). Southern Democrats were between 35 and 42 percent of their Caucus during the 1950s, but only about 30 percent in the 1980s.

8. This corresponds to figure 3.2 for the Democrats.

9. The largest difference was in the Ninety-second Congress, when Democrats were 11 points lower.

10. In the nine Congresses from the Eighty-ninth to the Ninety-seventh, Democratic cohesion on unity votes was higher than Republicans' in only one Congress (the Ninety-third, by 2 points).

11. The Eighty-fifth, Ninety-first, Ninety-second, and Ninety-sixth; the maximum difference in these cases was 7 points.

12. The Eighty-seventh, Eighty-eighth, and Ninety-eighth through One Hundredth. It is also worth noting that Democratic cohesion on unity votes was lower than for nonunity votes for six consecutive Congresses (Ninetieth through Ninety-fifth), while this was true for Republicans only in the Ninety-first and Ninety-third.

13. Republican support is still necessary when Democrats divide (either in committee or on the floor), and is desirable when the majority wants to present a bipartisan front behind an initiative, which can be useful to help persuade a Republican president to accept it. It is, of course, also usually necessary when extraordinary majorities are required, as on suspensions or veto overrides.

14. In those instances where bipartisan activity does still operate, there is pressure from some Republicans to end it. For example, on the Appropriations subcommittees dealing with the Energy and Water and Interior appropriations bills, there is often wide consensus. Both Democrats and Republicans who draft these bills fight efforts (often by Republicans) to cut them on the floor. This has caused intraparty conflict. See *CQWR,* Aug. 1, 1987, p. 1720.

15. In his memoirs, O'Neill said that his move made Walker "look like a fool," and admitted that he should have warned the Republicans first (O'Neill and Novak, 1987, p. 354).

16. The reader will also note that the average support for rules was somewhat higher among Republicans than among Democrats in the Ninety-first. These

average figures reflect the fact that the Rules Committee was still independent of the party and its leadership. Sometimes it would produce rules that were highly satisfactory to Republicans and less so to Democrats, and sometimes vice versa. Rules that garnered greater Republican support usually produced conservative coalitions on the floor vote; that is, they also tended to be supported by southern Democrats and opposed by northern Democrats. They also frequently involved closed rules which prevented northern Democrats from proposing amendments. (Some examples from the Ninety-first Congress include closed rules for bills dealing with tax reform and selective-service reform, and a resolution dealing with the Vietnam War.) After the Democrats passed the closed-rule reform and put the Rules Committee under leadership control, rules with higher Republican support became very rare. For evidence on this point, see Rohde (1990a).

17. This exchange appears in the *Congressional Record,* Apr. 1, 1987, pp. H1723–24.

18. This exchange appears in the *Congressional Record,* May 6, 1987, pp. H3198–99.

19. More graphically, in an interview with *National Journal* Cheney referred to Wright as a "heavy-handed SOB" (Cohen, 1988a, p. 238).

20. Gingrich's negative characterizations were returned by Wright, who said that his feelings toward the Republican "are similar to those of a fire hydrant to a dog" (Kenworthy, 1988, p. A1).

21. Jones (1970, p. 160) states, "The organizational changes in the House Republican Party since 1959 are the most important developments in the role of the minority party in policy making in this century."

22. The Meyers committee recommendations resulted in the first complete codified set of rules for the Republican Conference, which were modeled after the Democratic Caucus Rules. In fact the Democratic rules were used by the Meyers committee for markup purposes (Wolfensberger, 1988, p. 40).

23. Under Conference rules, the eight elected leaders are: the party leader; the whip; the chairman, vice chairman, and Secretary of the Conference; and the chairmen of the Policy, Research, and Congressional (i.e., campaign) committees. The four designated leaders are the ranking Republicans on the four top committees: Appropriations, Rules, Budget, and Ways and Means. Note the similarity to the Democrats designated to the members of Steering and Policy.

24. These provisions are all part of Rule 2 of the Republican Conference Rules, and the quotations are from that rule. I am grateful to Michael Malbin for making a copy of these rules available to me.

25. Kemp's behavior as the motivation for these changes was first brought to my attention by Michael Malbin.

26. Jerry Lewis (R, Cal.), a member of the GOP leadership, said that his party had not developed a way of countering Wright's control of the Rules Committee. Republican cohesion had increased in response, but it didn't matter. "As for influencing what happens inside the House," he said, "we have just enough votes to be irresponsible" (Barry, 1989, p. 304).

27. Recall Majority Leader O'Neill's statement to John Rhodes, quoted above, that Republicans were not going to write legislation. A decade later, in 1986, Tony Coelho was offering his view of what the One Hundredth Congress would be like after (he predicted) the Democrats made gains in the 1986 House elections. He said, "Republicans will continue to be non-players in the legislative arena" (*CQWR*, June 21, 1986, p. 1396).

28. The literature on congressional-presidential interactions is quite large. For some starting points, see the discussion in Rockman (1985), the analyses of Edwards (1980, 1989), and the works cited therein, as well as the specific pieces cited below.

29. Authors vary in their use of the term *agenda* in this connection. Some include both issues and the alternatives regarding them, while others apply it only to the former. We use it here to encompass both, while maintaining the distinction between the two aspects. See Rohde (1990a).

30. Of course, the case of Jim Wright's speakership provides a counterexample to this generalization, a point to which we shall shortly return.

31. Jones (1988b, p. 82) says that Carter's campaign staff "kept a record of campaign promises, which was actually published."

32. There is disagreement among analysts in the characterization of the size of Reagan's agenda. Edwards (1989, p. 216) terms it "the smallest policy agenda of any modern president," while Light (1983, p. ix) calls it "remarkably large." The difference may be largely semantic because of the omnibus packaging of some Reagan successes, like the 1981 reconciliation bill. That contained a wide range of domestic-spending changes, but was only one bill.

33. They were, of course, starting from heavy majorities in both bodies.

34. See Hook (1986a). We discuss this point more extensively later in this chapter.

35. At the margin, at least, presidents can potentially exert considerable influence on members' preferences. See Edwards (1980, 1989) and Kingdon (1989, chap. 6).

36. As David Mayhew wrote (1974a, p. 71), "Nothing is more important in Capitol Hill politics than the shared conviction that electoral returns have proven a point."

37. Especially during the One Hundredth Congress, and the feeling was often returned by Wright and the Democrats. See Barry (1989, pp. 108, 174, 304, 387, and 400) for some examples.

38. Thus we exclude all votes on amendments and all procedural votes. "Initial" passage excludes votes on conference reports and veto overrides. This limits consideration to the House's judgment on content before disagreements with the Senate have been bargained away. "Regular" passage excludes passage by suspension of the rules, the incidence of which we know varied greatly over time. "Bills and joint resolutions" excludes simple and concurrent resolutions, which don't involve presidential approval. Similarly, we exclude those few joint resolutions that involve passage of constitutional amendments. With that one exception, bills and joint resolutions are equivalent (Oleszek, 1989, pp. 296–97). In the rest of this discussion, therefore, we will use only the term *bills*.

39. Strictly speaking, the House has not "endorsed" the alternative unless the bill actually passes. This is, however, almost always the case. Of the votes on initial passage analyzed here, the House approved the bill on 96.7 percent of them.

40. Data on presidential positions were taken from roll-call data in *CQWR*.

41. This is a somewhat different overall pattern than that shown for all votes in figure 5.5, but it reflects the varying circumstances when presidential position votes are separated out.

42. With consensual votes excluded, there are no instances of bills opposed by the president in the Eighty-seventh, Eighty-eight, or Eighty-ninth Congresses, and in the Ninetieth through the Ninety-second there are only two, two, and one such instances, respectively. In the One Hundredth Congress there were only five bills endorsed by the president. The only other situations with fewer than ten cases are: *president for:* Ninety-ninth Congress (eight); *president against:* Eighty-fifth Congress (seven), Ninety-fifth Congress (six), and Ninety-sixth Congress (five).

43. The minority, however, cannot afford to be so magnanimous, which is another source of their frustration.

44. To avoid artificially inflating Democratic success in the Ninety-ninth and One Hundredth Congresses, votes on approval of the House *Journal* and votes related to the contested Indiana House seat are excluded. As noted in chapter 3, they are also excluded from calculations of party-unity scores.

45. There were 204 northern Democrats in the House in the eighty-ninth Congress, only fourteen votes short of a majority by themselves.

46. For example, on the fiscal 1988 defense bill, Lyn Martin (R, Ill.) sponsored an amendment to delete funds for two aircraft carriers. It was supported by 36 percent of Democrats, but only 20 percent of Republicans.

47. Timothy Penny (D, Minn.) sponsored an amendment to cut discretionary funding in the fiscal 1988 Labor–Health and Human Services appropriations bill by 2 percent. He was supported by 81 percent of Republicans and 16 percent of Democrats.

48. Before the Ninety-second Congress (and recorded voting) there are too few record votes to provide any meaningful comparisons.

49. This pattern is even stronger when one controls for the issues involved. Those data show that the Democrat-supported proportion was below the Carter years in both the Ninety-ninth and One Hundredth Congresses. See Rohde (1990a).

50. Actually this generalization is true for domestic- and foreign-policy issues, but not for defense. There the Democrats still offer most of the amendments, but partisanship has increased on those votes as well. See Rohde (1990a).

51. We will not present data on passage controlling for which party favors bills since, as noted, virtually all bills pass. Those small differences that do exist, however, generally support what one would expect from our theory: Republican-supported bills were more likely to pass until the reform era (specifically, through the Ninety-second Congress). The rate reversed in the sec-

ond Nixon-Ford term and reversed again under Carter. Then in each Reagan Congress, Democrat-favored bills were more successful.

52. See n. 38 for details on this subset of votes.

53. Actually, if we confine the analysis to domestic policies, the proportion of Democrat-favored bills was equal or higher in each of the Ninety-eight, Ninety-ninth, and One Hundredth Congresses than any preceding Congress in the series, including the Eighty-seventh and Eighty-ninth (Rohde, 1990a).

54. The number of bills in the Ninety-ninth Congress was nine, three on domestic policies and six on defense matters. The level of party difference for the domestic bills was consistent with those of earlier years, while conflict was much higher on defense. In the One Hundredth Congress there were only four cases, three of which involved defense issues.

Chapter 6

1. These arrangements include party control of nominations and of the electoral power base, and the need to sustain a cabinet; see Mayhew (1974, pp. 25–27).

2. This was once stated by John Ferejohn, although it may not have been original with him.

3. Actually, the budget resolution, which was one of the priorities, did not "become law," since it didn't involve presidential assent. However, a Democrat-favored conference report was passed.

4. Democrats voted 239 to 7 for the report; Republicans 62 to 108 against.

5. Northern Democrats voted 145 to 23; southerners 67 to 11.

6. The Republican vote was 44 to 130. As in the case of the budget resolution, Democratic opposition came from both wings of the party: the northern Democratic vote was 134 to 34, and among southerners it was 59 to 17.

7. All data cited here through 1988 are taken from Ornstein, Mann, and Malbin (1990, pp. 198–99). Recall that these data employ all votes, and do not remove the effect of protest votes in the House.

8. The four Senate committees are Appropriations, Armed Services, Finance, and Foreign Relations. The four House Committees are Appropriations, Budget, Rules, and Ways and Means. The committee assignment data are taken from *CQWR*, May 6, 1989.

9. Again, these figures are not directly comparable to those in table 5.3 because they include procedural protest votes.

10. One Republican strategy that could prove significant if successful is the attempt to ally with blacks to support the creation of more black majority districts. This is a classic gerrymandering strategy which seeks to concentrate the opposition's support in a few districts where they will have overwhelming strength. Such a device would not only weaken other Democrats, but would also mitigate the liberalizing effects of black enfranchisement in the South. See *CQWR*, June 2, 1990, pp. 1739–42.

11. Author's interview, May 1990.

12. Author's interview, May 1990.

13. Author's interview, May 1990.

14. Author's interview, May 1990.

15. Author's interview, May 1990.

16. Author's interview with a member of the whip organization, May 1990.

17. The data on presidential position votes are taken from *CQWR,* Dec. 30, 1989, p. 3563, and from various issues during the year.

18. These included matters like the congressional ethics reform–pay raise package and the compromise on Contra aid.

References

Abramson, Paul R., John H. Aldrich, and David W. Rohde. 1990. *Change and Continuity in the 1988 Elections.* Washington, D.C.: CQ Press.

Aldrich, John H. 1989a. "On the Origins of the American Political Party: The Endogeneity of the Party in the Legislature." Paper presented at the annual meeting of the Public Choice Society, Orlando, Florida.

———. 1989b. "Power and Order in Congress." In Morris P. Fiorina and David W. Rohde (eds.), *Home Style and Washington Work: Studies in Congressional Politics.* Ann Arbor: University of Michigan Press; 219–52.

Arieff, Irwin B. 1980. "Carter-Congress Relations Still Strained Despite Gains." *CQWR,* Oct. 11: 3095–97.

———. 1981a. "Conservative Southerners Are Enjoying Their Wooing as Key to Tax Bill Success." *CQWR,* June 13: 1023–26.

———. 1981b. "'Gypsy Moths' Poised to Fly against Reagan's New Cuts; Charge Pledges Were Broken." *CQWR,* Oct. 10: 1950–52.

Asher, Herbert B., and Herbert F. Weisberg. 1978. "Voting Change in Congress: Some Dynamic Perspectives on an Evolutionary Process." *American Journal of Political Science* 22: 391–425.

Bach, Stanley. 1986a. "Suspension of the Rules in the House of Representatives." Congressional Research Service Report 86-103.

———. 1986b. "Suspension of the Rules, the Order of Business, and the Evolution of Legislative Procedure in the House of Representatives." Paper presented at the annual meeting of the American Political Science Association, Washington, D.C.

———. 1988. "Patterns of Floor Consideration in the House of Representatives." Paper presented at the Center for American Political Studies of Harvard University, Dec. 9.

Bach, Stanley, and Steven S. Smith. 1988. *Managing Uncertainty in the House of Representatives*. Washington, D.C.: Brookings Institution.

Baker, Ross K. 1985. "Party and Institutional Sanctions in the U.S. House: The Case of Congressman Graham." *Legislative Studies Quarterly,* 10: 315–38.

Barry, John M. 1989. *The Ambition and the Power*. New York: Viking.

Bolling, Richard. 1966. *House Out of Order*. New York: Dutton.

Brady, David W., and Charles S. Bullock III. 1980. "Is There a Conservative Coalition in the House?" *Journal of Politics* 42: 549–59.

———. 1981. "Coalition Politics in the House of Representatives." In Lawrence C. Dodd and Bruce I. Oppenheimer (eds.), *Congress Reconsidered,* 2d ed. Washington, D.C.: CQ Press; 186–203.

Brady, David W., Joseph Cooper, and Patricia A. Hurley. 1979. "The Decline of Party in the U.S. House of Representatives, 1887–1968." *Legislative Studies Quarterly* 4: 381–407.

Brady, David W., and John Ettling. 1984. "The Electoral Connection and the Decline of Partisanship in the Twentieth Century House of Representatives." *Congress and the Presidency* 11: 19–36.

Brady, David W., and Barbara Sinclair. 1984. "Building Majorities for Policy Change in the House of Representatives." *Journal of Politics* 46: 1033–60.

Broder, David S. 1971. *The Party's Over: The Failure of Politics in America*. New York: Harper and Row.

———. 1981a. "The Gypsy Moths." *Washington Post,* July 27: A1.

———. 1981b. "Hill Democrats Grant Amnesty to Boll Weevils." *Washington Post,* Sept. 17: A1.

Burns, James McGregor. 1963. *The Deadlock of Democracy*. Englewood Cliffs, N.J.: Prentice-Hall.

Cain, Bruce, John Ferejohn, and Morris Fiorina. 1987. *The Personal Vote*. Cambridge: Harvard University Press.

Calmes, Jacqueline. 1986a. "'Boll Weevils' Now Welcome in House Democratic Fold." *CQWR,* Apr. 26: 909–13.

———. 1986b. "Class of '82: Redefining Democratic Values." *CQWR,* June 7: 1269–73.

———. 1987a. "Aspin Makes Comeback at Armed Services." *CQWR,* Jan. 24: 139–42.

———. 1987b. "Aspin Ousted as Armed Services Chairman." *CQWR,* Jan. 10: 83–85.

———. 1987c. "Four Battling for Armed Services Chairmanship." *CQWR,* Jan. 17: 103–4.

Carmines, Edward G., and James A. Stimson. 1989. *Issue Evolution: Race and the Transformation of American Politics*. Princeton, N.J.: Princeton University Press.

Carter, Jimmy. 1981. *Keeping Faith: Memoirs of a President*. New York: Bantam Books.

Cheney, Richard B. 1989. "An Unruly House: A Republican View" *Public Opinion,* Jan.–Feb.: 41–44.

Clubb, Jerome M., and Santa A. Traugott. 1977. "Partisan Cleavage and Cohesion in the House of Representatives, 1861–1974." *Journal of Interdisciplinary History* 7: 375–401.

Cohen, Richard E. 1980. "House GOP Conflicts May Surface If Party Gains in Fall Elections." *NJ*, July 12: 1142–46.

———. 1981. "They're Still a Majority in the House, but Are Democrats Really in Control?" *NJ*, Jan. 31: 189–91.

———. 1983. "Strains Appear as 'New Breed' Democrats Move to Control Party in the House." *NJ*, June 25: 1328–31.

———. 1984. "Frustrated House Republicans Seek More Aggressive Strategy for 1984 and Beyond." *NJ*, Mar. 3: 413–17.

———. 1985. "Moderates in the Middle." *NJ*, May 4: 998.

———. 1987 "Quick-Starting Speaker." *NJ*, May 30: 1409–13.

———. 1988a. "Full Speed Ahead." *NJ*, Jan. 30: 238–44.

———. 1988b. "We Changed Nation's Priorities." *NJ*, Jan. 2: 26–27.

———. 1989 "Foley's Honeymoon." *NJ*, July 15: 1799–1802.

Cohodas, Nadine. 1989. "Rep. Mazzoli Loses Immigration Chairmanship." *CQWR*, Feb. 4: 226.

Cohodas, Nadine, and Diane Granat. 1985. "House Seniority System Jolted; Price Dumped; Aspin Elected." *CQWR*, Jan. 5: 7–9.

Collie, Melissa P. 1986. "New Directions in Congressional Research." *Legislative Studies Section Newsletter* 10 (Nov.–Dec.): 90–92.

———. 1988. "Universalism and the Parties in the U.S. House of Representatives: 1921–80." *American Journal of Political Science* 32: 865–83.

Collie, Melissa P., and David W. Brady. 1985. "The Decline of Partisan Voting Coalitions in the House of Representatives." In Lawrence C. Dodd and Bruce I. Oppenheimer (eds.), *Congress Reconsidered*, 3d ed. Washington, D.C.: CQ Press; 272–87.

Collie, Melissa P., and Joseph Cooper. 1989. "Multiple Referral and the 'New' Committee System in the House of Representatives." In Lawrence C. Dodd and Bruce I. Oppenheimer (eds.), *Congress Reconsidered*, 4th ed. Washington, D.C.: CQ Press; 245–72.

Committee on Political Parties, American Political Science Association. 1950. "Toward a More Responsible Two-Party System." *American Political Science Review* 44: supplement to the March issue.

Congressional Roll Call. Various years. Washington, D.C.: Congressional Quarterly.

Conlon, Richard P. 1982. "Response." In Dennis Hale (ed.), *The United States Congress: Proceedings of the Thomas P. O'Neill Symposium.* Chestnut Hill, Mass.: Boston College; 239–45.

Cooper, Ann. 1978. "House Democratic Whips: Counting, Coaxing, Cajoling." *CQWR*, May 27: 1301–6.

Cooper, Joseph, and David W. Brady. 1981. "Institutional Context and Leadership Style: The House from Cannon to Rayburn." *American Political Science Review* 75: 411–25.

Cooper, Joseph, David W. Brady, and Patricia A. Hurley. 1977. "The Electoral Basis of Party Voting: Patterns and Trends in the U.S. House of Representatives, 1887–1969." In Louis Maisel and Joseph Cooper (eds.), *The Impact of the Electoral Process.* Beverly Hills: Sage Publications; 133–65.

Cox, Gary W., and Mathew D. McCubbins. 1989. "Political Parties and the Appointment of Committees." Paper presented at the Conference on Congressional Structure and Elections at the University of California at San Diego, Feb. 11.

———. 1990. *Parties and Committees in the U.S. House of Representatives.* Manuscript.

Crook, Sara Brandes, and John R. Hibbing. 1985. "Congressional Reform and Party Discipline: The Effects of Changes in the Seniority System on Party Loyalty in the House of Representatives." *British Journal of Political Science* 15: 207–26.

Cummings, Milton C., Jr. 1963. "The Decision to Enlarge the Committee on Rules: An Analysis of the 1961 Vote." In Robert L. Peabody and Nelson W. Polsby (eds.), *New Perspectives on the House of Representatives.* Chicago: Rand McNally; 167–94.

Davidson, Roger H. 1981. "Subcommittee Government: New Channels for Policy Making." In Thomas E. Mann and Norman J. Ornstein (eds.), *The New Congress.* Washington, D.C.: American Enterprise Institute; 99–133.

———. 1988. "The New Centralization on Capitol Hill." *The Review of Politics:* 345–64.

Davidson, Roger H., and Walter J. Oleszek. 1977. *Congress against Itself.* Bloomington: Indiana University Press.

———. 1987. "From Monopoly to Interaction: Changing Patterns in Committee Management of Legislation in the House." Paper presented at the annual meeting of the Midwest Political Science Association, Chicago, Illinois, Apr. 9–11.

Davidson, Roger H., Walter J. Oleszek, and Thomas Kephart. 1988. "One Bill, Many Committees: Multiple Referrals in the House of Representatives." *Legislative Studies Quarterly* 13: 3–28.

Deckard, Barbara, and John Stanley. 1974. "Party Decomposition and Region: The House of Representatives, 1945–1970." *Western Political Quarterly* 27: 249–64.

Deering, Christopher J., and Steven S. Smith. 1981. "Majority Party Leadership and the New House Subcommittees System." In Frank H. Mackaman (ed.) *Understanding Congressional Leadership.* Washington, D.C.: CQ Press; 261–92.

Dodd, Lawrence C. 1979. "The Expanded Roles of the House Democratic Whip System: The Ninety-third and Ninety-fourth Congresses." *Congressional Studies* 7: 27–56.

———. 1987. "Woodrow Wilson's *Congressional Government* and the Modern Congress: The 'Universal Principle' of Change." *Congress and the Presidency* 14: 33–50.

Dodd, Lawrence C., and Bruce I. Oppenheimer. 1981. "The House in Transition: Change and Consolidation." In Dodd and Oppenheimer (eds.), *Congress Reconsidered,* 2d ed. Washington, D.C.: CQ Press; 31–61.

Downs, Anthony. 1957. *An Economic Theory of Democracy.* New York: Harper and Row.

DSG Staff. 1969. "Voting in the House." *Congressional Record,* Mar. 19: H6749–52.

———. 1970. "The Seniority System in the U.S. House of Representatives." *Congressional Record,* Feb. 25: H5169–72.

Edwards, George C., III. 1980. *Presidential Influence in Congress.* San Francisco: W. H. Freeman and Co.

———. 1989. *At the Margins: Presidential Leadership in Congress.* New Haven: Yale University Press.

Erenhalt, Alan. 1983. "The Unfashionable House Rules Committee." *CQWR,* Jan. 15: 151.

———. 1986. "Media, Power Shifts Dominate O'Neill's House." *CQWR,* Sept. 13: 2131–38.

Fenno, Richard F., Jr. 1966. *The Power of the Purse.* Boston: Little, Brown.

———. 1973. *Congressmen in Committees.* Boston: Little, Brown.

———. 1978. *Home Style.* Boston: Little, Brown.

Ferejohn, John. 1977. "On the Decline in Competition in Congressional Elections." *American Political Science Review* 71: 166–76.

Ferejohn, John, Morris Fiorina, and Richard D. McKelvey. 1987. "Sophisticated Voting and Agenda Independence in the Distributive Politics Setting." *American Journal of Political Science* 31: 169–93.

Fessler, Pamela, 1990. "Senate Plan Faces Uphill Fight; Exploratory Talks Are Set." *CQWR,* May 5: 1329–32.

Fiorina, Morris P. 1974. *Representatives, Roll Calls, and Constituencies.* Lexington, Mass.: Lexington Books.

———. 1977. *Congress: Keystone of the Washington Establishment.* New Haven: Yale University Press.

Fiorina, Morris P., and Kenneth A. Shepsle. 1989. "Formal Theories of Leadership: Agents, Agenda-Setters, and Entrepreneurs." In Bryan D. Jones (ed.), *Political Leadership from Political Science Perspectives.* Lawrence: University of Kansas Press; 17–40.

Fishel, Jeff. 1985. *Presidents and Promises.* Washington, D.C.: CQ Press.

Fowler, Linda L., and Robert D. McClure. 1989. *Political Ambition: Who Decides to Run for Congress.* New Haven: Yale University Press.

Froman, Lewis A., Jr., and Randall B. Ripley. 1965. "Conditions for Party Leadership: The Case of the House Democrats." *American Political Science Review* 59: 52–63.

Galloway, George B., and Sidney Wise. 1976. *History of the House of Representatives,* 2d ed. New York: Thomas Y. Crowell.

Granat, Diane. 1983. "Democratic Caucus Renewed as Forum for Policy Questions." *CQWR,* Oct. 15: 2115–19.

———. 1984a. "The House's TV War: The Gloves Come Off." *CQWR*, May 19: 1166–67.

———. 1984b. "Junior Democrats Gain a Louder Voice . . . Leadership Panels Will Serve as Forum." *CQWR*, Dec. 8: 3054–55.

———. 1984c. "Televised Partisan Skirmishes Erupt in House." *CQWR*, Feb. 11: 246–49.

———. 1985. "Deep Divisions Loom behind House GOP's Apparent Unity." *CQWR*, Mar. 23: 535–39.

Hager, Barry M. 1977. "Carter's First Year: Setbacks and Successes." *CQWR*, Dec. 24: 2637–42.

Hagstrom, Jerry. 1983. "Business Tax Breaks, Low Farm Prices Spur Revival of 'Pocketbook Populism.'" *NJ*, Mar. 12: 554–57.

Hall, Richard L. 1986. *Participation in Committee Decision Making*. Ph.D. diss. University of North Carolina.

———. 1987. "Participation and Purpose in Committee Decision Making." *American Political Science Review* 81: 105–27.

Hook, Janet. 1986a. "House Leadership Elections: Wright Era Begins." *CQWR*, Dec. 13: 3067–72.

———. 1986b. "Liberal Democrats Adapt to a Hostile Climate." *CQWR*, Aug. 9: 1797–1801.

———. 1987. "Speaker Jim Wright Takes Charge in the House." *CQWR*, July 11: 1483–88.

———. 1988. "House's 1980 'Reagan Robots' Face Crossroads." *CQWR*, Aug. 13: 2262–65.

———. 1989. "Bush Inspired Frail Support For First-Year President." *CQWR*, Dec. 30: 3540–45.

Hook, Janet, and Congressional Quarterly Staff. 1988. "One Hundredth Congress Wraps Up Surprisingly Busy Year." *CQWR*, Oct. 29: 3117–39.

Hurley, Patricia A. 1989. "Parties and Coalitions in Congress." In Christopher J. Deering (ed.), *Congressional Politics*. Chicago: Dorsey Press; 113–34.

Jacobson, Gary C. 1985. "Money and Votes Reconsidered: Congressional Elections, 1972–1982." *Public Choice*, 47: 7–62.

———. 1987. *The Politics of Congressional Elections*, 2d ed. Boston: Little, Brown.

Jones, Charles O. 1968. "Joseph G. Cannon and Howard W. Smith: An Essay on the Limits of Leadership in the House of Representatives." *Journal of Politics* 30: 617–46.

———. 1970. *The Minority Party in Congress*. Boston: Little, Brown.

———. 1981. "Can Our Parties Survive Our Politics?" In Norman Ornstein (ed.), *The Role of the Legislature in Western Democracies*. Washington, D.C.: American Enterprise Institute; 20–36.

———. 1988a. "Ronald Reagan and the U.S. Congress: Visible-Hand Politics." In Charles O. Jones (ed.), *The Reagan Legacy*. Chatham, N.J.: Chatham House; 30–59.

———. 1988b. *The Trusteeship Presidency: Jimmy Carter and the United States Congress*. Baton Rouge: Louisiana State University Press.

Jones, Charles O., and Randall B. Ripley. 1966. *The Role of Political Parties in Congress*. Tuscon: University of Arizona Press.

Kenworthy, Tom. 1988. "72 in GOP Ask for Probe of Wright." *Washington Post*, May 27: Al.

Kessel, John H., John A. Clark, John M. Bruce, and William G. Jacoby. 1989. "I'd Rather Switch Than Fight: Lifelong Democrats and Converts to Republicanism among Campaign Activists." Paper presented at the annual meeting of the American Political Science Association, Atlanta, Georgia.

Kiewiet, D. Roderick, and Mathew D. McCubbins. 1990. *The Spending Power*. Chicago: University of Chicago Press.

Kingdon, John W. 1973. *Congressmen's Voting Decisions*. New York: Harper and Row.

———. 1984. *Agendas, Alternatives, and Public Policies*. Boston: Little Brown.

———. 1989. *Congressmen's Voting Decisions*. 3d ed. Ann Arbor: University of Michigan Press.

Knudsen, Patrick L., and Julie Rovner. 1987. "Amid Democratic Dissension, Welfare Bill Is Delayed Again." *CQWR*, Dec. 12: 3036–37.

Kravitz, Walter, and Walter J. Oleszek. 1979. "A Short History of the Development of the House Committee on Rules." Congressional Research Service Report No. 79-87 Gov.

Krehbiel, Keith. 1989. "A Rationale for Restrictive Rules." In Morris P. Fiorina and David W. Rohde (eds.), *Home Style and Washington Work: Studies in Congressional Politics*. Ann Arbor: University of Michigan Press; 165–98.

Kweit, Mary Grisez. 1986. "Ideological Congruence of Party Switchers and Nonswitchers: The Case of Party Activists." *American Journal of Political Science* 30: 184–96.

Lemann, Nicholas. 1985. "Conservative Opportunity Society." *Atlantic*, May: 22–36.

Light, Paul C. 1983. *The President's Agenda*. Baltimore: Johns Hopkins University Press.

Loomis, Burdett. 1988. *The New American Politician*. New York: Basic Books.

Lyons, Richard L. 1975. "Freshmen Assess House Chairmen." *Washington Post*, Jan. 14: A2.

Maisel, Louis Sandy. 1982. *From Obscurity to Oblivion*. Knoxville: University of Tennessee Press.

Malbin, Michael J. 1977. "House Democrats Are Playing with a Strong Leadership Lineup." *NJ*, June 18: 940–46.

———. 1981. "Remember the Caucus." *NJ*, Sept. 9: 1642.

Manley, John F. 1970. *The Politics of Finance: The House Committee on Ways and Means*. Boston: Little, Brown.

———. 1973 "The Conservative Coalition in Congress." *American Behavioral Scientist* 17: 223–47.

Mann, Thomas, and Raymond Wolfinger. 1980. "Candidates and Parties in Congressional Elections." *American Political Science Review* 74: 617–32.

Matsunga, Spark M., and Ping Chen. 1976. *Rulemakers of the House*. Urbana: University of Illinois Press.

Mayhew, David R. 1974a. *Congress: The Electoral Connection.* New Haven: Yale University Press.

———. 1974b. "Congressional Elections: The Case of the Vanishing Marginals." *Polity* 6: 295–318.

Nesbit, Dorothy Davidson. 1988. "Changing Partisanship among Southern Party Activists." *Journal of Politics* 50: 322–34.

Oleszek, Walter J. 1989. *Congressional Procedures and the Policy Process,* 3d ed. Washington, D.C.: CQ Press.

Oleszek, Walter J., Roger H. Davidson, and Thomas Kephart. 1986. "The Incidence and Impact of Multiple Referrals in the House of Representatives." Congressional Research Service. Mimeo.

O'Neill, Thomas P., Jr. and William Novak. 1987. *Man of the House.* New York: Random House.

Oppenheimer, Bruce I. 1977. "The Rules Committee: New Arm of Leadership in a Decentralized House." In Lawrence C. Dodd and Bruce I. Oppenheimer (eds.), *Congress Reconsidered.* New York: Praeger; 96–116.

———. 1981. "The Changing Relationship between House Leadership and the Committee on Rules." In Frank H. Mackamen (ed.), *Understanding Congressional Leadership.* Washington, D.C.: CQ Press; 207–25.

———. 1985. "Changing Time Constraints on Congress: Historical Perspectives on the Use of Cloture." In Lawrence C. Dodd and Bruce I. Oppenheimer (eds.), *Congress Reconsidered,* 3d. ed. Washington, D.C.: CQ Press; 393–413.

Orfield, Gary. 1975. *Congressional Power: Congress and Social Change.* New York: Harcourt Brace Jovanovich.

Ornstein, Norman J. 1975. "Causes and Consequences of Congressional Change: Subcommittee Reforms in the House of Representatives." In Norman Ornstein (ed.), *Congress in Change.* New York: Praeger; 88–114.

———. 1985. "Minority Report." *Atlantic,* Dec. 30–38.

Ornstein, Norman J., Thomas E. Mann, and Michael J. Malbin. 1990. *Vital Statistics on Congress, 1989–1990.* Washington, D.C.: CQ Press.

Ornstein, Norman J., and David W. Rohde. 1974. "The Strategy of Reform: Recorded Teller Voting in the U.S. House of Representatives." Paper presented at the annual meeting of the Midwest Political Science Association, Chicago, Illinois.

———. 1975. "Seniority and Future Power in Congress." In Norman J. Ornstein (ed.), *Congress in Change.* New York: Praeger; 72–87.

———. 1977. "Shifting Forces, Changing Rules, and Political Outcomes: The Impact of Congressional Change on Four House Committees." In Robert Peabody and Nelson Polsby (eds.), *New Perspectives on the House of Representatives,* 3d ed. Chicago: Rand McNally; 186–269.

———. 1978. "Political Parties and Congressional Reform." In Jeff Fishel (ed.), *Parties and Elections in an Anti-Party Age.* Bloomington: Indiana University Press; 280–94.

Palazzolo, Dan. 1989. "The Speaker's Relationship with the House Budget Committee: Assessing the Effect of Contextual Change and Individual

Leader Discretion on a 'Leadership Committee.'" Paper presented at the annual meeting of the Midwest Political Science Association, Chicago, Illinois.

Patterson, Samuel C. 1963. "Legislative Leadership and Political Behavior." *Public Opinion Quarterly* 27: 399–410.

Patterson, Samuel C., and Gregory A. Caldeira. 1988. "Party Voting in the United States Congress." *British Journal of Political Science* 18: 111–31.

Peabody, Robert L. 1963. "The Enlarged Rules Committee." In Robert L. Peabody and Nelson W. Polsby (eds.), *New Perspectives on the House of Representatives*. Chicago: Rand McNally; 129–64.

———. 1967. "Party Leadership Change in the United States House of Representatives." *American Political Science Review* 61: 675–93.

———. 1976. *Leadership in Congress: Stability, Succession and Change.* Boston: Little, Brown.

Pianin, Eric. 1987. "House GOP's Frustrations Intensify." *Washington Post*, Dec. 23: A1.

Pitney, John J., Jr. 1988a. "The Conservative Opportunity Society." Paper presented at the annual meeting of the Western Political Science Association, San Francisco.

———. 1988b. "The War on the Floor: Partisan Conflict in the U.S. House of Representatives." Paper presented at the 1988 annual meeting of the American Political Science Association, Washington, D.C.

Plattner, Andy. 1983. "House Panel Seats Assigned: Democrats Tighten Control" *CQWR*, Jan. 8: 4–5.

———. 1985a. "Republicans Seethe over Indiana Eighth Decision." *CQWR*, Apr. 27: 773–75.

———. 1985b. "Republicans Walk Out in Protest after House Seats McCloskey." *CQWR*, May 4: 821–25.

———. 1985c. "Rules under Chairman Pepper Looks Out for Democrats." *CQWR*, Aug. 24: 1671–75.

Polsby, Nelson W. 1968. "The Institutionalization of the House of Representatives." *American Political Science Review* 62: 144–68.

Polsby, Nelson W., Miriam Gallaher, and Barry Spencer Rundquist. 1969. "The Growth of the Seniority System in the U.S. House of Representatives." *American Political Science Review* 63: 787–807.

Poole, Keith T., and Howard Rosenthal. 1991. "Patterns of Congressional Voting." *American Journal of Political Science* 35: 228–78.

Price, David E. 1978. "The Impact of Reform: The House Committee on Oversight and Investigations." In Leroy N. Rieselbach (ed.), *Legislative Reform*. Lexington, Mass.: Lexington Books; 133–57.

———. 1984. *Bringing Back the Parties.* Washington, D.C.: CQ Press.

Ragsdale, Lyn. 1985. "Legislative Elections." In Gerhard Loewenberg, Samuel C. Patterson, and Malcom E. Jewell (eds.), *Handbook of Legislative Research*. Cambridge: Harvard University Press; 57–96.

Rapoport, Ronald B., Alan I. Abramowitz, and John McGlennon (eds.). 1986. *The Life of the Parties.* Lexington, KY.: University Press of Kentucky.

Reid, T. R. 1984. "Outburst." *Washington Post*, May 16: A1.

Rhodes, John J. 1976. *The Futile System*. Garden City, N.Y.: EMP Publications.

Rice, Stuart. 1928. *Quantitative Methods in Politics*. New York: Knopf.

Rieselbach, Leroy N. 1982. "Assessing Congressional Change, or What Hath Reform Wrought (or Wreaked)?" In Dennis Hale (ed.), *The United States Congress: Proceedings of the Thomas P. O'Neill Symposium*. Chestnut Hill, Mass.: Boston College; 167–207.

———. 1986. *Congressional Reform*. Washington, D.C.: CQ Press.

Ripley, Randall B. 1964. "The Party Whip Organizations in the United States House of Representatives." *American Political Science Review* 58: 561–76.

———. 1967. *Party Leaders in the House of Representatives*. Washington, D.C.: Brookings Institution.

Roberts, Steven V. 1983a. "Democrats Reward Loyalty in Giving Committee Assignments." *New York Times*, Jan. 6: A25.

———. 1983b. "The Democrats Get Even." *New York Times*, Jan. 9: section 4, p. 1.

Robinson, James A. 1963. *The House Rules Committee*. Indianapolis: Bobbs-Merrill.

Rockman, Bert A. 1985. "Legislative-Executive Relations and Legislative Oversight." In Gerhard Loewenberg, Samuel C. Patterson, and Malcom E. Jewell (eds.), *Handbook of Legislative Research*. Cambridge: Harvard University Press; 519–72.

Rohde, David W. 1974. "Committee Reform in the House of Representatives and the 'Subcommittee Bill of Rights.'" *Annals* 411: 39–47.

———. 1988. "Variations in Partisanship in the House of Representatives, 1953–1988: Southern Democrats, Realignment, and Agenda Change." Paper presented at the annual meeting of the American Political Science Association, Washington, D.C.

———. 1989a. "Democratic Party Leadership, Agenda Control, and the Resurgence of Partisanship in the House." Paper presented at the annual meeting of the American Political Science Association, Atlanta, Georgia.

———. 1989b. "'Something's Happening Here; What It Is Ain't Exactly Clear:' Southern Democrats in the House of Representatives." In Morris P. Fiorina and David W. Rohde (eds.), *Home Style and Washington Work: Studies in Congressional Politics*. Ann Arbor: University of Michigan Press; 137–63.

———. 1990a. "Agenda Change and Partisan Resurgence in the House of Representatives." Paper presented at "Back to the Future: The United States Congress in the Twenty-First Century," a conference at the Carl Albert Center at the University of Oklahoma, Norman, Oklahoma, Apr. 11–14.

———. 1990b. "'The Reports of My Death Are Greatly Exaggerated': Parties and Party Voting in the House of Representatives." In Glenn R. Parker (ed.), *Changing Perspectives on Congress*. Manuscript.

———. 1991. *Legacy of Realignment: Southern Democrats and the Resurgence of Partisanship in the House*. In preparation.

Rohde, David W., and Kenneth A. Shepsle. 1987. "Leaders and Followers in the House of Representatives: Reflections on Woodrow Wilson's *Congressional Government*." *Congress and the Presidency* 14: 111–33.

Rules Committee. 1983. *A History of the Committee on Rules*. U.S. Government Printing Office.

Schlesinger, Joseph A. 1985. "The New American Political Party." *American Political Science Review* 79: 1152–69.

Sheppard, Burton D. 1985. *Rethinking Congressional Reform*. Cambridge: Schenkman.

Shepsle, Kenneth A. 1978. *The Giant Jigsaw Puzzle*. Chicago: University of Chicago Press.

———. 1989. "Congressional Institutions and Behavior: The Changing Textbook Congress." In John E. Chubb and Paul E. Peterson (eds.), *American Political Institutions and the Problems of Our Time*. Washington, D.C.: Brookings Institution; 238–66.

Shepsle, Kenneth A., and Barry R. Weingast. 1981: "Political Preferences for the Pork Barrel: A Generalization." *American Journal of Political Science* 25: 96–111.

Sinclair, Barbara. 1978. "From Party Voting to Regional Fragmentation, 1933–1956." *American Politics Quarterly* 6: 125–46.

———. 1981a. "Coping with Uncertainty: Building Coalitions in the House and Senate." In Thomas E. Mann and Norman J. Ornstein (eds.), *The New Congress*. Washington, D.C.: American Enterprise Institute; 178–220.

———. 1981b. "Majority Party Leadership Strategies for Coping with the New U.S. House." In Frank H. Mackaman (ed.), *Understanding Congressional Leadership*. Washington, D.C.: CQ Press; 181–205.

———. 1982. *Congressional Realignment, 1925–1978*. Austin: University of Texas Press.

———. 1983. *Majority Leadership in the U.S House*. Baltimore: Johns Hopkins University Press.

———. 1989a. "The Changing Role of Party and Party Leadership in the U.S. House." Paper presented at the annual meeting of the American Political Science Association, Atlanta, Georgia.

———. 1989b. "House Majority Party Leadership in the Late 1980s." In Lawrence C. Dodd and Bruce I. Oppenheimer (eds.), *Congress Reconsidered*, 4th ed. Washington, D.C.: CQ Press; 307–30.

Smith, Steven S. 1989. *Call to Order: Floor Politics in the House and Senate*. Washington, D.C.: Brookings Institution.

Smith, Steven S., and Christopher J. Deering. 1984. *Committees in Congress*. Washington, D.C.: CQ Press.

Smith, Steven S., and Forrest Maltzman. 1989. "Declining Committee Power in the House of Representatives." Paper presented at the annual meeting of the American Political Science Association, Atlanta, Georgia.

Smith, Steven S., and Bruce A. Ray. 1983. "The Impact of Congressional Reform: House Democratic Committee Assignments." *Congress and the Presidency* 10: 219–40.

Stampen, Jacob O., and John R. Davis. 1989. "The Policy Role of Subparty Coalitions." Paper presented at the annual meeting of the American Political Science Association, Atlanta, Georgia.

Stevens, Arthur G., Jr., Arthur H. Miller, and Thomas E. Mann. 1974. "Mobilization of Liberal Strength in the House, 1955–1970: The Democratic Study Group." *American Political Science Review* 68: 667–81.

Sundquist, James L. 1980. "The Crisis of Competence in Our National Government." *Political Science Quarterly* 95: 183–208.

———. 1981. *The Decline and Resurgence of Congress.* Washington, D.C.: Brookings Institution.

Tate, Dale. 1984. "The Budget at House Rules: A Foregone Conclusion." *CQWR,* Apr. 7: 761.

Towell, Pat, 1983. "MX Gains Narrow House OK, but Further Battles Expected." *CQWR,* July 23: 1483.

———. 1986. "House Approves Defense Authorization Bill." *CQWR,* Aug. 16: 1869–75.

———. 1987a. "House Rebuffs Reagan Views on Defense Spending, Policy." *CQWR,* May 9: 900–902.

———. 1987b. "House Slashes President's SDI Request in Move to Slow Push for Deployment." *CQWR,* May 16: 974–75.

Truman, David B. 1959. *The Congressional Party: A Case Study.* New York: Wiley.

Turner, Julius, 1951. *Party and Constituency: Pressures on Congress.* Baltimore: Johns Hopkins University Press.

Uslaner, Eric M. 1978. "Policy Entrepreneurs and Amateur Democrats in the House of Representatives: Toward a More Party-Oriented Congress?" In Leroy N. Rieselbach (ed.), *Legislative Reform.* Lexington, Mass.: Lexington Books; 105–16.

Waldman, Sidney. 1980. "Majority Leadership in the House of Representatives." *Political Science Quarterly* 95: 373–93.

Walsh, Edward. 1986. "New Speaker Quickly Asserts Style and Agenda." *Washington Post,* Dec. 17: A1.

Wehr, Elizabeth. 1987. "House Panel Abandons Public Budget Sessions." *CQWR,* Mar. 21: 517–18.

Weingast, Barry R. 1979. "A Rational Choice Perspective on Congressional Norms." *American Journal of Political Science* 23: 245–62.

———. 1989a. "Fighting Fire with Fire: Amending Activity and Institutional Change in the Post-Reform Congress." Hoover Institution Working Papers in Political Science, P-89-11.

———. 1989b. "Floor Behavior in Congress: Committee Power under the Open Rule. *American Political Science Review* 83: 795–816.

———. 1989c. "Restrictive Rules and Committee Floor Success In the Post-Reform House." Paper presented at the annual meeting of the American Political Science Association, Atlanta, Georgia.

Wilson, Woodrow, 1885. *Congressional Government.* Boston: Houghton Mifflin.

Wolfensberger, Don. 1988. "The Role of Party Caucuses in the U.S. House of Representatives: An Historic Perspective." Paper presented at the annual meeting of the American Political Science Association, Washington, D.C., Sept. 1–4.

Index

Abramowitz, Alan I., 196
Abramson, Paul R., 181, 206
Agenda(s): defined, 43, 208; variable, 43, 44, 52–54
Albert, Rep. Carl, 39, 66, 77, 82, 84, 105
Aldrich, John H., 181, 194, 206
Anderson, Rep. John, 121, 123, 205
Andrews, Rep. Michael A., 116
Appropriations Committee, 27, 28, 33, 71, 75, 80, 108, 195, 206
Arieff, Irwin B., 78, 124, 141, 199
Armed Services Committee, 18, 33, 63, 72, 74, 89, 117, 119, 134
Armstrong, Rep. William L., 121
Asher, Herbert B., 198
Aspin, Rep. Les, 23, 65, 72–75, 89, 117, 119, 134, 182, 205
Atari Democrats, 48
Au Coin, Rep. Les, 73

Bach, Stanley, 25, 32, 33, 99–104, 109, 111, 133, 203–5
Baker, Ross K., 80, 81
Banking and Currency Committee, 80, 109
Barnard, Rep. Doug, Jr., 80
Barry, John M., 88, 89, 92, 93, 106–8, 114, 119, 135, 137, 204, 205, 207, 208
Bates, Rep. Jim, 69
Beilenson, Rep. Anthony C., 100

Bennett, Rep. Charles, 72, 74, 118
Black Caucus, 74, 85, 89, 115, 187
Blanchard, Rep. James J., 48, 199
Boggs, Rep. Hale, 84
Bolling, Rep. Richard, 5–8, 18, 19, 25, 26, 95, 99, 164
Boll Weevils, 45, 73, 74, 103; and Democratic leadership, 47, 69, 71, 78–81, 152, 202; and Reagan's policies, 50, 60, 87, 159; pivotal role shattered, 50. See also Conservative Democratic Forum; Southern Democrats
Boner, Rep. Bill, 80
Bonior, Rep. David E., 88, 107
"Boss" model of leadership, 35, 37, 81
Boxer, Rep. Barbara, 70
Brademas, Rep. John, 86, 87
Brady, David W., 4–6, 9, 10, 12, 13, 23, 36–38, 66, 138, 198, 171, 172, 193
Breaux, Rep. John B., 80
Broder, David S., 79, 124, 193, 202
Brooks, Rep. Jack, 107
Budget Committee, 27, 28, 33, 49, 60, 80, 114, 182
Budget policy, 49, 50, 60–63, 114, 115, 182
Budget reconciliation bill of 1987, 115, 116
Budget resolution of 1987, 114, 115
Bullock, Charles S., 5

Burke, Edmund, 141
Burns, James McGregor, 193
Bush, George, 180, 183, 187, 189–92

C-SPAN, 129
Cain, Bruce, 13
Caldiera, Gregory A., 139
Calmes, Jacqueline, 50, 62, 73, 74, 144
Cambodia, 66
Cannon, Rep. Joseph G., 4–6, 8, 9, 14, 36, 37, 65, 172
Carmines, Edward G., 59, 201
Carper, Rep. Thomas R., 116
Carr, Rep. Robert, 66
Carter administration, 140, 147
Carter, Jimmy (James E.), 86, 94, 156, 209, 210; and House Democrats, 145, 146; and partisanship in the House, 146–51, 153, 157, 158, 161, 168, 169; policy agenda, 141–45, 161, 208
Catastrophic health insurance bill (1987), 175
Chapman, Rep. Jim, Jr., 107, 108, 116
Chen, Ping, 203
Cheney, Rep. Richard B., 122, 134–36, 207
Christian Right, 123
Civil rights issue, 183, 201; and Democratic divisions, 11, 58–60
Clean Water Act (1987), 113, 119, 175
Class of 1958 (Democrats), 7
Class of 1964 (Democrats), 7
Class of 1978 (Republicans), 122
Class of 1980 (Republicans), 122
Class of 1982 (Democrats), 49, 50
Closed rules, 28, 99, 113, 119
Clubb, Jerome M., 193
Coelho, Rep. Tony L., 48, 71, 88, 92, 114, 180, 185, 186, 199, 208
Cohen, Richard E., 48, 77, 108, 122, 124, 129, 137, 138, 204, 207
Cohodas, Nadine, 27, 72, 201
Collective control of power, 26–28, 165, 166, 168; and Boll Weevils, 78–81; and Democratic Caucus, 69–81
Collie, Melissa P., 1, 9, 12, 13, 23, 25, 93, 94, 170, 198, 200, 203
Committee assignments, Democratic, 24, 25, 65, 77–80, 107, 108
Committee chairmen, selection of, 22

Committee Democratic caucuses, 26, 27, 68, 69
Committee government, 7, 12
Committee on Political Parties (APSA), 6
Committee on Standards of Official Conduct, 135
Committee of the Whole, 21, 54, 91, 196
Committees, and committee system, 32, 33. *For party committees, see under party names; for House committees, see under committee name*
Complex rules, 99
Conable, Rep. Barber B., 95
Conditional party government, 31–34, 118, 119, 129, 165, 166, 169
Conlon, Richard P., 21, 27, 29, 194
Conservative coalition, 5, 10, 11, 24, 121, 163
Consensual vote, defined, 200
Conservative Democratic Forum (CDF), 80, 185, 199, 202; and Reagan's policies, 50, 60; formation, 47, 78. *See also* Boll Weevils; Southern Democrats
Conservative Opportunity Society (COS), 122, 123, 128, 130, 134, 205
Constituencies, concentric, 42; heterogeneity and homogeneity, 42
Contextual theory of party leadership, 35–39, 171, 172
Consumer Protection Agency, 142
Contras, 73
Cooper, Ann, 87, 202
Cooper, Joseph, 4–6, 9, 10, 12, 13, 25, 36–38, 66, 93, 94, 138, 171, 172, 193, 203
Cooper, Rep. James, 49
COS. *See* Conservative Opportunity Society
Cox, Gary W., 197, 198
Crook, Sara Brandes, 75
Cummings, Milton C., 195

Dannemeyer, Rep. William E., 115
Davidson, Roger H., 12, 25, 38, 93, 94, 195, 203
Davis, John R., 124
Deckard, Barbara, 193
Deering, Christopher J., 26, 27, 29, 33, 77, 94, 194, 196, 197

Defense authorization bill of 1987, 117, 118

Defense policy, 62–65, 89, 117, 118, 181, 182; and Armed Services Committee chairmanship, 72–75, 89

DeLay, Rep. Thomas D., 188

Democratic Caucus, 7, 18, 35, 40, 49, 88, 98, 182, 186, 195, 206, 207; and Boll Weevils, 78–81; and committee assignments, 77, 78, 80, 202; and party leadership, 69–71, 165, 189, 204; and selection of committee chairmen, 11, 21–23, 71–77; control of prestige committees, 25–28, 114, 196; historical development, 65, 66; preference homogeneity within, 82, 90, 105, 106, 117; revitalization in 1980s, 67–69, 83; taking policy positions, 66, 67, 201

Democratic Committee on Committees, 24

Democratic Committee on Organization, Study, and Review, 19

Democratic Committee on Party Effectiveness, 68, 201

Democratic Congressional Campaign Committee, 28, 71, 92, 187

Democratic leadership: and committee autonomy, 119; and media relations, 92; and partisanship, 16, 152, 168, 170–72, 184–89; and Rules Committee, 100, 101; and suspension of the rules, 97, 98; service activities of, 90–93. See also Speaker, Democratic; Party whip; House reform and leadership powers

Democratic party: task forces, 87, 88, 93, 108; victories on House votes, 151–54, 156, 157, 159, 160. See also House Democrats; Democratic leadership

Democratic party unity, 50–58, 152–54; and committee chairmen, 75–77, 79, 80

Democratic party whip, 28, 196. See also Democratic Whip Organization

Democratic Steering and Policy Committee, 35, 47, 67, 85, 98, 106, 202, 207; and Democratic committee assignments, 11, 28, 77–80, 91, 107, 108, 165; and selection of committee

chairmen, 72, 74; and Speaker Wright, 107, 108, 113; as communication channel for leadership, 83, 84; declaring votes to be party votes, 113, 168; reasons for creating, 24

Democratic Study Group (DSG), 7, 30, 31, 34, 66, 83, 84, 95, 106, 116, 193, 194; and collective control of power, 26; and Subcommittee Bill of Rights, 22, 26; Executive Committee of, 17, 18, 24; motives for reform proposals, 18–20, 23, 26, 29; staff reports, 18, 19, 29

Democratic Whip organization, 83–90, 107, 187, 202; and communications within party, 88–90; development of, 84–86; growth in 1970s and 1980s, 86–88

Democrats. See House Democrats

Department of Education, 142

Derrick, Rep. Butler, 108, 138

Dickinson, Rep. William L., 134, 205

Divided government, impact on partisanship, 10, 139–41, 146–51, 161, 168, 169, 174–77, 189–92

Dodd, Lawrence C., 12, 25, 85, 193, 194, 198, 202

Dole, Sen. Robert, 122

Dorgan, Rep. Byron L., 186

Downey, Rep. Thomas J., 49

Downs, Anthony, 29

DSG. See Democratic Study Group

Eckart, Rep. Dennis E., 116

Eckert, Rep. Fred, 196

Education and Labor Committee, 33

Edwards, George C. III, 92, 145, 208

Edwards, Rep. Mickey, 130

Eisenhower, Dwight D., 140; administration of, 147, 152

Energy and Commerce Committee, 108, 116

Erenhalt, Alan, 104

Espy, Rep. Mike, 177

Ettling, John, 10

Farm credit bill (1987), 175

Fenno, Richard F., Jr., 27, 29, 30, 42, 46, 117, 178, 194, 198

Ferejohn, John, 13, 43, 210

Fessler, Pamela, 182

Fiorina, Morris P., 13, 42, 43, 46, 198
Fishel, Jeff, 139, 143
Fisher, Joseph, 202
Flippo, Rep. Ronnie G., 80
Floor amendments, party victories on,
    154–58
Foley, Rep. Thomas S., 66; as Democratic
    whip, 86, 87; as Majority Leader, 92,
    106, 137, 138; as House Speaker, 172,
    180, 182, 184–89, 192
Ford, Gerald R., 143; administration of,
    156, 157
Foreign Affairs Committee, 107
Fowler, Linda L., 196
Fowler, Rep. Wyche, 78
Frank, Rep. Barney, 74, 75, 186
Fraser, Rep. Donald, 18, 19, 24, 26, 165
Frenzel, Rep. Bill, 95
Froman, Lewis A., 84
Frost, Rep. Martin, 80

Gallaher, Miriam, 5, 76
Galloway, George B., 66, 193, 201
Gephardt, Rep. Richard A., 48, 69, 70, 71,
    199, 205
Gingrich, Rep. Newt, 122, 123, 129–31,
    135, 137, 181, 188, 205, 207
Goals of representatives, 29–33; and
    policy preferences, 40–43
Gramm, Rep. Phil, 79, 80
Gramm-Rudman-Hollings, 50, 61, 62,
    115
Granat, Diane, 67, 69, 70–72, 129, 130,
    201
Gray, Rep. William H. III, 63, 74
Great Society, 8
Gregg, Rep. Robert, 112
Grove City v. Bell, 59
Gypsy Moths, 123, 124, 206

Hagar, Barry M., 145
Hagstrom, Jerry, 199
Hall, Rep. Sam, 78
Hall, Richard L., 198
Hansen committee, 19, 22, 194
Hansen, Rep. Julia B., 19
Hebert, Rep. F. Edward, 22, 23, 72
Hibbing, John R., 75
Highway reauthorization (1987), 113, 175
Hook, Janet, 106–8, 117, 119, 129, 191,
    204, 208

House Administration Committee, 131
House Democrats: factions among, 45–
    50; homogeneity and heterogeneity
    on issues, 8, 11, 34, 35, 45–50, 172. *See
    also* Democratic party unity; Civil
    rights; Budget policy; Defense policy;
    Democratic leadership
House Ethics Committee, 135
House *Journal*, votes on approval, 131,
    199, 200
House reforms: and committee chairmen,
    11, 12, 18, 19, 20–23, 31, 41, 75–77,
    79, 80, 164–66; and committees, 11,
    12, 33, 164–66; and decline of
    partisanship, 14; and Democratic
    leaders' powers, 11–13, 21–25, 163,
    165, 166; and member goals, 28–33,
    163; and recorded votes, 11; and
    resurgence of partisanship, 14–16,
    162, 173, 174; and seniority, 11, 19,
    21–23, 29, 76–77; and
    subcommittees, 31 (*see also*
    Subcommittee government); factors
    limiting impact, 34–39, 164–66;
    motives for, 17–20, 164–66
House Republicans: and committees, 127,
    128; and restrictive rules, 112, 132–
    35, 138, 188, 189; and Speaker Foley,
    186–88; changes in party rules, 136–
    38; conflict with Speaker O'Neill, 129,
    130; conflict with Speaker Wright,
    135; factions among, 120–27;
    frustrations of minority status, 128–32
Howard, Rep. James, 204
Hurley, Patricia A., 9, 10, 138, 193

Index of cohesion, defined, 9
Iran-Contra scandal, 107

Jacobson, Gary C., 13, 194
Johnson administration, 140, 147, 148,
    152
Jones, Charles O., 1, 5, 36, 127, 141, 143,
    145, 193, 196, 207, 208
Jones, Rep. James, 69, 202
Judiciary Committee, 27, 33

Kemp, Rep. Jack F., 136, 207
Kennedy, Sen. Edward M., 142
Kennedy, John F., 148; administration of,
    140, 147, 148

Kenworthy, Tom, 135, 207
Kephart, Thomas, 25, 94, 203
Kessel, John H., 30
Key votes, 18
Kiewiet, D. Roderick, 197, 198
King Caucus, 65
Kingdon, John W., 29, 30, 117, 139, 196, 208
King-of-the-mountain rules, 103, 104, 115, 118, 187, 188
Knudsen, Patrick L., 116, 205
Kravitz, Walter, 203
Krehbiel, Keith, 204
Kweit, Mary G., 30

LaFalce, Rep. John J., 99
Lagomarsino, Rep. Robert J., 136
Latta, Rep. Delbert, 60, 61
Leath, Rep. J. Marvin, 63, 73, 74
Legislative Reorganization Act of 1970, 21, 154
Lemann, Nicholas, 123
Lewis, Rep. Jerry, 207
Light, Paul C., 139, 140, 143, 208
Long, Rep. Gillis, 67–70, 80, 83
Loomis, Burdett, 30, 196
Lott, Rep. Trent, 130, 133, 135, 178
Lowery, Rep. Mike, 63, 116, 204
Lungren, Rep. Daniel E., 129
Lyons, Richard L., 23

McCain, Rep. John, 128
McCloskey, Rep. Francis X., 131
McClure, Robert D., 196
McCormack, Rep. John, 5, 18, 39, 66
McCubbins, Mathew D., 197, 198
McCurdy, Rep. Dave, 72
McFall, Rep. John, 85
McGlennon, John, 196
McGovern, Sen. George, 142
McHugh, Rep. Matthew F., 106
McIntyre, Richard, 130
MacKay, Rep. Buddy, 63
McKelvey, Richard D., 43
McMillan, Rep. J. Alex, 195
Maisel, Louis Sandy, 196
Malbin, Michael J., 15, 67, 68, 91, 92, 142, 153, 207, 209
Manley, John F., 5, 28
Mann, Thomas E., 13, 15, 84, 153, 193, 209

Martin, Rep. Lynn, 188, 209
Matsunaga, Rep. Spark M., 203
Mavroules, Rep. Nicholas, 74
Mayhew, David R., 13, 29, 96, 170, 208, 209
Mazzoli, Rep. Romano L., 27
Merchant Marine and Fisheries Committee, 32, 33
Meyers committee (Republicans), 207
Meyers, Rep. Jan, 136
Michel, Rep. Robert H., 130, 137, 186, 188
Miller, Arthur H., 84, 193
Miller, Rep. George, 73
Moakley, Rep. John Joseph, 185, 186, 189
Montgomery, Rep. G. V., 62, 79, 80
Moody, Rep. Jim, 62
Moore, Rep. W. Henson, 95
Moynihan, Sen. Daniel Patrick, 186
Multiple referral of bills, 25, 93–95, 101, 102
MX missile, 69

Neoliberals, 48
Nesbit, Dorothy Davidson, 30
New Breed Democrats, 48, 50, 60, 69
"New" conservatives (Republicans), 122
92 Group (Republicans), 124
Nixon, Richard M., 150, 191; administration of, 140, 147, 152, 156, 157
Northern Democrats, 55, 56, 60, 61, 64, 152, 207
Novak, William, 143, 206

Obey, Rep. David R., 77
Oleszek, Walter J., 21, 25, 93, 94, 195, 203, 208
Omnibus Trade Bill, 175
O'Neill, Rep. Thomas P., Jr.: as Speaker, 13, 37, 39, 62, 94, 98, 105, 168, 171, 172; and committee assignments, 77, 79; and committee chairmen, 71, 72; and Democratic Caucus, 67, 70–72, 204; and Democratic Whip organization, 86–89; and House Republicans, 128–30, 206, 208; and President Carter, 142; and Ronald Reagan, 143; and Rules Committee, 100, 101, 104; and southern Democrats, 47, 78, 79; and Steering and Policy Committee, 83; services for members, 91, 92

Operative preferences, 41–44, 144, 163, 168
Oppenheimer, Bruce I., 12, 98, 99, 104, 178, 194, 198
Orfield, Gary, 139
Ornstein, Norman J., 15, 21, 49, 124, 128, 136, 153, 179, 194–96, 201, 209

Palazzolo, Dan, 205
Panetta, Rep. Leon E., 48, 71, 182, 187, 199
Parliamentary parties, 3
Parties in the House: before reform, 3–8; general, 1, 2
Partisanship: defined, 2; and electoral forces, 9–11, 13, 16, 45–48, 162–64, 166, 167, 170–72, 179–83
Party difference (in floor voting), 146; defined, 8; on amendments, 157, 158; on passage of bills, 149–51, 158–60; on special rules, 102, 103, 132, 133; on suspension of the rules, 96, 97
Party government. See Conditional party government
Party leaders: and personal orientations, 37–39, 189; as agents of party, 35–37, 83, 198, 205
Party reform proposals, 6, 7
Party-unity index, defined, 9
Party voting, and institutional arrangements, 9–11; decline of, 8–11, 13, 14; defined, 8; resurgence, 13, 14. See also Democratic party unity; Republican party unity
Passage of bills, party victories on, 159, 160
Patman, Rep. Wright, 23, 195
Patterson, Samuel C., 1, 139
Peabody, Robert L., 1, 195, 198
Penny, Rep. Timothy J., 209
Pepper, Rep. Claude, 104, 112, 185, 203
Personal preferences, 41–44, 163
Peyser, Rep. Peter, 78
Pianin, Eric, 135, 137
Pitney, John J., Jr., 122, 123, 131, 205
Plattner, Andy, 80, 101, 102, 131, 203
Poage, Rep. W. R., 22
Polsby, Nelson W., 5, 76
Poole, Keith T., 200
Post Office and Civil Service Committee, 33

Presidents and House partisanship, 10, 138, 139, 146–51. See also Divided government
Presidents' agendas, 139–44, 174–77; Carter's agenda, 141, 142; Reagan's agenda, 142–44
Price, Rep. David E., 193, 196
Price, Rep. Melvin, 72
Public Works Committee, 107, 113

Quillen, Rep. James H., 102

Racial issues. See Civil rights
Ragsdale, Lyn, 194
Rangel, Rep. Charles B., 89
Rapoport, Ronald B., 196
Ray, Bruce A., 77, 195
Rayburn, Rep. Sam, 5, 6, 25, 36, 37, 84, 98, 172
Reagan, Ronald W., 67, 86, 94, 121, 210; administration of, 140, 147; administration compared with Bush administration, 189–91; agenda of, 16, 142-46, 161, 176, 208; and budget policy, 60, 62, 63, 103; and defense policy, 64; and Democratic policy agenda, 109, 113, 176; and partisanship in the House, 146–51, 153, 157, 159, 169; and southern Democrats, 60, 62
Recorded (teller) votes, 21, 54, 154, 195
Reed, Rep. Thomas F., 4, 6, 9, 36, 138, 172
Reform. See House reform
Reid, T. R., 130
Republican Committee on Planning and Research, 136
Republican Committee on Committees, 137
Republican Conference, 121, 136, 137, 205, 207
Republican Congressional Committee, 207
Republican Research Committee, 207
Republican party unity, 124–27, 152–54
Republican Policy Committee, 136, 207
Republican Study Group, 121
Republicans. See House Republicans
Responsible parties, 6. See also Conditional party government
Restrictive rules, 99–105, 109–18, 132–

35, 138, 186–89; and Democratic
agenda, 103–5, 109–13
Reuss, Rep. Henry, 66
Rhodes, Rep. John J., 82, 122, 128, 208
Rice, Stuart, 1
Rieselbach, Leroy N., 12, 23, 35, 173, 194,
195, 196, 203
Ripley, Randall B., 1, 84, 193, 202
Rivers, Rep. Mendel, 18
Roberts, Steven V., 80
Robinson, James A., 5, 203
Rockman, Bert, 208
Roemer, Rep. Buddy, 69, 80
Rohde, David W., 34–36, 45, 119, 136,
179, 181, 193–96, 198–202, 206,
207, 209
Rosenthal, Howard, 200
Rostenkowsi, Rep. Dan, 107, 114, 205
Rovner, Julie, 116, 205
Rowland, Rep. J. Roy, 118
Rules Committee, 4, 5, 7, 28, 165, 187,
195, 197, 205; and House
Republicans, 102, 103, 133–35, 138;
and multiple referrals, 101, 102, 203;
and partisan advantage from special
rules, 103, 104; and restrictive rules,
99, 100, 103; and Speaker O'Neill, 70,
100, 101; and Speaker Wright, 109–
18; changed relationship to
leadership, 98–99; closed rules and
Democratic Caucus, 28, 66;
conservative dominance of, 5, 24, 25,
207; Democratic assignments to, 24–
27, 93; Republican assignments to,
137. See also Speaker, and Rules
Committee; Special rules; Closed
rules; Restrictive rules; Self-executing
rules; King-of-the-mountain rules
Rundquist, Barry Spencer, 5, 76
Russo, Rep. Martin A., 73, 89

SALT II treaty, 64, 70, 117
Savings and loan rescue, 175
Schlesinger, Joseph A., 199
Self-executing rules, 103, 115
Senate, partisanship in, 177–79
Sheppard, Burton D., 17, 18, 22–25, 35,
66, 77, 94, 165, 173, 194–96
Shepsle, Kenneth A., 34–36, 169, 193,
196, 198, 200
Sikes, Rep. Robert, 196

Sinclair, Barbara, 11, 34, 43, 45, 67, 77,
81, 83, 84, 86, 87, 89, 90, 92, 100, 105,
108, 109, 121, 142, 143, 145, 175, 194,
198, 202, 203, 206
Slattery, Rep. Jim, 63
Smith, Rep. Howard W., 36, 195
Smith, Steven S., 26, 27, 29, 33, 64, 77, 94,
99–103, 104, 105, 109, 111, 119, 133,
154, 155, 178, 194–97, 203, 205
Social policy, and Democratic divisions, 11
Solomon, Rep. Gerald B. H., 186, 188
South Vietnam, 66
South Africa, 59, 109
Southern Democrats, 164, 172, 173, 206;
and budget policy, 60–63; and civil
rights issue, 59, 60; and defense policy,
63–65; and Reagan's policies, 145;
and party unity, 10, 11, 54–58, 89, 90,
152; electoral forces and changing
party loyalty among, 45–48, 145, 167,
171. See also Boll Weevils; Conservative
Democratic Forum
Speaker: and committee chairmen, 82;
and Democratic party agenda, 105–7;
and multiple referral of bills, 93–95,
101, 102, 108, 109; and Rules
Committee, 24, 25, 98–105, 109–13,
184; before Progressive revolt, 4, 5. See
also Democratic leadership
Speaker's Cabinet, 71, 202
Special rules, 28, 99, 206, 207;
Republican responses to, 132–35, 138.
See also Rules Committee; Restrictive
rules; Closed rules; Self-executing
rules; King-of-the-mountain rules
Stampen, Jacob O., 124
Stanley, John, 193
Steering and Policy Committee. See
Democratic Steering and Policy
Committee
Stenholm, Rep. Charles W., 47, 185
Stevens, Arthur G., 84, 193
Stimson, James A., 59, 201
Strategic Defense Initiative, 64, 118, 123
Strategy of inclusion, 89
Subcommittee Bill of Rights, 22, 23, 26,
27, 128, 164, 194
Subcommittee government, 12, 197
Subcommittees, selection of chairmen, 26,
27, 196
Sundquist, James L., 139, 175

Supreme Court, 59
Suspension of the rules, 25, 95–98, 134, 203

Tate, Dale, 104
Teller votes. *See* Recorded (teller) votes
Towell, Pat, 70, 104, 117, 118
Traditional conservatives, 121
Traditional liberals, 48
Traugott, Santa A., 193
Truman, David B., 1
Turner, Julius, 1

Udall, Rep. Morris K., 194
Uslaner, Eric, 30

Veterans' Affairs Committee, 33, 79, 80
Veterans' issues, 32, 197
Voting Rights Act, 46, 59, 167

Waggoner, Rep. Joe, 67
Waldman, Sidney, 13, 85, 202
Walker, Rep. Robert S., 130, 134, 135, 138, 206
Walsh, Edward, 117, 204
Washington Post, 144, 206
Watergate Babies, 48
Waxman, Rep. Henry A., 30, 49, 128, 196
Ways and Means Committee, 33, 66, 180, 195; and closed or restricted special rules, 99; and Democratic committee assignments, 7, 24, 27, 28, 65, 77; and Wright's legislative priorities, 108, 109, 114–16, 205

Wednesday Group, 123
Wehr, Elizabeth, 114
Weingast, Barry R., 155, 196, 200, 204
Weisberg, Herbert F., 198
Welfare reform bill of 1987, 115, 116, 175
Whitten, Rep. Jamie L., 71, 75, 76
Williams, Rep. Pat, 74, 89
Wilson, Woodrow, 1, 3, 4, 193
Wirth, Rep. Timothy E., 48, 199
Wise, Sidney, 66, 193, 201
Wolfensberger, Don, 136, 137, 207
Wolfinger, Raymond, 13
Women's Caucus, 85
Wright, Rep. James: as majority leader, 62, 67, 69, 78, 80, 86, 87, 94, 95, 129, 131; as Speaker, 2, 16, 39, 90, 159, 172, 180, 208; and Armed Services Committee, 117, 118; and Budget Committee, 114, 115; and conditional party government, 118, 119; conflict with Reagan administration, 175, 176; contrast with Speaker Foley, 184, 185, 189; and Democratic committee assignments, 107, 108; and Democratic priorities in the 100th Congress, 105–7, 110, 111, 113–18, 168, 175, 176, 204; and Democratic whip system, 107; and House Republicans, 133, 135, 137, 205, 207; and media relations, 92; and multiple referral of bills, 108, 109; and Rules Committee, 109–18, 132, 133, 185, 207; and Ways and Means Committee, 115, 116, 205